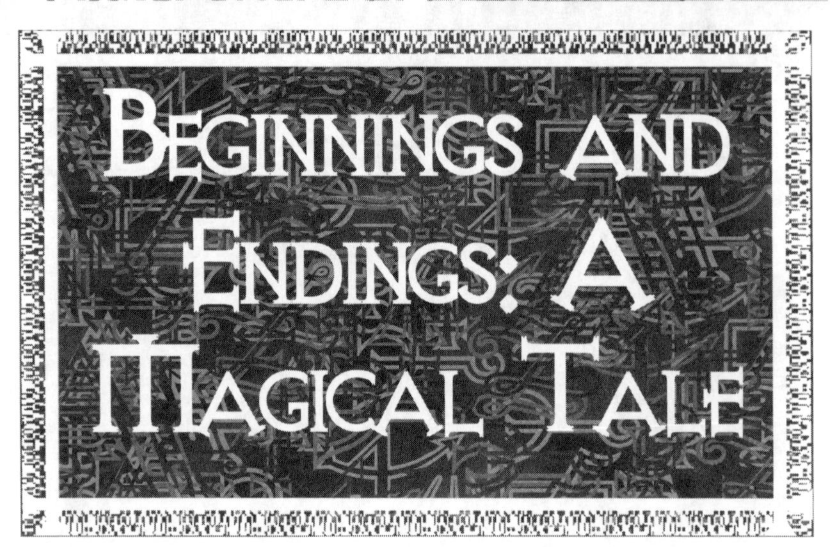

Beginnings and Endings: A Magical Tale

Little sound rattled through the Technocratic construct, other than the sussurations of the air conditioning. Deep in the ducts, something made an intermittent thumping.

"Seems like nothing works right these days," murmured Agent Graham. Pressing his identity card against the sealed door, he submitted to the quick DNA scan — none of this blood-drawing nonsense; the dead skin cells from his finger would suffice — and entered a moment later when the door whisked open.

"Any leads?" Graham barked with a stern, authoritarian voice. The woman in the doctor's coat barely turned her head; she looked tired and resigned. Quite unlike the Academy cadets who jumped at anything. *Probably already used to the authority*, Graham thought.

After a protracted sigh, the woman placed her stylus on her workbench and stood up. She unceremoniously shoved her hands into her coat pockets. "A few. Nothing major. A little bit of skin sampling, some extrapolation, protease matching, the usual. Three people, maybe with some friends that they didn't bring."

Graham peered over his sunglasses quizzically. "That's all?" he murmured quietly. His body language and voice inflection carried more to the question, though: Curiosity about those "friends", uncertainty over the techniques used, possibility of contamination.

"I'm sure. For now," the woman muttered. "No mistake. No attempts to stymie a trace or investigation. Almost as if they didn't care — or had bigger problems to worry about."

Graham nodded once to himself. His hand twitched slightly, carrying the subtext of *That's it, we're done*. The woman just nodded and turned back to her work.

Slipping back outside the lab, Graham headed to his gray mid-size car. Black sedans had been out for the better part of a year, and he was starting to prefer the better handling of the smaller vehicles. Checking his sidearm once, he paused to flip through the paperwork left on his seat. Even if he did track down the mysterious three who'd left their genetic fingerprints all over the agency's toys, what then? Arrest? Incarcerate them where? Shoot? The paperwork and the reports and the psych evals would have him tied up for months, keeping him from staying on the streets and doing good work.

Some days, Graham hated the bureaucracy. Then he remembered that it was the only thing that kept society functioning. *Better the devil you know*, he thought for a moment, and then started the car.

Credits

Authors: Mike Boaz, Scott Taylor and Jess Heinig
Additional Material: Ian Dunteman and Martin Hackleman
Development: Jess Heinig
Editing: Cynthia Summers
Art Direction: Aaron Voss
Interior Art: Laura Robles
Layout and Typesetting: Eric Ross

735 Park North Blvd.
Suite 128
Clarkston, GA 30021
USA

For a free White Wolf catalog call 1-800-454-WOLF.

Check out White Wolf online at

http://www.white-wolf.com;alt.games.whitewolf and rec.games.frp.storyteller

PRINTED IN USA.

Contents

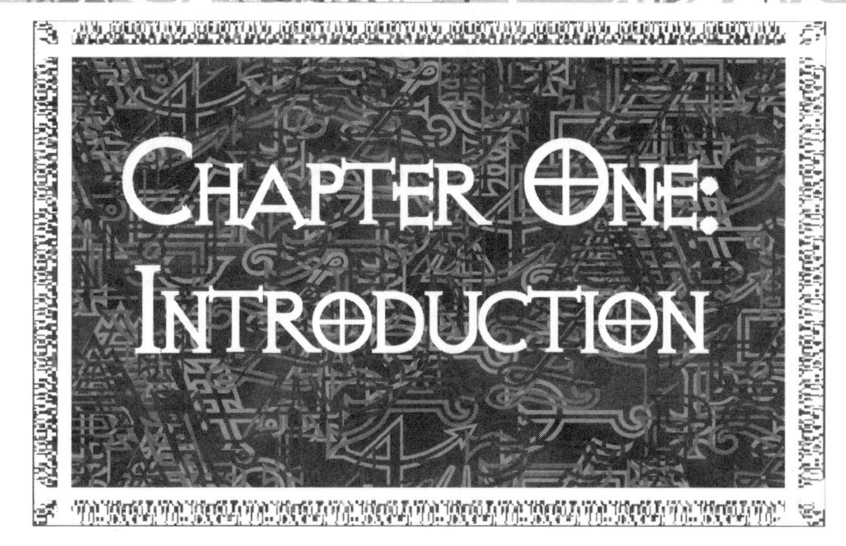

Chapter One: Introduction

Chances are, if you're reading this, you already have your copy of **Laws of Ascension** and you may have even run a game or two. You're probably champing at the bit for ways to expand your chronicle, or scratching your head over some rules that didn't quite click for you. In short, that's what this book is for: Everything you wanted to know about live-action **Mage** that couldn't fit in the first book.

Again, since there's no telling how *you* run *your* game and what works for *your* troupe, many parts of this book contain optional rules and potential ideas. Based on the same mechanics as the rest of the live-action system in **Laws of Ascension**, these rules provide different ways to expand your chronicle, but you can always pick and choose what works for you.

This **Companion** clarifies a few rules and adds many new ideas. You'll find that a lot of these spring directly from ideas presented by the original book, or from other sourcebooks for **Mage**. With this book, you should have just about all the guidelines you need to any of the **Mage** cosmology fully accessible.

So, without further ado, here's what you'll find in this **Companion**:

Chapter One: Introduction is this little stuff right here.

Chapter Two: The Technocracy covers in detail that most fearsome of organizations — the conspiratorial Technocratic Union. From Technocracy character recruitment to special Storytelling considerations to running a Technocracy-based game, it's all here.

Chapter Three: Character Additions expands upon all of your materials for making Mage characters, including new Backgrounds, Adversarial Backgrounds, Merits, Flaws, disparate types and more. It's everything from the advantages and disadvantages of playing a strange mage like an Ahl-i-Batin, to how to convert the Merits and Flaws from your tabletop supplement.

Chapter Four: Rotes and Wonders expands upon the sample rotes from the core book. This comprehensive list includes a lot more things for mages to do, and some clarifications on the uses of earlier rotes. Also, you'll find some rotes that show a wide range of capabilities, from shaking the world to just getting along in daily life, all suitable for inspiration.

Chapter Five: Rules Addenda updates and clarifies some of the rules from **Laws of Ascension** so that you can avoid headaches or minor mistakes. Also in here are a few additional optional rules, like how to build a Paradox deck with a deck of normal cards and how to deal with the headaches of crossovers with other World of Darkness games.

Chapter Six: Places of Stories covers the Umbra, spirits, Shallowings, hauntings, the Digital Web and the like all in detail. You'll find ideas on how to create new and compelling places for your stories. You'll also learn the rules governing those strange locations and how mages interact with them.

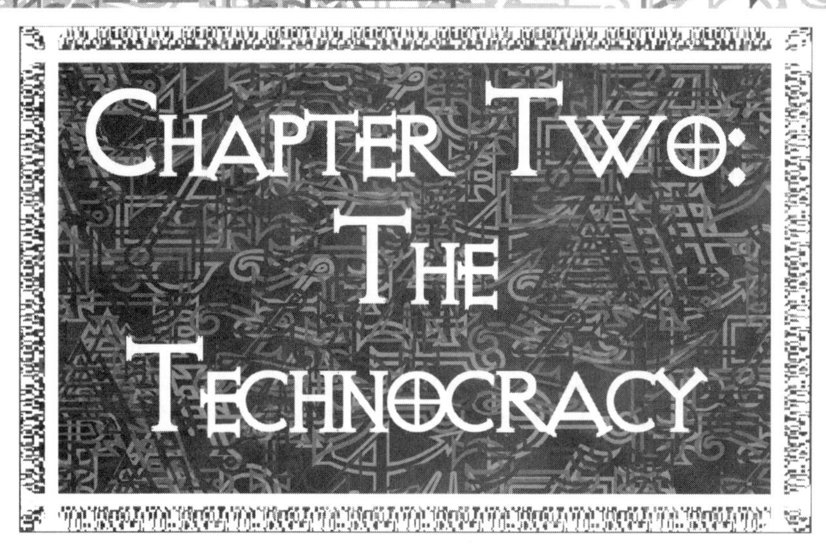

Chapter Two: The Technocracy

Every Tradition mage fears them. Every shadowy conspiracy is attributed to them. Every historical impetus to stamp out the mystical world in favor of reason is a victory at their feet. They are the Technocracy.

The Technocracy, or Technocratic Union, is often considered the greatest antagonist for any Tradition **Mage** game — or the greatest set of heroes and protagonists for a game centered around the Union.

To understand the Technocracy and use it in your games, you'll need to know a bit about where they come from. With the helpful indoctrination/education guide here, you'll have no problem getting in step with the Pogrom. You might even find yourself Conditioned to play a Technocracy-based game instead of a Tradition-oriented one!

The Technocracy Itself

Most Tradition mages see the Technocracy as a faceless megalith bent on domination not only of the Earth but all of Reality. They claim that the agents of the Technocracy are at best willing dupes, and most are actively evil. They see the philosophy of the Technocracy as abhorrent.

And the Technocracy doesn't mind one bit. Let their enemies underestimate them, they say. Technocracy members know better; they are the last, desperate bastion of hope against madness and chaos.

They just might be right.

Tradition Propaganda

The Technos are a bunch of fascist bastards. All they are doing is imposing their views on the world, strangling all choice and beauty. They want a sterile, clockwork universe where everything is totally regimented and precisely controlled. They want all magic gone from the world — no sense of wonder, no joy of discovery, just endless tedium and toil, forever.

That's what the Tradition mages will tell you.

The Technos no more see themselves as mustache-twirling villains bent on world subjugation than the Traditions see themselves as bomb-throwing anarchists bent on unmaking the laws of reality just so they can regain power. Members of the Conventions of the Technocracy see themselves as many things — employees of an advanced group of companies devoted to promoting scientific understanding of the universe, agents in a secret war against paranormal terrorists, defenders of humanity, or promoters of civilization and rational thinking. Their tools are not magic cloaked in the trappings of science and technology, they *are* science and technology; extremely advanced examples, to be sure, but nothing that humanity won't be able to use, in time.

All but the most devoted Technocrat will admit that the Technocracy has made mistakes, some of them quite heinous. Sometimes they have reasons why these mistakes were made, other times all they can say is that they screwed up. Still, overall, they can point to a world that is safer, cleaner and overall a better place to live than the one they inherited six centuries ago. People live longer, enjoy better lives, have more opportunity and more equality than ever before.

How true this image of the Technocracy is depends on the spin you want to give your story. The Technocracy could in fact be nothing more than mustachioed villains hiding their plans behind beeping computers and giant ray-guns, the black hats in a game more about beating ass than about complex issues and ideas. At the opposite end of the scale, the Technocracy really could be everything it thinks it is — an organization of dedicated men and women (and artificial creations) devoted to making the world a better place, and protecting humanity from dangerous paranormal infestations. The truth, as with all things, is somewhere in the middle.

History

The first members of the Technocracy, by some accounts, were the prehuman that grabbed a leg bone and bashed his opponent over the head with it, the Cro-Magnon that grabbed a burning hunk of tree from a lightning strike and used it to light his cave, and the Neanderthal that domesticated the wolf and the horse. Others trace the origins of the groups that would become the Technocracy to ancient Egypt, or to China, or suggest that the scientist-magi of early Arabia might have been their antecedents. Stll others credit Pythagoras, Archimedes, Hero and Daedalus of the Greeks. Any or all of these theories may be correct — it really depends on what interpretation of history you want to use.

The Technocracy truly began to get organized in the beginnings of the second millennium. A noble named Wolfgang von Reismann helped organize the Craftmasons, an organization of secret societies dedicated to the pursuit of knowledge, the betterment of Mankind and (secretly), a cure for death itself. The Craftmasons soon made contact with an organization of alchemists and herbalists called the Solificati, who joined them in an informal alliance. They were joined by the High Guild, a brotherhood of Enlightened tradesmen and merchants. As the loose coalition grew, they became increasingly concerned about the threats presented by the supernatural world. Mages and vampires ruled the civilized world, while the woods were home to all manner of fell beasts and monsters. Most people spent their lives wracked with fear. Something hadto be done.

The Order of Reason announced its presence to the world with a bang, at the Covenant of Mistridge. Mistridge was a large Hermetic Chantry located in southern France that had long since fallen into corruption and moral decay. The local peasants, tired of magical depredations and heavy taxation brought the tower of Mistridge under siege, and the Craftmasons showed up to help. Artificer artillery blasted down walls of stone, while prayers, sacred geometry and alchemically erected barriers in the Gauntlet prevented escape. By the time the siege was over, Mistridge Tower was no more, and the members of the Order of Hermes who had lived there were dead. In place of the tower, the Craftmasons raised a school and a church.

News of the events at Mistridge spread, and the influence of the Craftmasons and their allies soon followed. While their success was not universal — the disastrous events in Languedoc and the Cathar heresy being perhaps the most notable error — it was ever-present and growing. In 1325, the Convention of the Ivory Tower at Yossamy formalized the alliance between the Craftmasons, the Cabal of Pure Thought (a group of religious warriors that may be the predecessors of the modern NWO), the Artificers (a group of smiths, artisans, inventors and mechanics), the Celestial Masters and the Void Seekers (guilds of explorers and stargazers), the Cosians (healers, herbalists and alchemists), and the High Guild (financiers, traders, and merchants) into a new organization — the Order of Reason. The Solificati, one of the Craftmasons' first allies, were members of the Order for only a short time, quickly falling away from them, and eventually leaving the Traditions as well. Within a century, the Order wielded influence in every court in Europe and the Middle East, and its touch was felt as far away as China and South America. In many parts of the world, their advice came to be more important than that of the mages who had acted as advisors for years before. At first, this rivalry was nearly friendly, a disagreement between equals, but this was not to last. Eventually the Traditions and the Order would be locked in a secret war that has lasted until recently, when the Ascension War finally ended.

Even in the early days, the Order was not without internal strife. The Craftmasons were at odds with the Cabal and the High Guild on a number of subjects, and in 1670 they were betrayed and destroyed, apparently to a man. Today, only scraps of records exist to suggest that the Craftmasons ever existed, the result of some unknown cover-up or reworking of history.

Storytelling the Technocracy.

Members of the Technocracy can take many roles in your story, and different members can take on different roles at different times. The Man in White who is a covert source of information one week can be an implacable foe a month (and possibly some re-education) later.

Using the Technocracy in a Traditions game

In a story that concentrates on Tradition mages, the Technocracy are usually the antagonists, but what kind of opposition can impact immensely on the feel of the game. The Technocracy doesn't need to be played in any one particular style, but a trend or theme in their behavior can lend a sense of how the game is to be played. Some examples include:

Shadowy Nemesis

In this version, the Technocracy works from the shadows, using its influence and information to hamper your players' characters, but rarely taking an active role against them. The players may not even be aware that the Technocracy is actually out to get them, or may suspect, but not be able

Tradition Propaganda

The Technos are a bunch of fascist bastards. All they are doing is imposing their views on the world, strangling all choice and beauty. They want a sterile, clockwork universe where everything is totally regimented and precisely controlled. They want all magic gone from the world — no sense of wonder, no joy of discovery, just endless tedium and toil, forever.

That's what the Tradition mages will tell you.

The Technos no more see themselves as mustache-twirling villains bent on world subjugation than the Traditions see themselves as bomb-throwing anarchists bent on unmaking the laws of reality just so they can regain power. Members of the Conventions of the Technocracy see themselves as many things — employees of an advanced group of companies devoted to promoting scientific understanding of the universe, agents in a secret war against paranormal terrorists, defenders of humanity, or promoters of civilization and rational thinking. Their tools are not magic cloaked in the trappings of science and technology, they *are* science and technology; extremely advanced examples, to be sure, but nothing that humanity won't be able to use, in time.

All but the most devoted Technocrat will admit that the Technocracy has made mistakes, some of them quite heinous. Sometimes they have reasons why these mistakes were made, other times all they can say is that they screwed up. Still, overall, they can point to a world that is safer, cleaner and overall a better place to live than the one they inherited six centuries ago. People live longer, enjoy better lives, have more opportunity and more equality than ever before.

How true this image of the Technocracy is depends on the spin you want to give your story. The Technocracy could in fact be nothing more than mustachioed villains hiding their plans behind beeping computers and giant ray-guns, the black hats in a game more about beating ass than about complex issues and ideas. At the opposite end of the scale, the Technocracy really could be everything it thinks it is — an organization of dedicated men and women (and artificial creations) devoted to making the world a better place, and protecting humanity from dangerous paranormal infestations. The truth, as with all things, is somewhere in the middle.

to prove it. Characters may find their *Resources* diminished as the Syndicate works against them, the local police (at the behest of an FBI agent who unknowingly works for a cutout that works for the NWO) might start hassling them, their Chantry might be threatened by Eminent Domain and possibly seized. At every turn, anything that can go wrong involving local government, politics, criminals or society will go wrong. This kind of Technocracy can be amazingly effective… and insanely frustrating. Make sure you give your players some chances to finally make the connections, track down the leads and put paid to some of their tormentors, or they are going to hate not just the Technocracy, but you.

Technocracy Versus Scientocracy

Remember, the Technocracy *uses* science as a tool, but science itself is not the only end. While there are in fact many scientists in the Union who perform experiments, try to fit observed data into theories and look for ways to make the universe "make sense," these scientists usually aren't on the front lines, nor are they policy-makers. The Technocracy runs to propagate its own structure. Once upon a time, the Order of Reason tumbled to science as a tool to advance its agenda of protecting humanity. Now, that tool and others fall into the hands of agents who may still have that agenda or may have others.

So what, you say? This is why the Technocracy doesn't bother trying to figure out Tradition magic. Remember, since Technocratic researchers don't *believe* that magic should work, it doesn't, for them anyway. Empirical tests of Tradition techniques fail. The Technocrats are left with the notion that Tradition mages are aberrations, superstitionists, people playing with uncontrolled and incomprehensible forces. Maybe science *never* can explain the strange things these people do — and somewhere along the way, the Union stopped caring to explain. They decided that "magic" was dangerous, so it had to go.

The end result: The Technocracy doesn't really care where Tradition magic comes from, or how it works, or why. This isn't very scientific, but that's because the Union is not about science for science's sake. All the Union cares about is making a better tomorrow, *sans* Reality Deviants.

Overwhelming Force

This form of the Technocracy strikes without warning. Suddenly, combat cyborgs are chasing the players, NWO cutouts are everywhere, genetically engineered monsters are crawling out of the sewers, and space Marines in power-armor are coming through the roof of the Chantry! This kind of Technocracy can be very cathartic, a target-rich environment for the players to get all *Matrix* on. It can also ruin a story, kill off all the players if they aren't careful, and often is very much at odds with the feel of many **Laws of Ascension** chronicles. Care should be used in making this the standard version of the Technocracy in your chronicle, as it can be hard to manage, and is always available as an option when needed.

Beleaguered Hostiles

The Technocracy is spread thin, but the players don't know *how* thin. There are actually only a handful of agents in your local area, in this version of the Technocracy — they work through cutouts and unwitting pawns for the most part. While this can be similar to "Shadowy Nemesis", in this version the agents who are around are more out in the open. A Man in White might show up on the doorstep of the Chantry (carefully providing for plenty of defenses and lots of plainclothes officers about) to let the players know they are under surveillance, and if they step out of line….

Intimidation and misdirection are the tools of the Technocracy in this case. The agents on point know the only way to keep the Traditions off their backs until they can gather forces to definitively squash them is to keep them off-balance and guessing, never knowing when, or if, the Technos are going to strike.

Potential Allies

Especially suited for a game with a number of Sons of Ether and Virtual Adepts, or other technology- and science-friendly characters in it, this version of the Technocracy is surprisingly friendly. Oh, they'll stomp on anyone who gets too far out of line, but other than that, their primary focus appears to be elsewhere. You can let the players hear about operations against the shapeshifters in the nearby national park, or actions taken to stop the outbreak of some plague. These Technos might even ask for help, once in a while — working at stopping the machinations of a crazed Marauder, or eliminating a particularly nasty Nephandi cult.

But there should always be a glimmer of doubt, of hidden malice. Are the Technos really nicer than the characters' masters said they would be, or is that Lady in Gray with her not-quite-convincing smile just luring them into a trap? Things are rarely as they seem with the Technocracy, and wheels within wheels rule their agendas.

Technocracy-Centered Games

Of course, sometimes you have to put on your shades, play the good guys and kick some Reality Deviant ass. That's where Technocracy chronicles come in. A Technocracy chronicle is a chance for people to dress to the nines, pull out their scientific magazine subscriptions and go hunting for freaky Things that Should Not Be. It's a game about being the Man and part of the System, but also about being a hero.

The Technocracy has its flaws and problems. At heart, the machine of the Union plans to go on, with agendas hard-wired centuries ago and policies that are obsolete and contradictory. Even the New World Order can't completely eliminate bureaucratic inefficiency — and Paradox, it seems, even strikes to cripple social orders. So it is that Technocracy characters could range from the cold, heartless agents who cover up supernatural events and bring out the inhumanly heavy firepower, to sympathetic, insightful researchers and protectors who want to make the world a better place. It's up to you to decide which style of play you prefer, or whether to have elements of both.

Included in this book are all the Conventions of the Technocracy, as well as some of their specific abilities and tools. With these, you can build your own Technocracy characters, whether as protagonists or villains.

Technocracy Op Teams

When you're organizing Technocracy groups, the smallest group is the op team — a squad formed to deal with specific emergencies or problems. Sometimes they're formed "on the fly" in response to an issue. In other cases, they're long-standing groups of allied Technocrats who combine skills to complete tasks, in an *X-Files*-like fashion.

The Technocracy can and does use normal people in its work. Indeed, many of the Union's agents don't even realize the nature of the conspiracy for which they work. Player groups, however, if they consist primarily of Enlightened individuals, probably know at least passingly of the Union and its organization. While they have day jobs and normal lives, they also do special tasks for the Technocracy to accomplish things that normal governments and agencies can't or won't deal with. More importantly, while some players might enjoy playing an unEnlightened operative, for most games you'll want to forge entire groups of Enlightened agents.

A Technocratic op team is roughly equivalent to a Tradition cabal: A group of mages that all work together for common goals. Op teams in turn report to higher-level facilities, such as Technocratic Constructs (bases). In many cases, higher-level administrators in the Union hand down specific goals and instructions. Some op teams, though, have wide leeway to investigate and resolve cases of Deviants on their own. As a Storyteller, you can be as controlling or as free-handed as you wish with your players, either keeping them in rigid lockstep or assuming that their superiors don't have the time or inclination to watch over them heavily.

Ultimately, the Technocracy operates under the auspices of Control. This shadowy group of anonymous figures generally sends its missives and directives — including updates to the Time Table, the plan for world innovation and influence — down through the many layers of Enlightened bureaucracy. In dire cases, someone from Control may become more directly involved, but in modern eras this is not only very rare but very difficult. Representatives of Control use anonymity as a shield and source of power; they distance themselves from problem situations, so as to avoid repercussions. As many agents of Control are literally hundreds of years old, thanks to biological and bionic engineering, and they reside in Constructs on the other side of the Dimensional Barrier (the Gauntlet), they don't make trips to Earth frivolously. With communication sporadic due to the strength of the Dimensional Barrier, field agents usually hear of Control only third-hand.

Location

The locales of a Technocracy-centered story are often very different than those of an ordinary **Laws of Ascension** game, although there is substantial overlap (and in a mixed game, of course, there will be locations fitting both/all sides). Technocracy games take place in science labs and starship bridges, in submarines exploring the Marianas Trench and Wall Street trading floors. They are often the antithesis of Tradition sites; where a Hermetic library is dusty and cramped, overflowing with ponderous tomes, the research library in a Progenitor lab complex is clean and tidy. It may be tightly organized, with roll-out shelving units to store data tapes and research files, or open and spacious, with plenty of room to slide one's chair out from the computer while contemplating the wrapping of an artificial protein.

In terms of actual locations for play, almost any university contains a wealth of spots that can be used. Actual chemistry or other science labs can be very cool places, but keep in mind the fact that they are often filled with active experiments, or very breakable, very expensive research equipment. Actual computer labs, server rooms or wiring closets are also probably off-limits, lest the wrath of a *real* sysadmin come down upon your head!

If you can't use those kinds of areas, there is still a lot you can do to simulate them. An ordinary classroom can be turned into a lab with the help of some tubing, a burned-out oscilloscope (or better, a working one), and some miscellaneous widgets and gadgets. Some working (but not irreplaceable) computers, gotten for cheap at a computer show or donated/ borrowed from the computer interest floor can help make a lounge look like the computer center in a laid-back Iteration X front company.

Of course, the Technocracy's agents also spend time in the field. All of the burned-out buildings, street games and glitzy clubs are open to them, where they'll be watching over humanity, taking notes and hunting down their adversaries.

Lingo and Jargon

While on a rules-specific level the Technocrats are ultimately mages, they don't see themselves that way and would never refer to themselves in such a fashion. For those used to the terms from **Laws of Ascension**, this handy guide gives you the ways that the Technocracy sees everything.

Arcane: "Cloaking." Some agents are so unobtrusive that it's almost impossible to track them. Others have specific programs at work to remove their identities from databases and records.

Arete: "Enlightenment." The stream of high-level thought and intuition combined that allows the operative to understand the universe on a fundamental level imperceptible to the common man.

***Avatar* Background:** "*Genius*." The subconscious parts of the mind that whisper hints and offer dreams to help break through the barriers of mundane science.

Avatar Essence: "Eidolon." The form that dreams and inspirations often take when they suddenly bubble forth to give new ideas.

Awakening: "Empowerment." The fundamental spark of Genius when the agent realizes his ability to change the world.

Chantry: "Construct." A place for operatives to gather and a central information source.

Consors: "Citizens." Useful aides and confederates (although they may not know it).

***Dream* Background**: "*Hypercram*." Technocrats don't connect to any sort of universal unconscious. Instead, they call upon the densely impacted knowledge imparted with their training, and sometimes formulate amazing leaps of deduction from it.

Focus: "Apparatus." A technological device that assists in the performance of Enlightened Science.

Horizon Realm: "Colony." A place in extradimensional space where the Technocracy maintains a stronghold.

Magic: "Inspired (or Enlightened) Science." Magic is an aberration. It doesn't work in the lab; it shouldn't work at all. True agents use their phenomenal knowledge of science and technology to "bend" the rules of the cosmos.

***Mentor* Background**: "*Patron*." A higher-ranking figure who offers advice and occasional behind-the-scenes aid.

Quintessence: "Prime energy." The whole universe vibrates on a subquantum level with the raw energy of Creation's frequency. Enlightened personnel with the right tools can sense and manipulate that energy, thus reinforcing or reversing aspects of the cosmos.

Sanctum: "Laboratory." A clean room with controlled conditions where experimental Inspired Science is almost guaranteed to work without drawbacks or hindrances.

Sleepers: "The Masses." Common people, unEnlightened.

Sorcerer: "Extraordinary Citizen." An otherwise unEnlightened person who still manages to follow and grasp certain specific Enlightened procedures, and can thereby perform certain very limited feats of Enlightened Science.

***Spirit* Sphere**: "*Dimensional Science*." Spirits are useless rubbish from superstitious cultures. Quantum physics shows that "spirits" are really emanations and creatures from other dimensions.

Tradition mage: "Superstitionist." Someone who believes in and uses the power of superstition. That it works for a few people is irrelevant; that such power is dangerous to humanity is of paramount concern.

Wonder: "*Device*." A tool that uses Enlightened Science so far beyond mundane technology that it seems impossible is a special *Device*. Sadly, such devices are often prone to malfunction and require lots of maintenance (i.e., they suffer Paradox).

A Note on Technocracy Costuming

Costuming is, of course, half the fun of a **Mind's Eye Theatre** game; dressing up appropriately for your character's role or assignment is incredibly cool, and can really set the mood or tone of your game. Despite this, unless you have access to a very private location, it is strongly recommended that you place a restriction on costuming to avoid any outfits that might be misconstrued. Sure, the actors on *La Femme Nikita* dress up in armored vests, tactical gear and balaclavas, but they have security on their shooting site to make sure nobody is unduly alarmed and calls the cops to report a terrorist incident. You probably don't. And the boys in blue get nervous when they hear about such things.

This doesn't mean you can't ever have costuming like that — just that you have to be very careful, moreso than usual. A bunch of folks in disparate (if weird) clothing talking about weird stuff doesn't attract *nearly* the amount of attention that a couple of people dressed in ninja outfits will, especially in light of the events of 2001. So, if you are going to allow that kind of costuming, make sure the owners of the site know about it ahead of time, control access to the location as much as you can, and make sure that the site's security and/or the local police are very clear about what is going on. If you have a member of your group who is actually a police officer, or member of the campus security, they should be the ones to explain what is happening. In any case, you should have a representative (that will usually be *you*, as the chief Storyteller) who has been listed as the contact person, and who is ready to field questions if the police *do* show up. That means, by the way, that you should leave the Merlin robes at home — a conservative suit is a lot more presentable.

Enlightened Science

Loopholes. Enlightened Science is all about loopholes.

Reality has laws. Energy flows from areas of high potential to areas of low potential. A dropped item falls. Whether these laws are just beliefs so deeply ingrained in the subconscious of humanity that even the Awakened are unable to flaunt them indiscriminately, or are actual objective laws of reality, is a subject of great debate. In the end, despite what scholars in the Technocracy and the Traditions may believe or argue, they are real. The laws are there, and the Technocracy wrote the definitions, the case law and the majority opinions.

So the Technocrats know the loopholes and exceptions. They know the sub-paragraphs and exit clauses. This gives the Technocracy their greatest advantage, and their greatest weakness. The average Tradition mage is willing to flaunt the rules of reality, bend them and break them at will. A Technocrat must work within the laws — indeed, most are unaware that they *can* break the rules. Only those Technocrats with very high Enlightenment scores are truly aware that reality is consensual, and that technology is merely magic gone static.

For most Technocrats, their foci are more than just convenient tools for concentrating their will — they *are* the means by which they alter the universe. Just as a soldier relies on his rifle to kill, Technocrats rely on their foci to create the Effects they use. An Iteration X cyborg without his plasma gun can no more blow up the car across the street than a soldier without a grenade launcher can. Enlightened Scientists are able to wrap their minds around concepts and ideas most Sleepers find difficult or impossible to understand, granting them the ability to work with technologies most simply cannot make work, regardless of training, but they still must have access to those technologies. So a Technocrat can't just wave a magic wand, mumble a few incantations, and cause a bouquet of roses to appear in his other hand. But he could trigger a holographic generator, or activate a sub-space wrinkle transporter, or use nanoassemblers to create the roses out of the elements located nearby and the effect would be the same, or nearly so.

The most advanced Technocrats finally begin to understand what it is to be Awakened in a consensual universe, but even they find it difficult to perform Enlightened Science outside the paradigms of technology and science. Their own beliefs and doctrines get in the way of their magics — without their tools, any Effects they try are automatically vulgar with witnesses, or simply fail outright.

Paradox and Technical Systems

Although most Technocrats will hotly deny it (speaking instead of "system crashes", "hardware failures", "genetic incompatibilities" and even "subconscious use of anti-psi"), technological systems are just as prone to Paradox effects, although the manifestations are usually less flamboyant than those suffered by the Tradition mages. (This, of course, depends largely on the Effect and the device used; Iteration X mages are known for their rather… pyrotechnic Paradox backlashes, as when a laser's super-conducting power cells backfire.)

Tools of the Technocracy

Almost any science is of use to some arm of the Technocracy, but these are some of the more commonly encountered ones.

Nanotechnology: Use of molecular-scale devices and engineering. This can create amazingly perfect materials, assemble or disassemble objects out of (or into) seeming nothingness, heal impossible wounds and all manner of other "miracles." Its drawbacks are heat, and the possibility of the nanobots getting out of control.

Hyperphysics: The study of extremely advanced (and theoretical, to modern scientists) physics involving alternate universes; "imaginary" numbers, materials and sub-atomic properties; and gross manipulation of the space-time continuum. The drawbacks to this science include the massive power requirements, and the extreme danger of most of the effects; one wrong step usually means death for the subject, experimenter and everyone else within a couple blocks of the experiment site.

Computers: Computers are everywhere in the Technocracy, and are used for everything from record-keeping to doing predictive analysis on future trends and overseeing routine surveillance gear. Of course, computers are only as perfect as their programmers.

Chemistry: Including medicines, drugs, poisons and many other substances. Advanced fuels, plastics and other materials, neurotoxins, explosives and super-adhesives are all some of the tools chemistry makes possible. Drawbacks include the difficulty of synthesizing many of these compounds, the hazards in storing and shipping them, the sheer cost of manufacturing and their side-effects.

Memetics: The science of ideas and thought constructs. Memes are ideas or concepts that are infectious; they can spread, replicate, "breed" with other memes to create new ideas; they can even be inoculated against, engineered and isolated. Some examples are catchy songs, advertising logos, slogans, urban myths and ideologies (most -isms are complexes of interrelated memes). This is different from psionics, below, in that a meme doesn't have to be delivered telepathically, and someone with strong mental defenses may still be susceptible to attacks by hostile memes.

Physics: More conventional studies than hyperphysics, in general. Room temperature superconductors, high-energy lasers and plasma, magnetic acceleration systems, sonic fields, advanced aerodynamics and many other advances. Paradox tends to be messy and involve a lot of exploding stuff — most Technocracy physics devices pack a lot of power into a fairly small space.

Psionics: A controversial field of study in the Technocracy, but one with slowly gaining popularity. NWO agents use telepathy to ferret out secrets, projective empathy (and sub-sonic sound waves) to give themselves the sense of unease and dread that surrounds them, and mind shields to keep unwanted intruders out of their cerebrums. Progenitors hold up psionics as the ultimate perfection of the mind. Still, psionics smacks of magic in the eyes of many (including most in Iteration X), and its study, while not banned, is subject to more than the usual levels of oversight.

Genetic Engineering: Along with its close cousin cloning, genetics is the home ground of the Progenitors. With the right bit of resquencing, a Gengineer can create a new protein for use in nanotechnology, a microbe that deposits titanium in a particular pattern when it dies, or a supervirus. Larger-scale operations are also possible; cloned dinosaurs and other extinct creatures have been kept in isolated zoological research centers, and stranger creations (called Chimera) have been created, although their lifespans are usually quite short, for reasons that have yet to be determined.

Chaos Math/Complexity: Chaos math is the study of inherently unstable or unpredictable systems. The classic example of this is meteorology; the planet is so large, and so many factors involved in the weather, that it is impossible to predict it beyond a certain set of general trends, and very short-scale predictions of limited accuracy. Fractals are another example of chaos theory. An understanding of how complex systems work, what can be predicted and what can't, how trends work, and where the borderline between linear, predictable systems and nonlinear, complex systems falls is vital to almost all aspects of the Technocracy, but the NWO and Syndicate make perhaps the most direct applications of these theories.

Cybernetics: At its most fundamental level, cybernetics is the study of augmenting or enhancing the human body with mechanical systems; a pair of glasses might be considered a cybernetic device. More commonly, however, this field of study involves implanted systems, prosthetic replacements and augmentations.

Iteration X

The earliest legends speak of smiths and craftsmen able to build tools and weapons that were impossibly strong, light or sharp — these were the predecessors to the modern Iteration X. The Artificers (also known as the High Artisans) could be found building weapons of war for Thothmes in Egypt, steam-powered toys in Greece and the great waterworks of Rome. During the "Dark Ages", their wonders delighted the courts of Arabia and Persia, and fortified the walls of Byzantium. The coming of the Renaissance saw the High Artisans brought to new heights of power. They joined the Order of Reason, and their mechanisms, printing presses, gunpowder weapons, clockwork devices and mathematics helped create new ideas about civilization, science and technology, laying the groundwork for an ideal of science and rationality that persists to this day. The hidden lords of the Industrial Revolution, the High Artisans grew increasingly fascinated with the mechanical computing engines first prototyped by Charles Babbage, revising and improving them until, in an unknown iteration, one achieved sentience. In overjoyed celebration, the High Artisans renamed themselves "Iteration X", in honor of their success.

A Convention composed of engineers, mathematicians, physicists and computer scientists and programmers, for many years ItX provided the weapons (and weapon carriers) of the Technocracy. HIT-Marks and cyborgs provided shock troops, and ItX-designed sidearms and defenses provided more fragile agents (Enlightened or not) with the firepower they needed to pursue the Pogrom. Iteration X was one of the most fervent pursuers of the assault on the Traditions, tracking down and destroying mages and Chantries with a brutality that disturbed even their peers in the Union. Tradition rumors (and Technocracy turncoats) speak of massive slave labor camps outside the Barrier, and Tradition mages (or parts of them) being converted into killer cyborgs and turned against their former allies. On the flip side, the Iterators contend that they've neither the inclination nor the budget to pursue such tremendously costly and dubious ventures; besides, why turn someone into a slave in a Construct when a couple of simple chips in the head will let the person go back to a safe, normal, productive and non-Deviant lifestyle?

Iteration X theoretically follows a strict hierarchy of command and control, deviated from only in extreme situations. At the bottom of the Convention are the unEnlightened *proles*, who take care of most of the day-to-day tasks. Ranging from lab assistants, graduate students and some professors, IT professionals to secretaries, security officers, technicians and maintenance personnel (many of them not even aware of what they are part of), proles also form the core memberships of labor unions (particularly in technological fields), Internet discussion and special interest groups, and professional organizations. Especially gifted members (including Enlightened Scientists, but also Extraordinary Citizens and Sleeper scientists or researchers of unusual merit) are recruited as *Ciphers*, and placed in a grueling training program. Ciphers are often unaware they have been recruited; they find themselves working on demanding jobs in frustrating projects, sent to far-away cities and forced to live in motels, or stuck with incredible classloads under dictatorial professors. Those who persevere are promoted to the status of *Armature*, the lowest actual rank in the Convention. Until recently, all Armatures, regardless of their final position or calling, served for a time in a front line combat unit; while this practice has fallen out of favor, most Armatures receive at least some basic combat training.

Since Earth lost contact with the Union's extraterrestrial holdings, and the end of the Pogrom, Iteration X has undergone a change that many in the Technocracy see as for the better. Younger, more flexible programmers and Armatures are taking charge of the Union's Earthbound operations, bringing with them new ideas about how the Convention should proceed and what sciences are important. Where many of the higher-ranking members of the Convention frowned on nanotechnology, quantum physics and other esoteric studies, preferring the stability and predictability of Newtonian physics, younger members thrive on the new sciences. A subscription to *Paradigma*, (the newsletter and research journal of the Sons of Ether) has for many years been considered a minor breach of Protocol, but rumors circulate that some Armatures may be (or already are) seeking closer ties with their Tradition cousins, particularly the younger generation of Etherites, which is more concerned with cutting-edge sciences and alternate theories, and less with etherships and radium projectors. Another rumor, that a Virtual Adept is nothing more than an Xer on the weekends, may have more truth to it; the Virtual Adepts and Iteration X have always had common interests, even after the Adepts left the Union.

Roleplaying Hints: Not every Iteration X member is a rigid-thinking automaton under constant surveillance by her implants and following pre-programmed orders, despite what Tradition propaganda

and Technocracy lore would have some believe. The average Armature is a low-ranking scientist, computer technician, server administrator, programmer or other high-tech professional.

Specialty Sphere: *Matter*

Common Foci: Sensor gear, lab equipment, cybernetic systems, computers, robots, nanotechnology, hyperphysics, energy weapons

Convention Advantage: Hardware Supremacy

Iterators have access to the best hardware available — and if they don't have it, they can make it. All Iterators have two free levels to split between *Enhancements* and *Devices* as desired; these can be added to levels taken as Backgrounds or with free Traits or experience, up to the usual limit.

An Iterator's hardware familiarity and knowledge also translates into real competence in dealing with modern technology. Once per session, an Iterator can make a free special retest when coaxing performance out of some piece of technology, be it a Device or a mundane bit of tech. This doesn't apply to magical challenges (it can't be used to retest an Enlightenment test) but does give an Iterator an edge on *Computer* and *Technology* challenges, even if the Iterator doesn't have a lot of personal experience with the items in question.

Convention Disadvantage: Dimensional Incompetence

For many years, members of Iteration X were forbidden to learn the Sphere of *Dimensional Science* (*Spirit*). While the lack of contact with Autocthonia (the home of Iteration X's vaunted sentient Computer and controller) has allowed some adventurous members to take tutelage from members of the Void Engineers or the NWO, they still find this path of study a difficult one. Members of Iteration X may not begin game play with this Sphere, and pay double to acquire levels or rotes using it.

Additionally, Iterators typically have some sort of monitoring implant hand-in-hand with their usual technological wonders. Assume that at any time an Iterator's location can be found (unless magically shielded) by his superiors, so he'd better not screw up.

Methodologies

BioMechanics — Cybernetic researchers and bionic inventors. These Iterators create the hardware and implants that go into Technocratic operatives, especially in conjunction with the Progenitors.

Statisticians — Mathematicians and hyperphysicists who delve into abstract models of the universe.

Time- Motion Managers — Hyperefficient managers and overseers who compute time tables, determine ratios of labor to loss and resolve issues in projects, as well as working on some levels of macrotechnology. TM Managers use their sciences to keep projects working as well-oiled as the machines they build.

New World Order

Historically, the New World Order's functional roots seem quite recent compared to the rest of the Technocracy — records claim that Queen Victoria created the NWO by fiat as a bureaucracy to deal with the transition of government from a religious, divinely backed edifice to an enlightened, reasoned nation-state. Conspirators point out, though, that the Order has roots stretching back to such early groups as the Cabal of Pure Thought, a religious conspiracy devoted to the spread of orthodoxy under one united church. Noting the NWO's penchant for advanced planning and political manipulation, a few pundits claim that the group actually socially re-engineered itself from its roots as a religious conspiracy so that it could purge divisive or conservative elements and create its own rebirth. Regardless of the truth, NWO historians consider the matter closed. Drawing inspiration from such historical figures as Hammurabi and his famous legal code, or Confucius and his Analects, the NWO points out that so long as humans have organized in groups, they've always had governments, information disseminators, educators and secrets. From such roots comes the New World Order, but only the Order's highest academics can tell where it'll go.

The New World Order oversees the dissemination of information in all its forms and the structures that build around that information. Governments, academies and media outlets all hover along the NWO's fringe of influence. Let the Syndicate concentrate on the buying and selling — the NWO focuses on those things that people don't buy, on public goods and externalities like infrastructure or the moral ambiguity of legal codes. Other Conventions provide hard-tech while the NWO collates historical information, makes projections for future society, arranges hyperefficient bureaucracy and political communication, streamlines dissemination and education procedures, and locks away the things that people don't need to know about. Hand-in-hand with these programs are the editation projects to rewrite history to the Technocracy's liking, removing all "superstitious" viewpoints that would hinder the Union's goals, and the political projects to carefully balance world development in hopes of raising the Masses' intelligence and education to a less dangerous level. Tradition mages speak fearfully of NWO's practiced conditioning techniques: according to rumor, the appearance of black-suited agents means that someone will disappear soon after with no records left. Most fearsomely, the NWO does oversee psychological conditioning, and their special projects in the halls of

Room 101 provide whispered, terrifying stories. Those who return from such conditioning sessions don't need any technological alterations to their minds or bodies — the advanced psychology of the NWO turns traitors into loyalists, rebels into conformists and the most staunch Traditionalist into a Technocratic operative.

As the masters of bureaucracy, the New World Order oversees communication not only internally but among the other divisions of the Technocracy. New recruits and education programs most often form out of the NWO's advance planning. Of course, other Conventions suspect that NWO education indoctrinates agents with hidden loyalties, but the NWO's psychology also insures that such recruits often have very useful talents — the NWO knows how to pick them. UnEnlightened recruits fall into the category of *Sympathizers*, including everything from trained spies to the occasional janitor who keeps an ear out. Those who move up in the Convention gain prestige and influence according to their pursuits: Academics have limited pull but can set policy with their papers and reports, while media pundits exert their ties on the Masses subtly. The most infamous ranking agents are the Men in Black, Enlightened field operatives (or sometimes clones or constructs) who wear the signature black suit, black tie, black shoes and shades and have all the influence one would expect of a covert government operative. The top of the NWO hierarchy lies with the mysterious Gray Men and Men in White, who oversee the Convention as a whole and maintain orthodoxy (such as it is in a non-religious organization) among the entire Union.

The modern New World Order always rides the forefront of social change. Why not, with advanced social sciences 50 or a hundred years ahead of the current human condition? This isn't to say that they're perfect; after all, they couldn't predict the Technocracy's current problems, nor can they always model the vagaries of Tradition mages or even the occasional Deviant moving among the Masses. Some up-and-coming operatives suspect that perhaps humanity is simply too complex to understand completely; the human spirit can't be bounded so easily. With this in mind, field agents operate with greater personal discretion, so that they can bring their own intuition to bear on rapidly changing, unpredictable situations. Upper-level operatives — those that remain and keep in touch — offer the idea that the NWO should be guides, not police, in the quest to shepherd humanity to a better social state. Ethics, once considered a marginalized study that could be brought down to a calculable state, now demands that perhaps some compromises *aren't* worth it.

Roleplaying Hints: NWO operatives are savvy, alert and in charge. Although there's some room for personal eccentricities, all NWO operatives give off the impression that they've already laid plans and contingencies for every possibility. With their superlative understanding of ethics, social evolution and information flow, agents constantly and intuitively put together disparate pieces of a scene to arrive at an overarching picture of the dynamics at work behind it. NWO members include everything from teachers and reporters to historians, politicians, spies, spin doctors and psychologists.

Specialty Sphere: *Mind*

Common Foci: Government ID badges, black suits, authoritarian behaviors ("It's a matter of national security"), research papers, historical records, spy gadgets

Convention Advantage: Information is Power

New World Order agents have access to some of the best information sources in human existence, and some can even open rare files of historical import that have long since been sealed away from the public eye. Whether by calling in government favors or digging through academic paperwork, an operative can find information on nearly any topic. Every agent has two free levels in any combination of the following Backgrounds: *Contacts*, Influence: *Media* or Influence: *Espionage*.

Furthermore, the authoritarian and knowledgeable position of NWO agents places them regularly at the top of the chain for information retrieval. Information truly is power. Once per session, an agent can do a background check on a piece of information gleaned from a *Contact* or Influence (it doesn't even have to have been one of the agent's *Contacts* or Influences, if someone else cooperates). The agent automatically determines whether the information is true or a deliberate falsehood. This doesn't necessarily tell if it's *accurate*, but will immediately tell if a *Contact* or Influence is giving incorrect information or if the information has been tampered with.

Convention Disadvantage: Who Watches the Watchers?

Sometimes politicking gets in the way of free information flow. Other times, a superior determines that it's "for the greater good" that certain files don't make it out, or that a given agent winds up on a hit list for learning things better left unknown. NWO agents must step carefully, because their Convention monitors them just as much as it monitors everyone else. Somewhere, somebody has a record of everything an agent does on a mission — including every screw-up. Iterators might have some sort of locator beacon, but the NWO agent has something arguably worse: a permanent record.

Any NWO operative of higher rank than the character (typically, someone with higher Enlightenment and a commensurate posting in the Convention) can use *every Negative Reputation Trait the character has ever had* in any Social Challenge against the character.

Agents who rack up too many bad missions on their records (i.e., too many Negative Traits, at the Storyteller's discretion) may be retired to desk jobs (taken out of active duty and play).

Methodologies

Ivory Tower — Academics and historians who perform pure research and soft science. The Ivory Tower intellectuals may seem distant from worldly affairs, but have a firm handle on the history and psychology behind the world's events.

Operatives — The feared Men in Black work as troubleshooters, taking care of problem elements. Their higher-level Gray Men and Men in White coordinate government sub-agencies and special policing units to keep a net of legal influence throughout the civilized world.

Watchers — Mass media and instant information merge into a hyperattenuated picture of the world, one that the Masses consume readily. The Watchers observe and sometimes manipulate this process to keep an eye out for social developments and nudge the public's opinions.

PROGENITORS

Early man lived in constant fear of the mystery of death. Around every corner waited disease, accidental injury, age and eventually the inevitable end. At first, humanity sought spiritual recourse from rigors that couldn't be avoided, constructing elaborate mystical causes for sickness and life. The blossoming of reason, though, bent Mankind to study of the self, which in turn led to the realization that perhaps some elements of the life process could be controlled. Famine could be warded off with the cultivation of crops and animals. Disease could be halted with sanitation and treatment. Certain herbs and practices reversed symptoms and even brought wellness where before only slow death lay. From these beginnings sprang the Cosians, researchers into the process of life and all of its permutations. At first simple physicians, the Cosians quickly took to the study of all biological phenomena. As the Enlightened communities developed germ theory, cell theory, understanding of herbalism and pharmacology, and the repeatable benefits of trauma care, the science of medicine came to fruition. At length, these researchers reached for the ultimate question: Where does life come from? How does it persist? In seeking the answers, they became the Progenitors, the scientists and doctors who sustain — and create — life.

As one would expect of a medically oriented Convention, the Progenitors count doctors, research physicians, pharmacologists and psychiatrists among their numbers. Less common but no less important are paleontologists, xenobiologists, botanists and other researchers who contribute to the understanding of extinct creatures, extradimensional entities and the plants and animals that surround the human world. Through their studies, the Progenitors insure health and long life; their regular treatments can cure grievous injuries, and even field medicines greatly improve the survival chances of young Technocratic operatives. High-ranking Technocrats undergo special procedures to extend their lifespans, effectively renewing their flesh and returning youth to the mind. Even the Masses benefit; Progenitors working in research hospitals turn their talents to saving all lives, and their work often slowly filters into the medical community. Perhaps more frighteningly, the Convention experiments with the alteration and synthetic augmentation of living beings, and can and does create mutated animals, retroviruses that can re-engineer a human's protein processes to change the body's chemistry, or even clones sprung from a single sample of an individual. Rumor holds that many otherwise disabled agents or captured enemies are replaced with clones, and that the Progenitors hold a special protein combination that causes such copies to disintegrate quickly with a single application — or, equally disturbingly, that Progenitor projects might contain the secrets to reversing any of their biological engineering. Such thoughts do not comfort the agents who rely on Progenitor techniques for their continued health and youth.

Progenitor ranks follow the same academic mindset that rules the rest of the Convention. While it's possible for someone without a professorial appointment or formal advanced degree to hold authority, it's rare; such highly Enlightened individuals usually learn to work within the system, at least for appearance's sake. At the low end, *Street Ops*, *Recruiters* and *Technicians* handle the day-to-day maintenance of the Convention, doing everything from working at public clinics to maintaining hospital machinery or serving as interns. Enlightened operatives who show promise generally become *Students* under an experienced Progenitor; these students participate in fieldwork and hone a research thesis, just like any other graduate student at a university. The difference lies in the nature of the field work, which can include research on alien or Deviant creatures and high-security secret medical technology. A surviving Student whose thesis passes muster goes on to become a *Research Assistant*, usually posted to a specific Construct for continued training, but given greater discretion to pursue personal projects. Some RAs instead continue field work, to support their own theories, to gather specimens or just to stay out of the lab. *Primary Investigators* and *Research Directors* operate at the top rungs; the PIs follow through on important topics of research, using their formidable Enlightenment to bring unique solutions to bear, while the RDs decide on the up-and-coming technologies to study. RDs also handle all of the Technocracy-related political maneuvering, since they have the long overview of the Convention's work. The only ones above the RDs are the Progenitor elements associated with Control, the *Administration* — who have all the qualities one would expect of hospital administrators who're seen only through paperwork, intermediaries and their special operatives for dealing with emergency situations ("Damage Control" teams).

The Progenitors have fortunately undergone a hefty shift in policy over the last few years. Originally, the modern Administration seemed bent on the creation of genegineered creatures, augmented clones and tailored viruses almost purely out of some grotesque "pure research" directive. Doubtless some of this had to do with the fact that Progenitor Administrators had an effective life expectancy outstripping anything else in the Technocracy; the heads of the Convention were, quite literally, old-school physicians from the Renaissance, still obsessed with the creation of creatures and with raw experimentation as compared to logical, scientific medical development. With the Administration out of the picture, the Progenitor RDs and, in some cases, PIs have taken the initiative to re-organize their departments for specialized research in different areas of personal interest. A Progenitor Student is unlikely to see or engineer some sort of monstrous beast unless it's for specific study; disease programs initially made for bio-war have turned into pathogen control centers. While the Convention can and does still perform biological augmentation for combat operatives, the focus of the vast majority of Progenitor work now lies directly in line with improving the human condition and understanding the processes of life. Many Progenitors now openly assert that this is where it should've been all along.

Roleplaying Hints: Fully 95 percent of Progenitors hail from experienced medical academic backgrounds, and it shows. Most are affluent, fit and just a little bit nerdy — not too much contact with people outside the lab for 30 years, after all. Many have the glazed, stressed-out look of an overworked medical intern, but their Enlightenment makes them sharp and steady when it comes to medical matters.

Specialty Sphere: *Life*

Common Foci: Medical equipment, surgical tools, retroviruses, CHON (carbon-hydrogen-oxygen-nitrogen — the basis of living proteins) reservoirs, genegineering, grafts, psionic enhancements

Convention Advantage: Better Living Through Chemistry

Access to pharmacoepia, retroviral engineering, protease inhibitors and catalysts, grafts, cloned transplants and any number of minor medical miracles gives Progenitors a leg (or two) up on physical health and recovery. Due to minor enhancements, body tailoring and just darn good medical care, a Progenitor heals all damage as if it were one health level less severe for time purposes. (This is 10 minutes/ one hour for the Bruised level).

A Progenitor earns one level of *Medicine* Ability and one level of Influence: *Medicine* as a by-product of working in university medical departments for so long.

Convention Disadvantage: Stuck in the Lab

Progenitors, more than just about any other Conventioneers, spend their days (and nights, and weekends) stuck in the lab. Earning an M.D. is taxing enough, but Students must prove themselves above and beyond the "normal" medical crew. Progenitors cannot begin play with more than two Abilities outside their medical study profile. This effectively limits Progenitors to mostly having *Academics*, *Biotech*, *Hypertech*, *Medicine*, *Research*, *Science* and *Technology*. Furthermore, no Ability can ever be raised above the level of the highest of these — thus, if a Progenitor wants to learn five levels of an Ability, he must first learn five levels in one of his university disciplines (most likely *Medicine*).

Methodologies

Forced Adaptation and Clone Alteration Developmental Eugenecists (FAÇADE Engineers) — Cloning experts who produce tissue, organs and entire bodies. These clones can, with Enlightened Science, even take on the memories of their originals, thereby working as replacement bodies or spies, and also serve as raw meat for manufacture of HIT-Marks and low-grade Men in Black. FAÇADE Engineers also perform surgery and trauma care.

Genegineers — Specialists in genetic manipulation and protein recombination. The creations of the Genegineers are born better, faster and stronger, but often have unforeseen chaotic side-effects (from Paradox). Both monsters and supermen come from these labs. The sub-division of Damage Control specifically designs bio-weapons, especially for use against Reality Deviants.

Pharmacopoeists — Chemists and biologists who examine the interaction of the human body with outside influences and substances. Anything from herbalism to high-tech pharmaceuticals falls under this Methodology's purview. Some Pharmacopoeists have also started researching the interconnectedness of macro-scale ecology and the human place in the living world (or "Gaia-cosm," as some refer to it — out of earshot of the New World Order, of course).

Syndicate

"What do you want?" is a signature question of the Syndicate. It's all about money, this Convention claims — or, at least, about what passes for money. From crude barter to the innovation of coins, then paper money, and finally modern credit and debit, the traders and financiers have been the grease that lubricated human progress. Medieval guildsmen protecting their livelihood formed trade consortiums to guarantee their product quality and training; later, these High Guilds became powerhouses of the Renaissance, issuing letters of credit that could be cashed in faraway cities. Hard currency gave way to portable paper with no intrinsic value; only the value that people perceived in an otherwise worthless scrap propped up emerging economies. Finally, people accepted even invisible currency: the idea of notes or cards that symbolized not only a fixed amount but a potential to earn or a chance to spend. The transaction of humanity culminates in the Syndicate, which places a value on everything and pushes humanity to a society where every trade registers in ephemeral energy that tracks everyone's wants and needs.

Up front, the Syndicate sounds like a cartel — criminals and money men, shady dealers and con artists. The true Syndicate agent realizes, though, that only the desperate trade with criminals; to become a true connoisseur of money, one must earn trust. That makes the high-profile Syndicateers bond traders, international bankers and investors, but also marketing reps, empowerment speakers, even social commentators. Other Conventions make things, but it's the Syndicate that provides the luxury of doing so: Without the patronage of the purse-strings, there's no funding for expensive toys. The Syndicate knows who's buying what, be it mundane or Enlightened, and they hold the disbursements for many of the Union's most important projects. While some operatives might complain that this unfairly burdens their research with Syndicate agendas, the Syndicate itself wisely points out that money doesn't come from nowhere, even with Enlightened Science. The Syndicate's top representatives can smooth out even the most ruffled feathers, and in conjunction with the rest of the Union, influence the market pricing and introduction of new technology — as well as buying off politicians and leveraging out entire corporations or countries.

Corporate mentality dominates the Syndicate. As a result, the bottom ranks are those who rely on the good graces of the company: the *Providers*, who work indirectly for the Syndicate in return for a paycheck that goes back into the Syndicate's pockets through debts and bills. Those who manage to turn around their financial fortunes and realize their ability to control transactions may rise to become *Associates*, who are actual (very junior) partners in the Syndicate's pseudo-corporate hierarchy. Associates handle day-to-day business for the Syndicate, often working mundane jobs while occasionally doing side work coordinating larger projects or making sure that a specific account has just the right delay or expedite to meet the requests of a supervisor in the Convention. Associates who continually show not only financial acumen but also social skill move up to *Management*, and take on responsibilities for overseeing entire Syndicate accounts, including some of the funding for extra-Convention projects run by the Union. Managers have wide-ranging discretionary funding and connections throughout dozens of companies and projects of all sizes. Above Management are the *Chairmen* and *Vice-Presidents of Operations*; the former set continental policies and hold voting power over proposed projects, while the latter make up the Syndicate's contribution to Control and see to the continued financial development of human economic systems.

While some people might accuse the Syndicate of leeching off productive angles of society, the Syndicate itself points out that all human behavior comes down to trades. Energy is expended in the pursuits of survival, entertainment and procreation; that energy can be measured and traded, assigned to the same items that might fulfill those same desires. The modern Syndicate isn't about money or debt, argue its agents: It's about calculating that exchange of energy, figuring out how to evaluate efficiencies and place the most favorable transactions in places where they'll reap the most output. Forget leveraged buyouts with stocks and holding debt over the heads of unwilling accomplices — the real race now is to form an adaptable, imaginary currency that can describe everything humans might trade without needing any solid, stealable form.

Roleplaying Hints: Syndicate agents excel not only in the use of money, but also in the social circumstances of the transaction. That means they're poised, slick and able to sell anything — be it an item or a story — at a moment's notice. Syndicateers recognize the value of first impressions and surroundings, and tend to place themselves in situations where they can make an impression through the exercise of their incredible finances.

Specialty Sphere: *Entropy*

Common Foci: Credit cards, cell phones, wads of money, electronic debit systems, gadgets bought from other Conventions, financial reports, economic predictions

Convention Advantage: Money, Money, Money

Since the Syndicate's livelihood hinges on money, every Syndicate agent learns to handle and take charge of personal finance early on. A Syndicate operative has *at least* one level of *Finance* Ability and one level of the *Resources* Background; most have extensive *Resources* beyond this as well.

Because of their incredible money and their ability to use it well, Syndicate ops who have access to their *Resources* can cash in levels of that Background for extra Traits in a Social Challenge. Treat this as a normal expenditure of *Resources*, so money spent this way is used up for the game session. Each Background level grants one extra Social Trait, and this can be used to initiate a Social Challenge, too; even if the challenge is lost, the money is simply spent, and the *Resources* are used for the session but available again at the next game. The Syndicate op doesn't have to use all *Resources* at one time, but can only declare their use before the challenge is entered — no fair swinging the vote in mid-stride; you either committed your *Resources* or you didn't. (This typically takes the form of a challenge like "I use my incredible *Resources* to convince you to see things my way.")

Convention Disadvantage: Everybody Hates Marketing

Because of their rumored belief that everyone can be bought, many people consider the Syndicate's agents little more than sleazy hucksters (if well-dressed, well-mannered sleazy hucksters). Even the Syndicate's social acumen still only gives them the ability to put off this impression in person, and with effort; the Syndicate is often the target of all sorts of malicious rumors and slander when other Conventions think that nobody's listening.

Due to the Syndicate's extensive bad rep (a lot of it earned), all Syndicate agents count as having one less Reputation Trait with all other Conventions. A Syndicate op can never gain free access to other Conventions' materials and research — the operative must always use *Resources* or equivalent trade (probably calculated with the *Finance* Ability); none of the other Conventions will give anything away for free. They'll only grudgingly part with their hard work, and then only for the right price. Of course, a Syndicate agent knows that everyone has a price and excels in figuring it out....

Methodologies

Disbursements — As the credit holders for the entire Union, the Disbursements division sees to funding of all important projects and can halt or forward nearly anything with its stamp of approval. Every erg of transacted energy that makes its way to the Union traces through some accounting line at Disbursements. These financiers thus have the power to make or break Technocracy projects, regardless of what the other Conventions might consider critical or assured.

Enforcers — Any good company needs security, and any criminal organization needs muscle. The Syndicate is both, so the Enforcers serve double duty, from repo men to highly trained guards to simple thugs. Enforcers make sure that people respect the power of the Syndicate and of money, and that the bills are paid on time.

Financiers — While Disbursements handles internal Technocracy funding, the Financiers carefully adjust the world of the Masses. These super-economists see to the development of national policy, the fate of megacorporations and the future of banking. Their wide-ranging vision allows them to take in the economic state of the world and make subtle manipulations for long-term benefits.

Media Control — There's no sale when there's no market. Media Control handles the packaging and perception angle of everything that the Syndicate and Technocracy sells. From personal guarantees to blazing advertisements, Media Control ensures that people *want* to buy.

Special Projects Division — Money may not buy everything, but it buys a hell of a lot, including some impressive toys. Although the Syndicate must rely on the technologies of other Conventions for hardware, the Special Projects Division sees to the acquisition of promising and unique technologies from outside the Technocracy sphere. This gives the Syndicate access to strange devices or special patents that other Conventions don't invent. In some cases, this means dealing with companies that have decidedly Deviant bents, but as long as the money is good and the product is on time, nobody (in the Syndicate, anyway) is complaining.

Void Engineers

To touch the stars, to ascend the brightest heaven of invention (in a paraphrase of Shakespeare) — the motive of exploration is so deep that it touches a chord in the human soul that stirs poetry and grandeur. Whether from the first primal man who decided to see what was over the next hill, or the one who wanted to conquer the night with fire, the Void Engineers represent all the impulses to explore the world and make it safe for humanity. Travel, once a dire hazard and improbable difficulty, bent to the advent of maps, horses, sailing ships — and later, to the automobile, submarines and even spacecraft. The Void Engineers oversaw it all. As the Celestial Masters and the Void Seekers of the Renaissance, they sought the twin goals of expanding knowledge of the terrestrial sphere and reaching for the heavens. They achieved both goals; their early ships set down the oceans and islands into static form, making maps that anyone could use to aid travel. Their skyriggers and, later, aircraft reached up into the ether and the Void, and although they found many horrors, they also found the courage to continue exploring in places where Man had no right to tread. Be it in the depths of the ocean, the darkest recesses of the Earth, the coldest reaches of space or the chaotic realms of other dimensions, the Void Engineers have a system to map it, understand it and — perhaps — to some day make it safe and habitable for Mankind.

The split between support structure and field work is pronounced among the Void Engineers, but nobody enters the Convention without a passion for its work. Indeed, many Conventioneers relegated to support technologies and mission control long for the chance to explore and do so vicariously through their work. The actual explorers and fighters of the Convention are some of the toughest men and women around. They must be capable of surviving in environments inimical to humanity, of adapting and working with incredible precision, since the slightest error could be fatal. Worse still, terrible *things* lurk beyond the Dimensional Barrier, and it's the duty of the Void Engineers not only to seek out those other dimensions but to protect the Earth from the things that would come back. For this reason, the Convention includes not only the astronauts and technicians that so many associate with it, but also land-based travelers, cartographers, communications engineers, vehicle mechanics, soldiers, physicists and propulsion scientists.

Due to the irrepressible nature of the Engineers — everyone would be in the field, all the time, if they could — relations are relaxed;

protocol is informal, except when on task in the field. There's no room for questioning hierarchy when a single slip can kill everyone, after all. Internally, low-ranking personnel are *Cadets*; they learn the ropes, help with projections for future missions, study engineering and try to make themselves useful while they absorb the knowledge they'll need later. Cadets graduate into *Officers*, who're informally classed as *Enforcers* (who perform heavy combat and defense), *Explorers* (who head out to make maps of new places), *Investigators* (who look into the scientific repercussions of strange places) and *Researchers* (who develop new technology for travel). Those Engineers with a desire for greater responsibility move up to the rank of *Coordinators*, who act as command staff for entire mission teams, stations or ships. Above this is the "desk job" that all pilots dread, the *DSEATC: Dimensional Science Evaluation and Training Committee*. Since extradimensional travel is the most hazardous of the Void Engineers' jobs, only the most dedicated and experienced Engineers have the authority to oversee who undertakes *Dimensional Science* training and travel.

The Void Engineers have always had a spark of inspiration that sometimes seems lacking from other Conventions. Their maverick attitudes and drive to see new, wondrous things beyond human explanation paint them as loose cannons, but also as visionaries. Engineers often see the other Conventions as overly concerned with humanity — there's a whole cosmos out there, and it's too damn big to stay focused on such a small subject! On the flip side, the other Conventions argue that they must solve humanity's problems before the species is ready for the true jump into transplanetary (and transdimensional) civilization. Void Engineers also have contact with extra-planetary entities, and sometimes this leaves them a little bit changed, and usually not for the better. The rest of the Union keeps a close eye on the Engineers to make sure that the Deviants beyond the Barrier don't push the Engineers into wholesale uncontrollability.

Roleplaying Hints: Void Engineers run the gamut from science-oriented professor/ flight controller to heroic explorer/ captain. Most of them radiate a raw, tireless stamina. It's not enough to extrapolate; one must *see* for oneself all the variety the world and the universe has to offer. Of course, it's a dangerous world out there, so it's up to the Engineers to be ready as the first line of defense, too. No nonsense, no margin for error, but a whole lot of enthusiasm and attitude.

Specialty Sphere: *Correspondence*

Common Foci: Travel equipment, vehicles, space gear, measuring instruments, specially made jumpsuits, maps, planetary charts and programs, extrapolation models

Convention Advantage: Hardened Travelers

The irrepressible urge to explore causes Void Engineers to develop a strong survival instinct and a keen insight into their environment. Even those who stay behind often must react on a moment's notice to crisis situations, all the better to provide solutions to teams that could otherwise be stranded in inaccessible, hostile areas. A Void Engineer has two free Traits from the following list: *Alertness*, *Athletics*, *Computer*, *Influence: Transportation*, *Science*, *Survival* or *Technology*. The Void Engineer must take two separate Traits; both levels can't be used in the same one.

As the premier experts in *Dimensional Science*, all Void Engineers treat the Dimensional Barrier (the Gauntlet) as two Traits lower for themselves and their Effects.

Convention Disadvantage: Space Case

Long-term travel in strange conditions with highly technical equipment causes many Void Engineers to lose sight of what does and doesn't work quite right on Terra Firma. A Void Engineer in mundane society gains one Paradox for performing a coincidental Effect in front of Sleepers, although this penalty can't accrue more than once per scene (all further coincidental Effects really are coincidental). This is because the Void Engineer uses Procedures or Apparatuses that are obviously strange, responds to information he couldn't plausibly know, and otherwise exhibits mannerisms that clearly show to "normal people" that the Technocrat is up to something weird.

Methodologies

Border Corps Division — The vaunted "space Marines" who defend Earth against invaders from space or other dimensions. These tough-as-nails troopers also defend ships and Constructs; in contrast to the usual stereotype of soldiers, they're not only excellent combatants, but also must be fully skilled in all the technologies necessary to survive in hostile turf. The Border Corps Division's troops are well-trained crack survivors who can think with the best of them and outfight the best, too.

Earth Frontier Division — From the deep seas to the arctic reaches to the steaming jungles, the Earth Frontier Division explorers continue the job of mapping out the most inaccessible regions of the world. They experiment with novelties such as underwater habitations or long-range underground travel routes.

Neutralization Specialization Corps — Some extradimensional entities seem to be beings of pure energy, yet they manifest and molest humanity. The NSC specializes in wiping them out with custom-made tools and a good background in *Dimensional Science*. The NSC also runs facilities for the treatment of Technocrats unhinged by a close encounter of the spiritual kind.

Pan-Dimensional Corps — The vaunted extradimensional explorers of the Void Engineers sometimes run afoul of Horizon Realms and Chantries of the Traditions, which they dutifully map for later destruction. They also explore the reaches of the Umbra where more sensible mages don't travel, sometimes encountering Nephandi, Marauders or even more bizarre creatures. A rare few even explore time travel or the Digital Web. *Specialty Sphere: Dimensional Science.*

Research & Execution—With grants from the Syndicate and loaned tech from Iteration X, the R&E group (or "Q Division") handles all the hardware that makes travel possible—construction and maintenance of communications arrays, spacecraft and stations, as well as new technologies for experimental travel and mapping.

More on Technocrats

The preceding descriptions should give you the means to build Technocracy Conventioneers, and the equivalent terms for their magical capabilities. Their special character Traits, Backgrounds and Abilities are covered in Chapter Three; see Chapter Four for some sample Procedures and Devices.

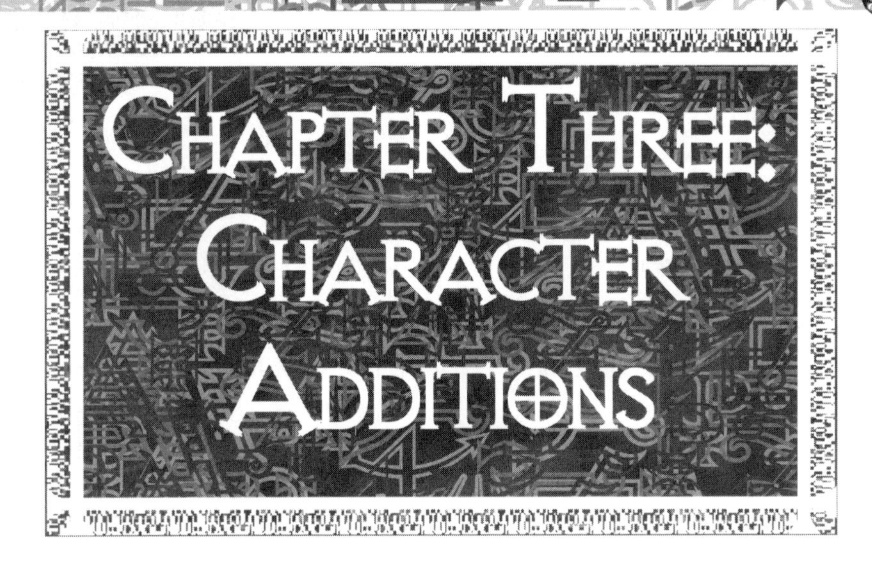

The character creation rules in **Laws of Ascension** provide plenty of options for building Tradition mages. But what about Disparates? Or the special Abilities of Technocrats? Wondering about how to translate some additional Backgrounds? It's all here. This is the meat and bones for your character systems: All of the Merits, Flaws, Backgrounds and Abilities from the **Guide to the Traditions** and **Technocracy**, plus the material from **Laws of the Ascension** that didn't make it before.

Abilities

The additional Abilities here not only give your mages some variety to play around with, they also allow you to explore the expanded training available to Technocracy characters. You can use these Abilities like any other Ability in your **Laws of Ascension** game, to perform specialized tasks. Most of them have a special benefit as well.

Abilities marked with "(Traditions)" are intended for mystically oriented mages. Abilities marked with "(Technocracy)" assume that the character has some level of training in Technocratic or Technomagical procedures; a mage can't simply learn *Energy Weapons* without having some way to practice it!

Important Note: Giving all Abilities some special capability isn't necessarily the best idea for all games. In many cases, the base Abilities presented in **Laws of Ascension** will more than cover the activities mages do, and any other Abilities added on could be considered *Hobby/ Professional/ Expert* Abilities. In such games, there's no need to complicate matters by adding on yet more rules, and the Abilities below therefore don't *necessarily* have to use all of the special benefits and challenges presented.

Acting

As a special form of *Performance*, you're particularly good at pretending to be something that you aren't, or having some emotion that you don't really feel. This is essential for a spy as well as for a stage performer. You can use a Social Challenge to put on a convincing display. *Performance* entertains; *Acting* allows you to convincingly portray a role and emotion (contrast a stand-up comic with a Shakespearean actor).

You can also use *Acting* to block an *Empathy* challenge against you.

Biotech (Technocracy)

While *Medicine* handles all sorts of techniques from mundane treatment to surgery, *Biotech* handles the organic machinery and hyperadvanced genetic projects of the Technocracy. Extraordinary citizens sometimes master a little bit of this Ability, and most Progenitors develop some skill in *Biotech* along the course of their career. *Biotech* covers the use of cloned organs, genetically engineered materials and all the machines that make, store and use them. Essentially, it's like a highly advanced version of *Medicine*, as far above *Medicine* as *Medicine* would be beyond simple first aid.

Progenitors use *Biotech* in conjunction with many specialty foci. *Biotech* is also necessary to understand and operate Technocratic biological machinery and living Devices.

Conspiracy Theory

Some would consider it a form of history or perhaps a type of politics. You know better: *Conspiracy Theory* explains the way that the world works, according to the hidden principles that They don't want you to know. You know enough to know about it — the question is, will you survive once They know you know?

Use *Conspiracy Theory* like a form of *Lore*: You can gather information about the tangled webs of networks and possible connections between shadowy organizations. While *Conspiracy Theory* never offers solid, concrete information, it can offer possibilities about who's behind a plot or why some groups are suddenly working together. As a rule of thumb, the *more* convoluted the plot, the more effective this Ability is at rooting it out. *Conspiracy Theory* doesn't necessarily grant knowledge of people's Reputation Traits (that's *Politics*); rather, it tells you about the ones who don't have a Rep because they want to remain hidden. The exact knowledge implied by this Ability is best left to the Storyteller; it may not be useful or appropriate for all games.

Construct Politics (Technocracy)

Unlike the politics of the Masses, the Technocratic Union relies on advanced sociology. Management is more efficient, bureaucracy is less wasteful, and the politics are less dangerous. Usually. The downside of this is that the structures often don't make immediate sense to the uneducated. You've survived long enough to know your way around the Constructs, though, and you know who's who.

Use *Construct Politics* to unearth the Reputation of Technocrats who're attached to a Horizon Construct. Since the Horizon Constructs have limited contact with Earth and often have their own (experimental) social structures, this Ability is invaluable for determining who's really in charge and how to go about getting things done. Essentially, this is a special form of *Politics* that works for Technocratic advanced bureaucracy in the same way that *Hypertech* compares to *Technology* or *Biotech* to *Medicine*.

Covert Culture

Spies, secret agencies and government ops are right up your alley. You don't waste your time on frivolous strange conspiracies or on the mundane aspects of police work. Rather, you concern yourself with the agencies that actually do things: Mossad, MI-6, the Readiness Agency and similar groups. And you know a *lot* about them.

Like *Conspiracy Theory*, this is a specific form of *Lore*. In this case, this is information regarding secret agencies, spies and (non-Technocratic) government operatives. You should use *Covert Culture* to navigate such groups and to understand Influence: *Espionage*. You also can probably look up information about the groups, what they do, who works for them and what range of jurisdiction they have, given enough time.

Cryptography

Public encryption keys are quickly becoming a thing of the past. Ciphers and substitution codes are laughable child's play. Through intuition, pattern recognition and large number theory, you can crack just about any code known to man — and maybe a few that aren't!

Use *Cryptography* to try to decipher coded messages that your Storyteller introduces. Even if you can't decipher it, you can usually tell a coded message from random static and maybe tell what sort of code was used (say, if you're picking up signals over a radio or computer). If your Storyteller decides to give you cryptographical puzzles, you can expend a *Cryptography* Ability to gain one of two benefits (depending on whether your Storyteller wants to stretch out the time to solve the puzzle): You can either gain more time to solve it, equal to the time you normally would have (so three *Cryptography* Traits turn a one-minute puzzle into a four-minute one), or you can choose a letter and have all instances of that letter revealed a la *Wheel of Fortune*.

You may need other Abilities for certain codes. For example, you might recognize a fractal pattern as a code because of your *Cryptography*, but without *Science: Fractals* you probably couldn't decipher it. Similarly, you would recognize Navajo code-talking but couldn't understand it without appropriate *Linguistics*.

Empathy

You're sensitive to people's emotions. This can be an upside, when you catch someone lying to you. It can also be a downer, when you find yourself sharing in the misery of one of your friends. Still, the ability to see where someone's coming from helps you to win trust and also to figure out the real motives behind the people you deal with.

You can use an *Empathy* challenge to determine the general emotional state of someone you're dealing with, if you can best the target in a Social Challenge. This might be agitated, angry, afraid, sad, moody, withdrawn or any number of other things; this can sometimes give you a clue to the subject's motives.

Energy Weapons (Technocracy)

Void Engineer space Marines and Iteration X grunts can't always rely on simple projectile weapons. Guns don't fire in space or underwater, and don't always have the power to take out threatening Deviants. Fortunately for humanity, the Union has and uses various forms of *Energy Weapons*: Lasers, plasma casters, shockers, particle beams and what-have-you. These weapons differ markedly from *Firearms*, and someone used to normal *Firearms* will find the advanced energy technology and the lack of recoil rather difficult to adjust to. Furthermore, *Energy Weapons* Ability covers the maintenance and minor repair of such weapons.

You can use Mental Challenges to attack with *Energy Weapons*, just like using *Firearms* with guns.

Note that while the Technocracy most commonly uses *Energy Weapons*, some Technomancers (especially Sons of Ether) occasionally build various "ray guns" as well, and could use this Ability.

Helmsman (Technocracy)

It's one thing to drive a car or pilot an airplane. It's another thing entirely to learn the three-dimensional tactics and incredibly complex operations necessary to pilot a Void Engineer spacecraft. This highly specialized Ability covers just such an occasion. While you probably won't spend a lot of time in spacecraft, getting from place to place can be difficult if nobody knows how to start the engines.

You must have *Helmsman* Ability to operate a Void Engineer spacecraft; guesswork isn't enough. The Storyteller may impose various challenges for piloting the craft through asteroids, into combat, landing and through other such hazards.

Sons of Ether can also use the *Helmsman* Ability with their etherships.

High Ritual (Traditions)

You're a master of pomp and circumstance. You know exactly where the candles go, how the invocation reads and which color of drapes to use for the best effect. You can take into account Resonance, the participants' personalities, your own knowledge and the limitations of your budget and still come up with a ritual that will not only succeed in amplifying your magic, but will look damn cool, too.

Play out your performance of *High Ritual* for a short time (assuming you're in a private location). You can expend a *High Ritual* Ability thereafter as a downtime action to extend your rite into the realm of Superhuman Ritual (see **Laws of Ascension** p. 140). Each level allows you to tack on one more grade of casting time, and thus one more grade of success. Of course, once you're done, you likely collapse from exhaustion and sleep for about 16 hours. Alternatively, you can use your *High Ritual* to grant a single retest to one *other* participant who fails a challenge when attempting to aid you in a cooperative rite.

Hypertech (Technocracy)

There's technology, and then there are *toys*. The Technocratic Union has at its fingertips access to some of the most amazing devices never seen by man. Of course, Enlightened Scientists can learn to use these incredible Devices by rote, but you actually understand some of the super-advanced abstractions of science that make them work. In theory, anyway.

You must have *Hypertech* Ability to design new Technocratic Apparatuses; otherwise, you're limited to using the equipment that your Convention supplies. With *Hypertech* you can puzzle out and possibly even repair damaged Technocratic equipment, subject to making a Mental Challenge (difficulty varies at the Storyteller's discretion, but usually eight or more Traits).

Interrogation

Sometimes you need information. Sometimes the informant doesn't want to talk. If you don't want to work over the target physically, this requires a level of psychological finesse. You may not be a psychologist, but you sure know how to read people. You can get them to talk, and more importantly, you understand how to draw conclusions from what they're *not* saying. Given enough time, you can crack some of the hardiest minds, but that's not even necessary — you're good enough that you can get them to betray themselves without breaking them.

Use *Interrogation* in a Social Challenge to gather information from a subject. You can ask one yes/ no question up to 10 words in length. Expend an *Interrogation* Ability and make the challenge; if you win, the subject must answer truthfully with "Yes," "No," or "I don't know." A question based on an assumption that's partially false counts as false (and generates a "No" answer). The subject can defend with *Acting*. Using *Interrogation* in this fashion requires a full scene/hour uninterrupted with the subject and can't be done under duress (that is, you can't *Interrogate* someone if you're both hanging from manacles in a prison or while you're being shot at; you must be in a situation of clear superiority).

Jetpack (Technocracy)

The Masses already have jetpack technology, but it's shaky, expensive, unreliable and just not very good. Technocratic jetpacks, of course, are much, much better. You're trained in the use of such jetpacks. Thanks to widespread televising of early jetpack experiments, most such jetpacks are now considered entirely coincidental and accepted by the Masses.

Use *Jetpack* as your piloting skill if you're flying with a jetpack and in a dangerous situation, such as trying to pull up from the last minute to avoid a building, or flying between tight canyons at high speed. Proper use of a *Jetpack* can give you great mobility advantages (see p. XX). Without this Ability, a character is limited to normal walking movement with a jetpack.

Jury-Rig

You may not know how things are put together or why they work, but you've got the knack of putting the right wires together and giving it a little duct tape to make things almost as good as new. Subject to having a few handy tools like a spool of metal wire and some chewing gum, you can often get one or two more uses out of the most crazily high-tech item.

When an item's destroyed (reduced to zero Traits or health levels), you can *Jury-Rig* it to bring it back to minimal functionality. Expend a *Jury-Rig* Ability and make a Mental Challenge with a difficulty of three times the object's normal Trait value — so an object that normally provides one bonus Trait has a difficulty of three. If you succeed, the item goes back up to one Trait. You can't *Jury-Rig* something above one Trait, and the item breaks again immediately after you use it. You can repeatedly *Jury-Rig* the same item, but the difficulty increases by one Trait each time. You can *Jury-Rig* just about anything that the Storyteller allows, subject to time and materials — some duct tape might *Jury-Rig* a knife back into functionality for one hit, but you probably couldn't *Jury-Rig* a Void Engineer space cruiser that rammed an asteroid.

Law Enforcement

Technocratic agents in the field often have to work with police or local law agencies. Tradition mages often find themselves on the run from those same groups. In either case, a working knowledge of the group is more than helpful, it's practical survival. Police don't like outsiders taking their cases, after all, so knowing how to appease them helps smooth along the transition. By the same token, if you know what the police are going to do, you have a better chance of getting away.

Law Enforcement acts again as a special type of *Lore* much like *Covert Culture*. You know the patterns of local law enforcement, their techniques, who'd be put on an investigation (a coroner, a detective or some other specialist), and what sorts of paperwork they fill out. You don't necessarily know specific people; that's the purview of Influence: *Police*. You do, however, have a good idea of what the reaction will be if you perform a specific criminal act, or need to work with the police, sheriff or other duly appointed badge-wearing representative.

Microgravity Operations (Technocracy)

The Void Engineers naturally spend a lot of time in space, and sometimes they bring other Conventioneers with them for specialty missions. You've been trained to handle the rigors of low gravity, and can handle spacewalking, ship operations and lunar travel with a minimum of fuss. While the greenhorns are floating away to the length of their umbilical tethers, you're floating upside-down and backward, getting a lovely view of the stars.

Normally, when in microgravity (that is, on the moon, in space, on a ship with no gravity and so on), characters can't use Abilities at all. You can use Abilities normally as long as you have at least one level of *Microgravity Operations*. You never lose your bearings and become confused by direction, nor do you suffer nausea due to microgravity (characters exposed to microgravity for the first time should make a Static Physical Challenge, six Trait difficulty, or be subjected to vertigo and incapacitating nausea for a full conflict/ 10 minutes). You use *Microgravity Operations* as your Ability to direct yourself in potentially hazardous free-fall situations, such as to slip out from between two slow-moving but heavy objects that might crush you or to avoid coming loose from the ship's hull and floating off into Jupiter.

Sons of Ether who spend a lot of time on etherships may also develop *Microgravity Operations* Ability.

Media

Talking to a lone individual is one thing. Reaching an entire audience is another. Preparing something to offend the least people and attract the most attention takes a lot of careful thought. Of course, sometimes you *want* to offend people in order to grab their attention. You know all of this, and how to do it, and when, and why. When it absolutely, positively has to have a sound bite, you're the one to do it.

You know how to best place and use media coverage. In conjunction with Influence: *Media*, this Ability allows you to make strong campaigns with the connections you have. Normally, when you invoke *Media* Influence, you kill a specific story, get an advance story or place a small publication. Using *Media* Ability in conjunction with your Influence, you can block an effort to kill a story (if you spend as many *Media* Ability Traits as the opposing individual), or you can guarantee that it shows up on everyone's doorstep (if you have at least one *Media* Ability left to use after canceling attempts to kill the story, you should ask the Storyteller to make sure that your story appears in a hand-out with all of the character sheets at the beginning of the appropriate game session).

Negotiation

The trick lies in making both sides feel like they got a good deal. Soothe egoes, make compromises and come out on top — that's the trick of *Negotiation*. You can tell when to put on pressure, when to ease off, when to play things up and when to look like you're on the losing end. Most importantly, this helps you in cross-dealings when you need tit-for-tat.

You can use *Negotiation* in conjunction with your various *Backgrounds* that normally garner aid (but not information). Your *Negotiation* Ability allows you a retest on the use of such a *Background*. For instance, if your *Mentor* refuses to help you, you can use *Negotiation* for a retest to see if you can convince her otherwise.

Networking

It's all in who you know. You can make contacts on the fly, figure out the power structures and milk your information sources for all the right dirt. With a few hours and a bunch of phone calls, you can usually dig up a little information about — well, just about anything.

Use *Networking* Ability in lieu of an established information network. If you don't have *Contacts* or a similar Background, you can rely on *Networking* instead. *Networking* has several disadvantages by comparison, though. It takes you a full scene/ hour to perform a use of *Networking*. You only gain information to answer one question or investigate one rumor. You must still make a Social Challenge with a difficulty determined by a Storyteller. Use of *Networking* does not generate a permanent social network; it just represents your ability to pull together bits and pieces of information from a few contacts and some hastily researched paperwork. Some information may be outside the scope of *Networking*. On the flip side, *Networking* doesn't count against your uses of *Contacts*, so you can potentially gain even more information if you spend enough time.

Newspeak

Control the language and you control the thoughts, Orwell asserted — and he was right. It's a known fact that languages drift, but you're plugged into the new jazz and spinning the verbage out faster than anyone can decrypt it. With *Newspeak*, you turn words to your advantage and make them mean what you *want* them to mean, instead of feeling constrained to formal, traditional vocabulary.

You can burn a *Newspeak* Ability to place a subtext into one sentence. Only other characters with *Newspeak* will gain this subtext. The subtext can only be two words. This can be in any mode of communication: You could blather out a sentence in person, over a megaphone, by computer, by Internet, written on paper — ultimately, anyone who reads or hears it may gain the subtext, subject to having *Newspeak* Ability. Deciphering a subtext doesn't cost a use of the Ability.

Pilot

Rotorhead, stick-jock, jetboy — you've heard them all, and if it has wings (fixed or rotary) you've flown it. You're familiar with how to handle planes, helicopters and hovercraft. Anything that floats on air is your baby.

Use *Pilot* in conjunction with dangerous maneuvers in a plane, jet, helicopter or hovercraft. You can't operate such a vehicle without the *Pilot* Ability.

Power-Brokering

Instead of making connections and wheedling with random people, you head straight for the top. By bullying your way past secretaries and slash-and-burning through red tape, you may not make friends, but you can certainly get things done. Of course, if your interpersonal skills aren't up to par, you might get into position to talk to someone who's just powerful enough to give you a swift kick to the head, but if you're suave enough, you can bring the *real* power players together.

Unlike *Negotiation*, this Ability doesn't represent interpersonal communication skills; unlike *Networking*, it's highly targeted. You specifically find the people who can get things done in an organization, and you bring them together to accomplish a task. When you invoke your *Power-Brokering* Ability, you can combine your Influence, *Contacts*, *Allies* and similar aiding Backgrounds with other characters. Each level of *Power-Brokering* expended (to call up people and burn a few bridges) lets you bring one additional person's Backgrounds into the group. You can add these Backgrounds as noted in the optional rule for Stacking Backgrounds on p. XX at double efficiency: That is, a character with one level of *Contacts* counts as having two levels for stacking purposes only.

Propaganda

You've run smear campaigns with the worst of them. You don't just sell things to the public — you get them to feel strongly about whatever you tell them, and you make them believe it.

By using your *Propaganda* Ability between games (it remains expended for the game in which it's set to take effect), you can briefly augment or hamper someone's Reputation Traits. Each expended *Propaganda* Ability allows the subject to recoup an expended Reputation

Trait, so that although it doesn't count as additional Traits, it's useable more than once because it refreshes immediately. Or, you can cause one (and only one) Negative Reputation Trait on a subject to count as two Traits.

Psychology

The workings of the human mind are laid bare to you. Behavior patterns and defenses are all clear. Well, perhaps not clear — humans are unpredictable and *Psychology* isn't an exact science. You do, though, have a better idea than average of what motivates people and why they do things.

You can use *Psychology* in conjunction with a Social Challenge to discern someone's current Demeanor. Given a full hour of time to study a subject, you can also use a Social Challenge to try to learn the subject's Nature, or to change the Demeanor for the next scene to a Demeanor of your choosing.

RD Data (Technocracy)

The Technocratic Union keeps files on all sorts of Reality Deviants — *extensive files*. You've read some. Maybe you've even encountered some of those Deviants. Be that as it may, you know about some of the dangers that humanity doesn't. Sometimes it makes you wish that you *were* blissfully ignorant.

RD Data is the Technocratic term for specific *Lore* regarding supernatural creatures. It's tightly controlled; the Union regards it as a "need-to-know" information resource.

Security

You fiddle with traps, electronic locks, scanners, motion sensors. In addition to knowing how to operate them, you know how to beat them. Whether it's with simple lockpicks or sophisticated electronic bypasses, odds are you can figure out a way around the system — or find a way to close an existing loophole.

Use your *Security* Ability to make challenges to set up or penetrate existing *Security* operations. For instance, you would use *Security* to set up a network of cameras in a building, with your Mental Traits as the difficulty that someone else would have to use *Security* to find a way to bypass it. *Security* with a Dexterity-related Physical Trait could pick a physical lock. You can also use *Security* to examine blueprints and look for holes in a building's security.

Subdimensions (Technocracy)

You've studied the myriad layers of quantum uncertainty and universal shear. Using string resonances and other obscure theories, you've come to a very basic understanding of some of the mysterious and nigh-unfathomable strangeness that exists beyond the Dimensional Barrier.

In game terms, this Ability works like *Cosmology* for Technocrats. Instead of granting knowledge of spirits and secret Umbral realms, it covers in detail areas that Technocrats frequent: Horizon Constructs, machine realms, parallel worlds and other "scientific" dimensions.

Terrorism

There's an art to fostering absolute, sheer, abject, mind-numbing terror. Sometimes it involves bombs and demonstrations. Other times, it's all about the subtlety of things that prey on the weak mind. From bomb-slinging to psychological warfare, you've practiced them all. To the wrong people, you *are* a monster.

The *Terrorism* Ability gives you specific knowledge of terrorist organizations and techniques, much like a *Lore* Ability. No specific mechanic or challenge applies; rather, you can gather information about what techniques would be effective in a given situation, what group might have something to gain from a specific action, or who's faking a terrorist attack in order to draw attention off.

Torture

First they beg. Then they scream. Then they bleed.

You understand how to drag out pain and punishment. Whether as an adjunct to interrogation or just because you're a sadistic bastard, you know the most effective ways to injure without killing, to keep someone alive through mutilation and to keep someone conscious for the whole procedure. You know how to take advantage of specific fears and how to stimulate suffering that your victims wouldn't believe possible.

Normally when you engage in physical torture, the victim suffers health levels of damage. With the *Torture* Ability, you can make a Static Mental Challenge (difficulty of the victim's Willpower Traits) to try to deliver agony without causing fatal damage. If you win, your "tender ministrations" cause the subject to lose a Willpower Trait instead of a health level. If you desire, after stripping all temporary Willpower Traits, you can even cause the victim to lose permanent Willpower with further applications. A subject reduced to zero permanent Willpower is little more than an utterly insane, vegetative lump (apply the derangement: *Catatonia*). Applying torture requires special equipment and can't be done in a hurry. Given enough time, though, you will either break or kill the subject.

Naturally, making someone lose permanent Willpower is pretty nasty, but if you've already got the subject in that position, you could have presumably killed him anyway, so....

Vice

There's an entire subculture to the criminal underworld, one that's not open to people who don't know the lingo. This isn't the penny-ante trade of the street hustlers and the signs of the gang-bangers, either. It's also in the high-class prostitutes, the secret gambling dens and the posh parties where stars come to get strung out of their minds.

Your *Vice* Ability works in a fashion similar to *Streetwise*, allowing you to make specific contacts and avoid trouble. Where *Streetwise* works with street culture, gangs and thugs, though, *Vice* deals specifically in the seedy elements that cater to illegal pleasures. You can find opium dens, strip joints that house prostitution, adult film stores that make their own porn in the back, and nastier, scarier things. Your *Vice* Ability can help you to navigate these places safely without seeming like a narc or becoming caught up in someone else's schemes.

Backgrounds

The additional Backgrounds presented here, like the Abilities presented previously, are sometimes marked (Technocracy) or (Traditions). Again, these delineate Backgrounds that are specifically appropriate to the group in question.

Backup (Technocracy)

Due to your rank in the Union, you have the ability to call up some additional muscle when the situation warrants it. This isn't exactly *skilled* muscle (they're not *Allies*), but rather a pool of faceless minions from the Union's rank-and-file proles — er, citizens.

Backup can be very hard to portray in a live-action game, because you'll typically need other people in order to represent the *Backup* that shows up. You can handle this in one of several ways. First, you can simply decide that *Backup* is too egregious and not allow it. Second, you can hold some Narrators in reserve, or use the recommended system of having some players take a little time each game to play Narrator characters, in order to represent *Backup*. Third, you can simply issue cards for *Backup*, which must be prominently displayed.

Backup typically takes a scene to arrive. Each level of *Backup* grants one additional warm body with normal human Attributes (you decide the character's strength in Mental, Physical or Social). You might suffer some repercussions if your *Backup* dies, but in general these are people expected to work in a dangerous job and to serve in the line of duty.

Stacking Backgrounds (Optional Rule)

This rule only works if you need a way to more realistically manage the combination of various Background factors.

When multiple characters get together they sometimes want to combine their Background benefits into a lump sum, especially for large and impressive actions. For instance, several mages with *Resources x3* might go in together to purchase an expensive estate.

Backgrounds do not add. Instead, they require cumulative outlay. *Resources x2* plus *Resources x2* is not equal to *Resources x4*; rather, it's about a two and a half.

The total value for combined Backgrounds equals the highest Background, plus a sum: Halve the value of the other Backgrounds. Then, if this is equal to or greater than the highest Background, add one to the total. If the remaining levels are still higher than the now-increased Background, add one again. Continue until no additional levels remain.

For example, if a character with *Resources x3* wants to perform something with the equivalent of *Resources x4*, he'd need the support of three people with *Resources x2* (total six levels, halved, equals his three) or two other people with *Resources x3*, or some other combination that added up to six levels.

The *Chantry* Background provides a special exception to this case.

Note that a character's still limited to handling Influence no greater than his total Attribute Traits. Donated Influence counts against this limit, making it very difficult to coordinate large-scale multi-Influence actions.

Adversarial Backgrounds

The **Guide to the Traditions** presents a sort of "negative Background," the adversarial Background. While this could be adapted into live-action play, it's a difficult proposition to do so. In a tabletop game, the Storyteller always has control of the story direction, and always has the chance to take such Backgrounds into consideration. In a live-action game, a single character's hindrance won't always come to the fore like this, especially if downtime action is sparse.

If you want to use adversarial Backgrounds, you treat them as negative versions of their corresponding Backgrounds. With a *Debt*, for instance, the mage must somehow raise money to pay of bills each month. With *Enemies*, the mage is guaranteed to have people out to ruin or kill him. The guidelines in **Guide to the Traditions** should suffice.

Adversarial Backgrounds will sometimes cause players to build characters with adversaries that they think will never come up in play, either because they revolve around events that don't happen or because they require too much Storyteller oversight. In such cases, simply don't allow them.

Blessing (Traditions)

You've got *it* — some natural, inherent magical quality. It's not an item you carry or a power from a familiar; it's just something in you. You might've been born with it, or maybe you gained a *Blessing* from a spirit or demon.

A *Blessing* functions just like a power in a *Wonder*, except that it's part of you. It has a cost equal to the level of Spheres required to make it work, doubled if it's always on. Subject to your Storyteller's approval, this could allow you to heal quickly, have a permanent supernatural sense, or just make you always manage to get a date when you go clubbing.

Cult (Traditions)

You have a group of people who support your magic and believe in its power. While they don't provide specific additional help — they're not competent to do special jobs, nor do they have access to unusual information — they are good for one thing: When you get them all together, they can help in the casting of ritual magic.

You must be able to access your *Cult* to claim the benefits of the Background. If you have access to your *Cult*, you can expend its levels for the session to treat this as gaining additional Sleeper helpers in a ritual (see p. 138 of **Laws of Ascension**). You don't have to use them all at once, or all in the same ritual. Remember, your *Cult* can desert you if you don't keep them motivated, and they can be hunted down, jailed or disbanded by your enemies if you don't protect them.

Chantry/ Construct

You're part of a group that holds territory in a place designed specifically for study and improvement. Your turf might have a *Library*, a resident *Mentor*, a small *Sanctum* for your style of magic or any number of other benefits. By sharing it with your friends, you all contribute and make the place better. It could be as simple as a small coffee shop that you all jointly own or as magnificent as a restored turn-of-the-century manor.

All of the mages in a given *Chantry* may contribute Background levels to it. Every two levels in the *Chantry* gives it one shared level of one of the following: *Arcane*, *Destiny*, *Library*, *Wonder*, *Sanctum*, *Mentor*, *Allies*, *Retainers*, *Cult*, Influence, *Fame* or a *Reputation* Trait. In this case, the *Chantry* itself hosts these benefits, but any contributing member (that is, a character with levels spent into it) may call upon these benefits. This allows the *Chantry* to collectively give the characters access to many more Backgrounds than they would have on their own.

Note also that a *Chantry* isn't always supported completely by the characters; a bunch of poor characters in a wealthy *Chantry* are probably members alongside a wealthy mage who subsidizes it.

The *Chantry*'s furnishings come out of its Background level. A *Chantry* with no *Resources* is little more than a ramshackle hut in some out-of-the-way park corner. A *Chantry* without a *Node* has no Horizon Realm.

Demesne (Traditions)

You have a stretch of dream-territory with which you're familiar. Whenever you sleep, you go there, and sometimes you can even control or shape it. The Dream Realm that you command is fluid and malleable to your will, and with the right magic you can even trap other dreamers there and subject them to your powers, or use it as a jumping-off point to enter the Umbra through dreams.

Your *Demesne* represents the area and control you have over a dream-realm that you visit whenever you dream. With *Mind* magic, you can pull other people into that realm; with *Spirit*, you can use it as a jump-off point. Your Dream Realm typically has an area of effect based on the grades of success for area, with your number of levels as the grades. Thus, a one-Trait *Demesne* is a single room, but a five-Trait *Demesne* stretches across an entire Dream continent. You can also add your *Demesne* Traits to all challenge resolution against other dreamers who enter your Dream Realm. Within your *Demesne*, the reality bends to your will, but if you're not careful, it is possible to spawn elements that can harm you as well. In all other ways the Dreamscape is essentially similar to a Mindscape (see **Laws of Ascension** p. 176).

Enhancement

Due to genetic engineering, grafts or bionic implants, you've been made… more than human. Or perhaps just different.

You can choose to be cybernetically or biologically enhanced — one or the other. A cyborg has bionic implants that provide weaponry, armor, replacements to organs and other such useful gadgetry. A genegineered human typically has superior physiological capabilities, often with enhanced mental ability as well.

Cyborg: Your cybernetic enhancements cause Paradox because they're not yet accepted in the Consensus. Each level of the Background grants one permanent Paradox Trait that counts for backlashes but never goes away. Each level allows you to purchase one additional Attribute Trait (which can take you above your normal maximum) or two Traits of implanted *Devices*. Naturally, you're still limited to *Devices* that can fit in your body, and no *Devices* above five Traits. Thus, you can have implanted armor or a plasma cannon, but not a car.

Biomod: Your biological modifications cause physiological disorders. Choose one Negative Trait for every level you take in the *Enhancement*, or one Derangement for every two levels. You gain one additional Attribute Trait (above normal human maximums) or two Traits of biological modifications.

Familiar/ Companion

Whether it's a traditional black cat, a ferret, a favored horse or even a tiny dragonet, you have some sort of bonded companion that shares a link with your very spirit. You may or may not realize the depth of this link (Technocrats often think their *Companions* are simply very clever pets), but you can gain many benefits from your *Familiar*'s presence.

You spend levels from your *Familiar* Background, when you choose it, to gain certain benefits for your *Familiar*. The *Familiar* is essentially a small physical creature invested with a spirit that has become bound to you.

A *Familiar* automatically serves as an arcane connection for you. Thus, you can affect with magic anything your *Familiar* touches, but the reverse is also true. The *Familiar* serves as part of a pact (perhaps unspoken) that requires your attention and perhaps some effort on your part; you can take elements of this pact as Flaws to reduce the cost of the *Familiar* (for instance, if your *Familiar* requires you to compose eccentric poetry to it and read it aloud at cabal meetings, this is probably an obnoxious one- or two-Trait Flaw). Your *Familiar* can take on your own Paradox and suffer the backlash from it, although this typically requires some level of incentive. Finally, a *Familiar* requires a supply of Quintessence; generally this is one Quintessence Trait per week per level of the *Familiar*, or else it fades away, loses its powers or otherwise becomes inert until fed.

For one Trait, the *Familiar* can talk; for two Traits, it can communicate with telepathy with anyone in sensory range, regardless of language.

The *Familiar* can have countermagic Traits equal to the Traits you place into that capability, and you gain this while you are physically in contact with the *Familiar*.

You can grant the *Familiar* special *Lore* on a one-Trait-for-one-*Lore*-level basis.

Your *Familiar* can nullify one Trait of Paradox per game session per Trait spent on Paradox nullification.

For one Trait, your *Familiar* can be an unusual form of an otherwise natural creature, like a dog with a prehensile tail. For two Traits, it can be clearly unnatural, such as a multicolored, six-legged frog.

For one Trait, your *Familiar* can have two extra health levels or two extra Physical Traits.

For one Trait, your *Familiar* can be larger than cat-sized, up to horse-sized.

Legend (Traditions)

You are literally a living legend. You're the reincarnation of some legendary ideal; when you live up to that ideal, you generate energy like a *Node*. Quintessence gathers from the strength of the Consensus and people's belief in the *Legend*.

Choose a specific *Legend* associated with your character. You might be a reincarnation of Jack the Ripper, or the home of all the legends associated with Achilles. When you behave according to your *Legend*, you generate Quintessence just like a *Node*. Someone else can tap this Quintessence by participating in your *Legend*. For instance, if you are a *Legend* of Jack the Ripper, you gain Quintessence by stalking and trying to kill prostitutes; the victim in question can gain Quintessence (if she survives) by playing out that role. If you are a *Legend* of Achilles, you would gain Quintessence for going on a mad rampage through an enemy fortification, especially if the enemies just defeated one of your friends.

Treat Quintessence generated in this fashion (including limits per session) the same as you would a *Node*.

Past Lives (Traditions)

Ancient days and half-remembered events flash before your eyes. Your Avatar carries memories, and sometimes they open up and reveal to you the lives that the Avatar has guided before. While this can be disconcerting, it can also be very helpful when you need to draw out specific knowledge of the past.

Spend a turn in concentration of your *Past Life* to bring forth images from it, then make a Simple Test. If you win or tie, you can expend a *Past Life* level to gain a level in one Ability appropriate to the life (for instance, you couldn't gain *Microgravity Operations* from a *Past Life* in Han Dynasty China). You can spend multiple levels of *Past Life* but must make a Simple Test for each. On a failure, you spend the Trait, but gain no benefit this time.

Requisitions (Technocracy)

A typical Technocrat can't afford energy weapons and hyperdense body armor — not to mention rooms full of surveillance equipment and spaceships. That's what *Requisitions* are for: An agent doesn't have to own these things. The Technocracy does, and it provides when necessary. If you fill out the right paperwork — and your bosses think it's worthwhile — you can get your hands on special gear for your missions.

When you invoke *Requisitions*, you can access special Technocracy equipment that's not normally available. Each level of *Requisitions* counts as two levels of *Influence* or *Resources* to garner a specific item. You must make a Simple Test (win or tie). If you lose, your request isn't granted in time, or the items aren't available, or for whatever reason you just don't get the goods. You may test separately for each item, though.

Sanctum/ Laboratory

Over time, a mage's influence can bend and warp the Tapestry in a specific place. That place becomes attuned to the mage and familiar with his magic. You have just such a place: a *Sanctum*. A *Sanctum* offers a hiding ground and, more importantly, a safe haven for magic. Within a *Sanctum*, all rules of magic are those of the owner. Your *Sanctum* follows your paradigm; your magic is coincidental there, while other magic is vulgar. Your years of work — often a decade or more in one place — have made it your mystical home.

A *Sanctum* is attuned to you and only you. Unless someone has a remarkably similar paradigm (perhaps an apprentice), the *Sanctum* won't work for the individual. In rare cases, old *Chantries* sometimes have small *Sancta* that act with a paradigm broad enough to encompass an entire Tradition's practices, and to work for any member of that Tradition. (Such *Sancta* are part of a *Chantry* package and not available to individual characters except through development in play).

Your magic is completely coincidental in a *Sanctum*. This trumps any other consideration: You can heal vulgar wounds, create elements, enchant weapons — anything you desire. You must still make all of the normal challenges and pay the normal costs. Magic that you send outside of your *Sanctum*, such as a ranged attack or enchanted item, is subject to Unbelief; the Paradox that you would normally garner from such an Effect applies to the Effect instead of you, and probably weakens or warps it. Thus, you can't easily send screaming bolts of death halfway across the world to coincidentally kill your foe, but you can repair your damaged foci, heal yourself and conjure a few spirits for advice.

The size of your *Sanctum* depends upon the level of the Background:

One Trait — A circle, one pace across

Two Traits — A small room, five paces

Three Traits — A workshop, 10 paces

Four Traits — A house, 30 paces

Five Traits — A manor, one hundred paces

Secret Weapons (Technocracy)

Q Division fills out the forms and hands you special *Devices* that're still on the drawing board. Instead of using the usual goods, you get to try out the new stuff. Sure, sometimes it's buggy as hell, but it's also stuff that nobody else will even *see* for a year.

You can use your *Secret Weapons* Background like *Requisitions*, except that it allows access specifically to *Devices*. In concert with your Storyteller, you can design special new *Devices* according to the usual rules for *Wonders*. Subject to this approval, you can then try out the *Device*. As with *Requisitions*, each level of *Secret Weapons* counts as two levels for the *Device*. In this case, though, the *Device* is untested; the Storyteller will always assign it some secret Flaw or Flaws equal to half its total value. You only get to use the *Device* for one session. (You also need to fill out paperwork about how it worked — or didn't — afterward, but that's a job for downtime.)

Spies (Technocracy)

You have a network of informants who watch your enemies' every moves. Just a couple calls and you can have your men keeping watch for specific actions or people, and returning to you with information about what's going on.

You use *Spies* in your downtime. Allocate your *Spies* to different characters (player or Narrator). Each *Spy* returns to you at the beginning of the next session with information about what the individual is doing with one Background. For instance, if you send two *Spies* after your nemesis who's using his *Influence: Health* and his *Contacts*, your *Spies* will come back and tell you that he's doing so, and what he's asked them to do.

Note that your *Spies* can be detected with other *Spies*, or by properly directed use of other Backgrounds.

Merits and Flaws (Optional Rule)

These rules only work if you want a crop of diverse mages at the risk of having some overused or abusive powers that you may not foresee.

Some heroic (or even otherwise mundane) individuals possess capabilities beyond the norm — twists of fate, chance knacks or advantages beyond usual skill and talent. Others have, like the Greek heroes, tragic flaws of character that impede or harm. These are Merits and Flaws.

You must have Storyteller permission to take Merits and Flaws.

A Merit is a special boon or benefit. It has a cost in Traits and is typically purchased with Free Traits equal to this cost. A Flaw, conversely, is a special problem. Taking a Flaw gives you a number of extra Free Traits equal to its rating. You can't take more than five Traits of Flaws normally, though you can take any *two* Flaws of *any* value (so you could be both blind and paraplegic, but we don't recommend it, and you couldn't have a whole host of problems all at once).

In some cases you may gain a new Flaw in the course of play. You generally don't gain points for this. You might be able to gain a Merit (at an Experience Trait cost of twice the Merit's rating), but this is unusual and should be specially worked into the story; generally, you either have a Merit or you don't.

Physical Merits and Flaws

Acute Sense (1 or 3 Trait Merit)

You have a naturally sharp sense, be it sight, hearing or whatnot. For one trait you have a one-Trait resolution bonus on all challenges involving that sense. For three Traits, you gain this bonus with *all* senses.

Ambidextrous (1 Trait Merit)

You can use both hands with equal facility. You suffer no Trait penalty when using an "off hand," because you don't have an off hand. If you use both hands at once, you still suffer a coordination penalty, as described on p. XX.

Catlike Balance (1 Trait Merit)

Balance comes naturally to you — you almost never slip or fall. You gain a two-Trait resolution bonus on all challenges of balance, like walking a ledge or tightrope.

Daredevil (3 Trait Merit)

Fortune favors the bold, and you're definitely one of them. Whenever you undertake a difficult or risky action — defined as one with a Static difficulty of eight or more Traits, or with damage as a possible result — you gain a one-Trait bonus to resolution. This only applies in combat if you are outnumbered or facing an opponent who can overbid you (Storyteller determines secretly).

Huge Size (4 Trait Merit)

Weighing in at over 400 lbs. and seven or more feet of height, you are *huge*. (If you aren't *really* this big, you should wear padded clothes, platform shoes and a special tag to indicate this). You have one extra Bruised health level, because you can take more damage without significant impairment.

Insensible to Pain (5 Trait Merit)

For whatever reason — burned-out nerves or an excess of amphetamines — you never feel pain. You suffer no wound penalties and may act normally until you die (go past the Mortally Wounded health level).

Addiction (1 to 3 Trait Flaw)

You have a physical addiction to some potent substance. For a trivial, legal or easily obtained substance like alcohol, this Flaw is worth one Trait. For an illegal, highly dangerous or expensive substance, the Flaw is worth three Traits. While under the effects of your substance of choice you typically suffer from an additional Negative Trait; perhaps *Impatient* for amphetamines or *Obnoxious* for alcohol. If you can't get your fix, you will likely become sick and/ or violent, with results up to the Storyteller (but usually at least a two-Trait resolution penalty on challenges).

Defective Sense (1 Trait Flaw)

One of your senses from abnormally poor functionality. In all challenges involving that sense, you suffer a two-Trait resolution penalty. You can temporarily overcome this with certain magics, but you cannot permanently repair this without permanent changes to your Pattern (i.e., spending experience and casting a powerful ritual). Obviously, you cannot take this in conjunction with an *Acute Sense* of the same type.

This problem may be correctable (wearing glasses, for instance), but the problem should be apparent if the correction factor is ever lost, damaged or removed. You can lose your hearing aid, for instance, or your enemy might break your glasses.

Short (1 Trait Flaw)

Wear a tag to note that your character is actually less than four and a half feet tall. You have trouble reaching countertops, doorknobs and similar height-based objects. You can only move two steps in each turn, instead of three.

Disfigured (2 Trait Flaw)

Some hideous disfigurement, scar or defect makes you look frightening. You suffer a two-Trait penalty on all Social Challenges not related to intimidation, and you cannot take any Appearance-related Social Traits.

One Ear/Eye (2 Trait Flaw)

Due to injury or defect, you lack an ear or eye. (Wear a tag or patch to indicate this.) You suffer a two-Trait resolution penalty on tests of the appropriate sense, just like someone with a *Defective Sense*. Additionally, if you are missing an eye, you suffer an *additional* one-Trait penalty on ranged challenges, while missing an ear causes an additional one-Trait penalty on sound location.

Primal Marks (2 Trait Flaw)

Potent mystical traits manifest in your physical appearance. You may have the features of a legendary Norse god, the look of a famous

family of reputed magicians, animallike characteristics or the mark of supernatural creatures (based on folklore and myth). These marks make you stand out to anyone with *Occult* Ability, who may recognize them. You almost certainly inherit a moniker to go with your traits: Your friends may call you "Badger" because you look like one, or "Thor" if you're tall and Nordic, or just refer to you as "that witchy woman."

If your inherited marks carry some sort of disfiguration, you have that as well, though you do get the Traits for it (for instance, if you seem to be a reincarnation of the god Hephaestus, you are automatically *Lame* in one leg but you get the Traits for it). Other than that, you're simply noticeable for your traits. Witch-hunters may recognize them, or other people may associate them with undesirable legends — if you resemble someone from the Bathory family, for instance, they'll remember tales of that ancestress who bathed in blood; if you look like a wolf, they may assume that you're dangerous, and so on.

Bad Sight (3 Trait Flaw)

You have a *noncorrectable* vision problem like astigmatism or severe cataracts. You suffer a two-Trait resolution penalty on all vision rolls, but you can only ever overcome this with extensive *Life* magic (i.e., spending experience and a long, probably painful, ritual).

Deformity (3 Trait Flaw)

A club foot, hunchback or similar problem cripples you. The specific deformity typically causes you three Traits' worth of problems. You might have a two-Trait penalty on movement and a one-Trait penalty on Social Challenges with a hunchback, for instance, or you could be completely unable to run if you have a badly malformed leg. The exact nature of these Traits is up to the Storyteller. You *must* wear a tag indicating your deformity and its Trait penalties unless you somehow conceal it magically. As with other biological problems, extensive *Life* magic might cure this, but only with lots of experience and time.

Degeneration (3, 6 or 9 Trait Flaw)

Without some sort of supernatural or super-scientific help, you will die. You could be necrotically falling apart, or perhaps you're an animated construct that needs magical energy to survive, or maybe you have a terminal disease.

For two Traits, you do not naturally heal from any wounds. This applies to all of the higher levels, as well.

For six Traits, you suffer wounds at the reverse of the healing chart: the amount of time it would take to heal the *Mortally Wounded* level is the amount of time it takes for you to suffer one level of damage, and you progress up the chart backward as you continue to take damage.

For nine Traits, you take damage as before, but it's *aggravated.*

Note that without a regular source of magical healing, your character is pretty much doomed. Good luck.

Diminished Attributes (Variable Flaw)

When everyone else got the good stuff growing up, you got the crappy end: You're living proof that you can be dumb, weak *and* ugly. You have fewer Attribute Traits than normal. For every two Traits that you *don't* take from your normal starting allotment, you gain back one free Trait. You still must have at least one Trait in each category, though. This doesn't prevent you from buying more Traits, later, nor does it affect your Trait maximums.

Lame (3 Trait Flaw)

You have a badly injured or misshapen leg or legs. Use something to show this Flaw — a cane, leg braces or the like. You should take the Negative Physical Trait *Lame* as well (though you gain Traits for it). You cannot run and you can only take one step per action.

Monstrous (3 Trait Flaw)

You have a thoroughly hideous visage — perhaps covered completely in scars, wracked by Paradox or whatever. You may not take Appearance-related Social Traits. You cannot initiate any Social Challenges, except those relating to intimidation, while your true form is apparent. Yes, this includes empathic senses with *Mind* magic — nobody *feels* normal around you!

Permanent Wound (3 Trait Flaw)

Like the proverbial wound in the side, you have some injury that never properly heals. This could be stigmata, a Paradox injury or some sort of permanent Pattern damage. At sunrise or sunset of each day (your choice, though once chosen it's set), you drop to the *Wounded* health level with lethal damage, if you aren't already there or worse.

Slow Healing (3 Trait Flaw)

You heal all injuries at half speed — double the healing times on the chart on p. 192 of **Laws of Ascension**. All healing magic heals only half damage to you (round down).

Deaf (4 Trait Flaw)

As you cannot hear at all, you cannot understand spoken language (unless you take *Linguistics: Lip Reading*), and you certainly can't hear people sneaking up on you. You suffer a three-Trait resolution penalty to challenges of alertness and sensitivity to your surroundings. Anyone who approaches you from outside your line of sight automatically surprises you.

Mute (4 Trait Flaw)

Talk about a pain for any mage who relies on language. You may not speak in character, at all, nor may you break character to explain your motives to anyone but a Storyteller. You can use *Linguistics: Sign Language*, though of course this does you no good if you don't have the Ability or you don't know anyone else with it.

Aging (5 Trait Flaw)

You're just not a teenager anymore. For each decade over the 40-year mark, you take the Flaw once and you lose one from both your starting and maximum Physical Trait total. You may also take this if you're underage: Once at 11-14, twice at 7-10 and up to three times for 4-6, with the same penalties (though you must buy off the Flaw with experience as you age, in the latter case). You must also take the *Child* Flaw if you're "underage." Obviously, you'll need makeup or a special tag to indicate your apparent age.

Mayfly Curse (5 or 10 Trait Flaw)

You age at an accelerated rate — and death comes soon. For five Traits, you age one physical year for every two real months. For 10 Traits, you age one physical year every single real week! You may take this Flaw in conjunction with *Aging* (above), based on your physical age, to represent decrepitude that has already caught up with you. You cannot take this Flaw if your chronicle won't outlast your projected lifespan, though (generally, it's only appropriate for long-term games).

Blind (6 Trait Flaw)

You can't see, and you automatically lose all challenges that rely on sight. On a test where sight can help but isn't strictly necessary (like finding a door by touch), you lose on ties. Wear a special tag or dark glasses to indicate your condition.

Paraplegic (6 Trait Flaw)

Confined to a wheelchair, bed or crutches, you can't move at all without extreme effort. You can only move one step per action, and doing so is very painful — take one level of bashing damage from exhaustion each time you move this fast. Anyone who relies on maneuverability (striking with a sword, kicking you or just running away) automatically bests you on all ties.

Social Merits and Flaws

True Love (4 Trait Merit)

You have found (and possibly lost) a *True Love*. This love buoys you even in the worst of times and gives you strength to continue against all odds. You gain one *True Love* Trait, which you may use each game session just like a Willpower Trait. (This Trait cannot be saved up from game to game.) Of course, your *True Love* may require rescuing, or perhaps you have to quest to find him, her or it.

Child (1 to 3 Trait Flaw)

The Awakening can strike nearly anyone — in your case, it struck during early life. *Very* early. You're a young child, with all of the attendant problems: Small size, inability to get into certain places, never taken seriously by adults and so on. You gain one Trait if you're 11-14, two if you're 7-10 and three if you're 4-6. See also *Aging* if your child isn't very physically adept or precocious.

Playing an Awakened child isn't an excuse to carry a teddybear, act cute and derelict yourself of responsibility. You're a child thrust into the middle of a war for belief, subjected to supernatural enemies that don't care about your age and at risk of blowing your mind due to magical stresses before you ever even have a life. This isn't funny or cute; it's a child thrown into a situation of horror.

Dark Secret (1 Trait Flaw)

Something terrible from your past haunts you and surfaces from time to time to make you miserable. You might have done something *very* naughty or perhaps you have a discredited past. Either way, you'll suffer significant social consequences (like ostracism, hatred or being hunted by new enemies) if your secret comes out. Perhaps you were taught by a mage who was later learned to be a Nephandus, or maybe you participated indirectly in the Gilgul of an innocent. Your secret could come up at any time and the Storyteller will be sure that it haunts you. If it gets out, you'll either gain an immediate Negative Trait (*Untrustworthy* is a good one) or lose a Trait of Reputation — and you may suffer other in-game repercussions.

Mistaken Identity (1 Trait Flaw)

You're not a reincarnated god, an Oracle descended from the Umbra, a miracle-worker or prophesied hero — but you sure look the part. People may automatically assume that you have some capabilities or significance beyond your actual abilities, or may even think that you're someone you aren't. You should wear a tag that indicates the individual you resemble. This could be troublesome if your look-alike is particularly well-known or infamous for some notorious deeds.

Shy (1 Trait Flaw)

Large groups of people make you uncomfortable. It's not that you don't get along with people; rather, crowds just cause you to become nervous. You suffer a two-Trait resolution penalty on social interaction with groups of three or more people; this goes up to three Traits for crowds of 10 or more.

Witch-Hunted (4 Trait Flaw)

Some hunter is out to get you, whether for religious reasons, for some perceived injustice, as a member of a secret cabal or just plain due to craziness. However, this hunter knows about your magics and has some idea of your capabilities. The hunter won't rest and takes steps to prepare for and counter your skills, and tends to show up at the most *inconvenient* times. Worse still, since the hunter keeps an eye on you, your friends and allies might be in danger as well if they're seen associating with you. Even if you defeat or convert the hunter, another will take up the crusade unless you buy off the Flaw. The Storyteller makes up this hunter and has a Narrator play the role anytime the hunter comes into play.

Probationary Member (4 Trait Flaw)

Perhaps you defected from the Technocracy, or maybe you split from a Craft, studied early on under an Orphan or switched Traditions with some bad blood left behind. Your current Tradition doesn't trust you, and your old group remembers you none too fondly. Although you may have Reputation and a powerful *Destiny*, nobody trusts you and nobody wants to risk you turning coat again to become a new enemy. Thus, you're treated by everyone above you as if you had only one Reputation.

Mental Merits and Flaws

Ability Aptitude (1 Trait Merit)

You have a natural aptitude for some Ability that goes beyond simple proficiency. With one non-combat capability (such as *Computer* or *Drive*) you gain a two-Trait resolution bonus. This can't apply to a combat skill or an exotic/esoteric Ability like *Firearms* or *Vampire Lore*.

Common Sense (1 Trait Merit)

Simple wisdom just comes naturally to you. When you're in a bind, you can think of any number of proverbs and you just have an instinct for "the right thing to do" — or at least you know better than to stir up any hornets' nests. When you're about to do something *stupid*, the Storyteller or Narrator should stop you and say, "Do you *really* want to do that?" This is a good Merit for novice players, as it allows them to play characters who know better or to help them learn the ropes of the game.

Concentration (1 Trait Merit)

When you shut out distractions and focus on a task, you can overcome any outside disturbance. It doesn't matter if you're in a firefight, in sleet or hail, hanging upside down — these annoyances just don't bother you. You never suffer any penalty Traits for deleterious circumstances, though you can still be distracted by *Mind* magic or wounds, and you still suffer penalties if you're actually mentally or physically restrained from performing your task completely.

Light Sleeper (1 to 3 Trait Merit)

Whether due to magical boon or just a quirk of physiology, you subsist on less sleep than the average person. For one Trait, you need sleep only four hours a night. You don't take penalties for sleep deprivation, unless you get less than this. For two Traits, you need sleep only two hours a night — you can remain functional even on the run or while holding down multiple jobs at once. At a cost of three Traits, you never sleep naturally; you can still be physically exhausted, but you don't require rest for your mind, and you only go to sleep if you choose to, if you are magically influenced or just plain knocked out.

Lightning Calculator (1 Trait Merit)

You're a whiz with numbers. You can perform all manner of complex math in your head instantly with incredible accuracy. You're allowed to carry and use a calculator, which isn't considered "in play" (it's just there so that you can do your calculations "in your head").

Time Sense (1 Trait Merit)

You have an unusual acuity for the passage of time. Although you're still susceptible to *Time* magic manipulation, you have an internal sense for time that's accurate to about a minute and, barring magical compression or time travel, always correct. This can be useful in determining *exactly* when a given spell will wear off or in calculating time differences for strange Umbral Realms.

Berserker (2 Trait Merit)

The killing fury lurks within you. When you're injured, a red haze seems to obscure your vision, and you kill… and kill… and kill. Each time you're injured in combat, make a Static Challenge pitting your permanent Willpower against a difficulty of six Traits plus one Trait for each health level of damage you've suffered. If you fail, you enter a berserk frenzy. While berserk, you suffer no penalties for wounds (though you still collapse when Mortally Wounded), and you immediately attempt to engage the nearest enemy target in close combat. You must make the same test each time you wish to snap out of the frenzy, unless there's nobody left (*including* your friends and allies!) around you.

If you have the Flaw: *Short Fuse*, you suffer a two-Trait resolution penalty on all challenges to resist or snap out of your berserk state.

Code of Honor (2 Trait Merit)

A specific code of behavior and ethics guides your actions. Your personal experiences and beliefs shape this code, so it's guided by your own nature, not some arbitrary list of external injunctions. You must work with the Storyteller to delineate the nature and limits of your code, and you must roleplay living up to it. However, you gain one free retest on any Mental or Social Challenge that might result in you violating your *Code of Honor*.

Eidetic Memory (2 Trait Merit)

Your memory is nearly perfect, and you recall with incredible clarity almost everything you experience. A single turn of attention is sufficient to commit a page, picture or short conversation to memory. If you are involved in a combat or otherwise distracted, you must make a Static Mental Challenge, difficulty of six Traits, to successfully memorize the contents of your subject of scrutiny. You should keep a "cheat sheet" of your memories to aid you and the Storyteller in "recollection."

Iron Will (3 Trait Merit)

When your mind is set, your will is not easily broken. You gain three bonus Traits in resolution of challenges where the outcome would affect your rational thoughts (most *Mind* manipulation counts, including manipulation of your senses with illusions or invisibility) but not against emotional alteration. Should you run afoul of a vampire with the *Dominate* Disciple (a set of hypnotic vampire mind-control powers), you may spend a Willpower Trait to gain a retest against it (as usual), but if you win, you gain total immunity to *all Dominate* powers of that vampire for the next five minutes.

Compulsion (1 to 4 Trait Flaw)

Whether by psychological, physical or supernatural impairment, you find yourself forced to do (or not do) a specific thing or class of things. The action could be just about anything; by its very nature, it can make your existence uncomfortable at the very least.

With a psychological *Compulsion*, you *might* be able to overcome your difficulty with a Static Challenge of your permanent Willpower Traits versus a difficulty of the Flaw's value plus six Traits. (If you lose, you *do* lose a temporary Willpower Trait — you fought and failed.) With a supernatural or physical *Compulsion*, you're stuck: Your body or soul just can't cope. Even if you manage to overcome your *Compulsion* briefly in some fashion, you don't escape it without extensive work (and Experience Traits).

The value for a *Compulsion* varies with its severity. Storytellers, take note of players who look for loopholes to take a *Compulsion* and then use the letter of the *Compulsion* to suffer no real hindrance for it. That's a violation of the spirit of the rules and should be disciplined appropriately.

Flaw	Compulsion
One Trait	Do not cross a threshold without permission, never show fear to the enemy, never contradict a superior, always keep your hands clean
Two Traits	Never refuse a reasonable bet, never betray any emotion, do not touch anything hold or consecrated to a particular faith, never harm a child
Three Traits	Never refuse a duel, never strike a woman, never refuse an offer of sex, never tell a lie, never take a life, always check for fire hazards before you leave the house
Four Traits	Never tell the truth, dance whenever you hear music, become entranced by the beauty in mirrors or books, never refuse a dare, do no harm *ever*

Deep Sleeper (1 Trait Flaw)

Snore, toss and ignore the alarm — you sleep like a force of nature. When you *must* wake up to deal with something, you're *stuck*. If you just

woke up, roleplay it: You stagger, stumble and look bleary-eyed, and rest up against anything vaguely pillowlike in an attempt to return to Dreamland. Take a one-Trait resolution penalty on *all* challenges for the scene, after which you *finally* wake up.

Ineptitude (1 Trait Flaw)

You just *suck* at something. Pick one Ability that you possess. You suffer a two-Trait resolution penalty on all challenges related to that Ability. The Storyteller has final say on which Ability you may limit in this fashion; taking *Ineptitude* with, say, *Computer* in a chronicle where you never use the things is not worth any Traits.

Nightmares (1 Trait Flaw)

Horrible nightmares wrack your sleep and prevent you from rest. You dread slumber as it may mean the return of the terrors, and you sometimes find yourself in such stunningly complex and real nightmares that you can't tell them from reality. If you suffer from *Nightmares* before a given game (Storyteller's discretion), you suffer a one-Trait resolution penalty on all challenges due to the fatigue. You might also find yourself involved in a short story that turns out to be a nightmare instead of reality, though you wouldn't know at first. You cannot take this Flaw in conjunction with the Merit: *Sleepless*.

Sleepwalker (1 to 4 Trait Flaw)

Magic? What a load of horse-puckey. No sane person believes in *that* — leastwise, not you. Or perhaps you don't believe in this high-fangled super-science — maybe you're from a backwater part of the world, or perhaps you have some reincarnation of a *Past Life* translocated to the present from the past, or just wound up coming from a non-technological background.

Since you don't believe in these things, you don't see them, and you certainly don't cause them. With the one-Trait version of the Flaw, you can only perform magic (or super-science) that would be coincidental, because you don't believe in it. For two Traits, you don't believe in either. This means that you count as a witness for Paradox purposes on other peoples' magic. For two extra Traits on top of this, you can still do vulgar magic but *you* count as a witness against your own magic, so it's *always* Paradox-prone.

Soft-Hearted (1 Trait Flaw)

You cannot abide suffering, because of the emotional disturbance or pain that it causes you. You must avoid causing pain or suffering to anyone; only by spending a Willpower Trait can you overcome this limitation for a scene/hour.

Speech Impediment (1 Trait Flaw)

A stammer, Tourette's Syndrome or other speech deficiency makes communication difficult for you. Roleplay your deficiency, and suffer a two-Trait resolution penalty on all verbal communication.

Amnesia (2 Trait Flaw)

You've got this problem, but damned if you can remember what it is.... You have no memory of your past, history, family or pretty much *anything*. This doesn't prevent you from having Abilities (you still know how to do things) but you may not know exactly *what* you can do, or how good you are. The Storyteller keeps your character record and never reveals to you your exact Traits, Spheres or the like until you try to use them.

Phobia (2 Trait Flaw)

Some object, creature or circumstance fills you with dread. This fear goes far beyond the normal level of phobias. You react with primal terror to the thing, treating it as a dire threat. When confronted by the object of your fear, you must make a Static Challenge of your permanent Willpower Traits against a difficulty of six Traits, risking a temporary Willpower Trait. Should you fail, you flee in terror. If you're out of Willpower, you simply curl up into a helpless ball, unable to act. If pressed into a corner and forced to defend yourself against the object of your fears, you suffer a two-Trait resolution penalty on all challenges against it.

Short Fuse (2 Trait Flaw)

Whenever someone ticks you off, you tend to fly off the handle. Make a Static Willpower Challenge (difficulty six Traits) when you're insulted or threatened. Failure means that you automatically take the offensive — this may mean responding in kind, be it with verbal abuse, social vendettas or physical violence. If you have the *Berserker* Flaw, you suffer a two-Trait penalty on your challenges to control your berserk rages, as well.

Vengeful (2 Trait Flaw)

You want to even a score, either from before your Awakening or with some group or individual encountered thereafter. You constantly plan ways to satisfy your revenge, and if presented with an opportunity for vengeance, you must spend a Willpower Trait to take any different action for the scene.

Ability Deficit (5 Trait Flaw)

You're not in tune with your natural Abilities; perhaps you lack an education, or maybe you're just not good with them. You start play with *no* Abilities other than those you take with Free Traits. Furthermore, you cannot purchase more than one level of any Ability, or any specialization at all, until you overcome this Flaw.

Supernatural Merits and Flaws

Conditional Magic (1 to 6 Trait Merit or Flaw)

Some specific condition either enhances or hinders your craft. Maybe you work your magic best in bright sunlight, or when affecting redheads, or on Halloween. Perhaps your magic has no effect on anything larger than you can hold, or anyone who's sworn to uphold justice.

The value for this Merit or Flaw varies with the scarcity of occurrence. If you gain a bonus against something really common, that costs several Traits; similarly, if your magic fails against a common fixture, that's a significant Flaw worth several Traits. As a base, this gives you a three-Trait resolution modifier to all Arete challenges where the condition is a factor. You may adjust this modifier downward; doing so reduces the value of the *Conditional Magic* by the same number of Traits.

Traits	Condition
One Trait	Unique: The Sword of Roland, the Matriarch of the MECHA construct, leap year
Two Traits	Scarce as hen's teeth: Current or former members of the Council of Nine, your former *Mentors*, once in a blue moon
Three Traits	Rare, but not unheard of: toadstones, Swedish royalty, werewolves, rowan and red thread, the holy days of the archangels
Four Traits	Special order: virgins, Middle Eastern eye-bead charms, any member of Iteration X, during a thunderstorm
Five Traits	Available without much trouble: cold iron, silver, Christians, any member of the Traditions, a windy day, holy ground
Six Traits	Common as dirt: men, anyone who's ever been baptised, the color purple, under cloud cover, Tuesdays

Example: *Melissa decides that she wants her character to be a "weather witch" — a Verbena with a knack for storms. She takes* Conditional Magic *as a Merit, with the four-Trait "during a thunderstorm" condition. When in thunderstorms, she'd gain a three-Trait resolution bonus to all Arete challenges! However, she feels that this is more than she wants to spend, so she lowers the bonus to two Traits. The Merit now only costs three Free Traits.*

Green Thumb (1 Trait Merit)

Flowers spring up in your footsteps, and trees burst into bloom at your touch. Your hands are as warm as sunlight or stones from a cheery hearth. A common Merit among Verbena.

Parlor Trick (1 Trait Merit)

You have some petty, not-very-useful-but-still-impressive magical feat that you can perform pretty much at will. This doesn't mean that you can duplicate the effects of the Spheres easily; it's just a little knack or trick that you've come by and which is so simple that it requires no challenge or risk of Paradox on your part.

You can use a *Parlor Trick* to conjure a dime with a twist of your wrist, make a spark with a snap of your fingers, turn around and cause motes of light to fly from the hem of your wardrobe, or perform some other simple feat. This doesn't give you bonus Traits, nor does it inflict any damage. The Storyteller has absolute discretion in the nature of what your *Parlor Trick* can or can't do. Note that you only get a single *Parlor Trick*; you can't do *all* of the above with this Merit, just one of them.

Circumspect Avatar (2 Trait Merit)

Avatar? What's that? You may believe in Avatars, but you've certainly never had any dealings with yours. You do not enter a Mindscape in order to undergo a Seeking; instead, you find enlightenment in mundane things. Your Avatar does not guide you directly or appear to you in dreams. At most, it simply gives you impressions or hunches.

Medium (2 Trait Merit)

You hear dead people. More specifically, you can hear the sounds of the Underworld. When a particularly fierce patch of storms races across the Deadlands, you hear the shrieking winds; when a ghost pleads for aid, you're aware. If this ability becomes known to the Dead, they may flock to you, begging for your aid and intercession in the living lands. Conversely, you don't have to rely on *Spirit* magic to speak with the departed, and occasionally they can provide useful advice or assistance.

Unaging (2 Trait Merit)

You never suffer the rigors of age. It's up to you and the Storyteller to decide whether you *appear* to age, or whether you just "stopped" somewhere along the line. You never suffer any penalties for old age (and you cannot take the *Aging* Flaw relating to old age).

Oracular Ability (3 Trait Merit)

No, you're not one of the strange and distant Enlightened masters living out beyond the Horizon, but you do have an uncanny knack for spotting signs and portents. Once per session, you may attempt to read a particular omen by making a Static Mental Challenge with a difficulty of eight or more Traits (Narrator's discretion). If you succeed, you receive some insight into the current situation, allowing you to claim one retest at some point during the night as you draw on the visions that you interpreted.

Cyclic Magic (3 Trait Merit)

Some natural phase ties directly into your magic. Perhaps you're in tune with the tides and your magic ebbs and recedes with them, or maybe you follow the pattern of seasons. Pick one cyclical phenomenon — phases of the moon, stock market patterns, Internet outages — and decide when your "high" and "low" points exist. Your Arete challenge resolution varies by up to three Traits depending upon the point of the cycle — plus three at your high point, minus three at the low. The timing should balance out, but this is an advantage because you can plan your most important and dangerous workings around your cyclical peaks.

Manifest Avatar (3 Trait Merit)

Your Avatar isn't content to sit idly by, whispering wisdom and urging you in dreams. No, it wants attention, and it wants it *now*! As a result, your Avatar actually manifests from time to time. When it appears, it does so as an illusory form that only you can see (though others who read your mind can also sense and see it). The Avatar may talk with you, order you around or just make cryptic mutterings. If you have the *Allies* Background, you may choose to specify that your Avatar is actually inside of a person or creature *Ally*, and it speaks and interacts through that entity. Destruction of that form doesn't hinder the Avatar; it simply finds a new home. If you have the *Phylactery* Flaw, your

Avatar may have a physical form that can interact with you (like a computer). With magic, you can even give your Avatar a separate form.

Natural Channel (3 Trait Merit)

You focus the spirit and material worlds together with your very presence. The Gauntlet is always considered one level lower for you.

Stormwarden (3 or 5 Trait Merit)

For some mysterious reason, the deadly veil that separates spirit from flesh has no effect upon you. While other mages must suffer terrible trials to quest in the spirit world, your magic can directly affect it without interference. You do not suffer any damage from the Avatar Storm. With the five-Trait version of this Merit, your protection extends to anyone touching you.

Unbondable (3 Trait Merit)

You're resistant to the blandishments of supernatural compulsion — well, maybe one such type of compulsion, anyway. You might be immune to cursed items that force you into servitude, or perhaps you are immune to the Blood Bond that befalls those who drink thrice of vampire blood. Pick one such condition of magically enforced slavery; you're immune to it. If, however, you are in a position to reap benefits as well due to it (say, you have a magical ring that normally corrupts the wearer but also gives him powers, or you want to be a ghoul without suffering the Blood Bond), you must pay double for this Merit.

Fae Blood (4 Trait Merit)

The blood of the fae runs in your veins. As a result, you can sense and interact with the faerie worlds, to a limited degree. You're considered kinain, a mortal who has a blood-relation to the fae and can thus learn some of their powers. Although you can't hold Glamour, you can learn changeling cantrips, and they're Paradox-free to you. You can also be easily enchanted to see the Dreaming worlds and interact with the fae. You have a naturally low Banality, so you aren't off-putting to many faeries.

For more about the kinain and their special gifts, see **The Shining Host Players Guide**.

Lucky (4 Trait Merit)

You're just plain lucky. You get three retests per story (for which you bid a *Lucky* Trait: "I got *Lucky* — you missed me last time."), though you may not use more than one to retest on any given challenge.

Shapechanger Kin (4 Trait Merit)

A cousin to wolves, or so it's said, you have a family relation (however distant) to the shapeshifter races. Even if you're not Awakened, you do not suffer the Delirium, the madness that overtakes humans who witness the Changing Breeds in their monstrous forms. You might even learn one of their spiritual tricks — Gifts — which gather no Paradox, but you cannot hold Gnosis, the innate connection to the spirit world shared by the true shifters. Some family or friends might know of shapeshifters, and you could perhaps learn a few rudiments about them, but you'd best be careful; the shapeshifters tread very carefully with mages. Still, you have a better standing than most with the changers.

For more about the Kinfolk of Garou and the Changing Breeds, see **Laws of the Wild** and the **Changing Breeds** books.

Twin Souls (4 Trait Merit)

Your Avatar sundered at some point, and you have a soulmate who has a similar piece of Avatar. This person could be anyone — a twin, a mage, a Sleeper, a stranger. The only thing you know is that when you two come in contact, your Avatar seems briefly whole. With your soulmate, you can share Quintessence and cast spells using the highest ratings for your Arete and Spheres. You gain an *additional* amount of Quintessence equal to the *Avatar* Background rating of the two of you combined, though this "bonus pool" is like any other pool in that it must be refreshed if you want it to continue to hold Quintessence for later junctures.

If you have Apprentice-level *Correspondence*, you always know where your soulmate is. With Apprentice-level *Life*, you know his exact state of health; with Apprentive-level *Mind*, you may share thoughts and emotions. If one member of the pair dies, the survivor must succeed in a Static Willpower Challenge (difficulty of eight Traits) or suffer a psychic shock leading to the loss of one permanent Willpower Trait. In any case, you won't have a soulmate to work with until the Avatar fragment returns through reincarnation.

Ghoul (5 Trait Merit)

The unholy blood of vampires gives you cursed power and sustains you. So long as you drink about a pint of vampire blood each month, you gain a multitude of inherent (Paradox-free) powers. You may refresh all of your Strength-related Physical Traits once per game at no cost, and you do not age.

If you use **Laws of the Night**, you gain the first Basic level of *Potence* and you can learn additional Basic Disciplines known to the vampire whose blood you drink (at twice the normal cost). You have a Blood Pool and can garner and use additional Blood Traits if they're given to you by a vampire.

On the downside, you're a parasite sucking on a parasite. You gain one extra Resonance Trait of both *Entropic* and *Static* Resonance. You risk the Blood Bond, and your Avatar is eclipsed by the curse of the blood, which may cause any of your Seekings to fail at a Narrator's discretion. If you fail to get your "fix," you lose your special powers and all of your skipped age catches up with you. Plus, vampires will fear or hate you and want to use you as a pawn. If they make you one of them, you lose your magical powers, *forever*. Step carefully.

Legendary Attribute (5 Trait Merit)

The might of Hercules, the wisdom of Solomon, the speed of Mercury — your mage inherits some phenomenal characteristic that exceeds normal human strengths. Pick one Attribute Trait category: In that category, your Trait maximum increases by three Traits. Actually *purchasing* these additional Traits still costs you the usual points, though. Furthermore, you have some sort of legendary capability tied to your improved Attribute. Work with your Storyteller to devise some passive (always on) or active (usable once per day) capability. Some examples include:

- With *Legendary Strength*, you might have the capacity to lift a tremendous weight once per game. You could heft a car, a boulder or a telephone booth, perhaps even staggering a few steps with it.
- With *Legendary Stamina*, you might heal one health level per day, regardless of the level of injury.
- With *Legendary Perception*, you might never be surprised.
- With *Legendary Charisma*, you might gain one free retest on any Social Challenge of first impressions, once per game.

Shattered Avatar (5 Trait Merit)

Some crisis in the past shattered your Avatar. This may have been before you were born, or perhaps a botched magical rite broke your Avatar to pieces after your Awakening. Although you start with only your basic *Avatar* Background, you have the potential to improve it during the course of the game. You need only hunt down the lost, shattered pieces of your *Avatar*, which could be anywhere — in some other dimension, trapped in an item, in another mage, etc. Liberate these pieces or claim them for yourself (by finding them, taking the item and breaking it or killing the other mages), and you gain the strength of that piece of your *Avatar* added to your own. You must seek these out on your own — some *Prime*, *Spirit* and *Correspondence* magic might help, but these pieces are flung across the whole of Creation with no telling where they're located or how they might be guarded against scrying or intrusion. Some might not even want to come back!

You may exceed the usual Background limit of Traits with this Merit, but of course only to the limit that your Storyteller allows. If the Storyteller decides that five Traits of *Avatar* is enough, he's not obligated to put in more quests for pieces of your *Avatar*.

Sphere Natural (5 Trait Merit)

Choose one Sphere. You have a natural affinity for this sort of magic. You pay one less Experience Trait for every level that you purchase in this Sphere.

Avatar Companion (7 Trait Merit)

Just as your Avatar cycles through many lives, so too does a lesser Avatar bound to yours by some skein of fate. Each time your Avatar is "reborn" to a new life, this other Avatar also returns to the mortal world with a body and soul. Your companion, though, retains many memories and past images of your earlier incarnations. This can be a great help in puzzling out *Past Lives*, working through problems that you've ostensibly solved before, and in recognizing works made by your Avatar in the past.

The Storyteller should create this companion, though another player's character *might* suffice if you trust the players sufficiently not to use this as an excuse to maximize their combined skills. The companion has no special characteristics other than its memories, unless you also take the *Allies* Background.

Dual Traditions (7 Trait Merit)

You trained early on in multiple styles: Perhaps your teacher was a maveric or Orphan, or maybe you swapped from one Chantry to a new mentor when your old instructor died or vanished, or maybe you just decided that you liked one Tradition better than the one that first inducted you. You may use the foci of both Traditions, and you gain a specialty Sphere from both.

True Faith (7 Trait Merit)

The light of God, Allah, Buddha or whatever name you use for the Almighty shines from your soul. You have one Trait of True Faith, which can be used in a variety of ways. Among mages, you gain one

extra Trait in defense against anyone else's magical Effects. Furthermore, you can use this Trait just like a Willpower Trait. However, retaining the compassionate, generous, honorable demeanor of one of the truly faithful requires you to uphold an exceedingly demanding code. You must *live and exemplify* all the best virtues of your religion: Charity, mercy, understanding and so on. Of course, you might also have some personal flaws — True Faith seems common among witch-hunters — but this is not often the case.

For more comprehensive information about True Faith, see **Laws of the Hunt**.

The Bard's Tongue (1 Trait Flaw)

When you mutter unpleasant imprecations, they have a nasty way of coming true. Once per session, some uncomfortable possibility that you mention — even sarcastically! — will come true. Anything from "It could only get worse if the car broke down" to "This guy's too good to be true — I bet he's a Nephandus" could come to pass. If you don't mention anything particularly noteworthy, a Storyteller or Narrator might whisper to you a cryptic pronouncement that simply comes upon you and blurts out. To quash this urge you must expend a Willpower Trait and suffer one health level of bashing damage as you bite down on your tongue.

Devil's Mark (1 Trait Flaw)

A small physical characteristic or deformity seems to lend credence to the belief that you're in league with infernal forces. While you may or may not really be an infernalist, this marking (which is otherwise not harmful or crippling) certainly *looks* like one of the signs out of folklore — a conspicuous, oddly shaped birthmark, an extra nipple, a set of burns that don't heal. Those who look for witches may recognize these signs.

(If you do happen to have a pet or consor of infernal origin, this familiar can draw Quintessence from you by contact with your mark, though this bonus is admittedly a slim one.)

Echoes (1 to 5 Trait Flaw)

Various legends and stories about magicians manifest around you. Perhaps your presence causes horses to sweat, or makes cows' milk curdle. Maybe wind chimes always ring when you're around, even if there's no wind. On the really nasty end, you might be vulnerable to nails driven through your footprints, or blocked by pure sea salt. Perhaps your shadow japes at you when you aren't looking, or your powerful chi energy causes you to float slightly when you sit. Pick one specific flaw based on folklore and seek your Storyteller's approval (and value).

Geasa (1 to 5 Trait Flaw)

Unlike a *Compulsion*, which is something that you deliberately have no choice to do or not do, a *Geas* represents a magical imperative that still gives you the choice, but requires you not to indulge in it. If you violate this *Geas*, you could suffer the loss of life, magic, perhaps even your soul. The *Geas* might be due to a curse, a particularly bad Paradox backlash, a special quest laid upon you or a hereditary condition.

You must attach your *Geas* to a specific Merit, Flaw or Background. The *Geas* represents a point-break, because it limits the final utility of that Trait. For instance, you could have the *Geas* of "If I ever entrap the souls of the dead with magic, I will lose their favor forever," linked to your Merit: *Sphere Affinity: Spirit*. Trapping the souls of the dead is a pretty easily avoided, unlikely circumstance — a four-Trait *Geas*, subtracted from the five-Trait value of the Merit, which yields a final result of one Trait. The *Geas* is thus a one-Trait Flaw. Conversely, if you stuck a very heavy prohibition on it ("If I ever see the full moon, I will lose my affinity for spirits"), that would be worth more: a five-Trait Merit, minus a one-Trait *Geas*, means that the final value of the *Geas* is a four-Trait Flaw. Or, say that you decided that if you ever eat red meat, you will sicken and die (gain the Flaw: *Degeneration*, six-Trait level). The condition is pretty unlikely (four Traits); take the four-Trait *Geas* from the six-Trait Flaw and you have two Traits — the final value of the Flaw with *Geas*, since it's unlikely to happen and thus not worth as many points. This means that a *Geas* on a relatively trivial boon is not worth much, but a *Geas* on a hefty power can heavily cut the cost of a power if the conditions are strict enough. Note that if the *Geas* Trait value exceeds the other Trait's value, you can still take the *Geas* but you'd get no Traits for it. For instance, you decide that if you ever bind the dead, you will lose your *Medium* Merit. The circumstance is a four-Trait *Geas*, pretty unlikely to happen, but the Merit itself is only two Traits; that would be a negative two Trait total, which would make the *Geas* a two-Trait Merit (you'd have to spend Traits for it!). Instead it's just not worth any Traits — the only way that you can cut the cost of an already-cheap Merit or Flaw is to take a very, very strong *Geas* with it.

A *Geas* cannot reduce a Merit, Flaw or Background cost to zero Traits.

The Trait values here are merely suggestions. The Storyteller, as always, has final say about appropriate *Geasa*.

Traits	**Geas**
One	Inevitable circumstance or incredible sacrifice: When you die, if you ever let the sun touch your skin, if you ever allow your feet to touch the earth, if you ever speak another word
Two	Almost unavoidable circumstance or significant sacrifice: Remain a virgin, never harm a living creature, never tell a lie
Three	Everyday circumstance or common sacrifice: Never back down from a fight, never tell a secret, never refuse hospitality, never marry, never have children
Four	Unlikely circumstance or a small sacrifice: Stop and pet every cat you see, never eat any animal product, never harm a certain type of animal or a certain type of person, never raise your sword in anger
Five	Easily avoided circumstance or trivial sacrifice: Never break bread with a red-haired man, say your prayers every night, take your vitamins, never harm the kind, don't eat ham, keep one small secret

Classic penalties for violating a *Geas* include suffering a *Dark Fate*, having luck turn from good to bad (like losing the *Lucky* Merit), being deserted by your familiar, losing your Avatar, losing a totem, losing all of your friends or losing all of your worldly possessions.

If you ever violate your *Geas*, you also become oath-marked. The patterns of fate determine that you have done so, and anyone with Apprentice-level *Entropy* who senses fate about you can tell that you are an oathbreaker.

Crucial Component (2 to 5 Trait Flaw)

Some special ingredient fuels your magic. This isn't just a focus — it's an absolutely essential material or prop that completes your magical castings for *all* of your spells. The value depends on the scarcity of the item:

Traits	Crucial Component
One	Sunlight, eggs, motor oil, tea, aspirin, electricity, emotion, ectoplasm
Two	Beeswax candles, blood, fresh lavender, grave dirt, holy water, rage, spectral residue
Three	Virgin's blood, hashish, dead humans, gold, platonic love, the fires of Hell
Four	Diamonds, live humans that you sacrifice, rare orchids, lightning strikes, transcendent joy, the tears of an angel, any variety of Tass

Dark Fate (5 Trait Flaw)

Some horrible end awaits you, and you cannot avert it. Worse still, you have glimpses or some foreknowledge of your demise or eternal torment. The Storyteller will determine a particular fate, which will invariably strike you, removing your character from play. Furthermore, in any particular session where the Storyteller deems it appropriate, you may receive a vision of your impending misery. You must spend a Willpower Trait to shake off the experience, or you are a Trait down on all challenge resolution for the rest of the session. This Flaw can be difficult to roleplay, and players are advised to think carefully before choosing it. Some may believe that this Flaw removes free will, but foreknowledge of one's demise can be quite liberating.

Sphere Inept (5 Trait Flaw)

You're just miserable with one of the Spheres. It simply doesn't work well for you. Maybe your Avatar is damaged, or perhaps your understanding is incomplete, or you may even labor under some karmic debt of a past life. The end result is the same: You must pay one extra Experience Trait for each level that you purchase in the Sphere. You may only choose this Flaw once.

Phylactery (7 Trait Flaw)

Your Avatar isn't tied directly to you — it's invested in some concept, object or location. So long as you remain in a place where that investiture is strong, you can tap your magical potential. If you lose the item, if the concept fades or if you leave the area, your ability to work magic vanishes until you can get back to your Avatar!

Your object, location or idea is essentially considered a part of you; that is, if your *Phylactery* happens to be your magic sword, you can affect it with *Correspondence* as if you have an arcane connection to it, and you can't be forced to discard it any more than you could be forced to discard your own hand. (It would still be affected with *Matter* instead of *Life* magic, though.) You must use your *Phylactery* in some way in all of your magic. If it's a magical staff, you must wave it grandly about; if it's the Pacific Ocean, you must hold up, splash and spray the ocean's water; if it's the idea of democracy, you must spout rhetorical dogma.

You can always sense the location of your *Phylactery*, so if you are teleported away or lose it, you can locate it. If it's damaged or destroyed, you can repair or replace it, but you can't have more than one.

If you are tied to a specific location, you can only work magic while you're there. Similarly, if you have a specific concept or group whose beliefs you espouse, your magic only works so long as you're a recognized part of that group (so destroying the group would also effectively snuff your *Phylactery*, unless you managed to rebuild the group from scratch or re-awaken the concept in people's minds.).

If you die, your Avatar may or may not go back into the cycle of being — the *Phylactery* might await you next incarnation, or it might crumble and vanish, or your Avatar might simply flee and return to the Wheel.

Technocracy Merits and Flaws

The following Merits and Flaws are from the **Guide to the Technocracy** and thus are especially appropriate to Technocrat characters.

Unobtrusive (1 Trait Merit)

This Merit allows you to be the person that no one ever notices. This is not as powerful as *Arcane* — you aren't invisible, people won't forget you were there, and evidence of you won't vanish. It does, however, allow you to not stand out of a crowd. Think of it as a perpetual "blandness" effect that you cannot turn off.

Add two Traits to all difficulties to recall your appearance, or your actions if you were not the center of attention.

Acute Senses (1 or 3 Trait Merit)

You have one or more senses that are above and beyond the human norm. While not superhuman, the amount your character can perceive is exceptional.

For one Trait, you have one sharp sense. This gives you a two-Trait bonus for resolution of challenges for tests involving that sense.

For three Traits, all your senses are enhanced.

Note that when your heightened senses are exposed to particularly powerful stimuli (such as spotlights, jet engines, a discharging skunk), you may, at your Storyteller's discretion, be rendered temporarily "numb" in that sense, resulting in severe penalties or lack of use of that sense for some time.

Factions

Zaotar: Many mages who have met Taftani see them as loud, brash, egotistical, obnoxious warmongers. The Zaotar very much resemble this remark. They live by the credo, "If it offends you, blow it up" and love nothing more than using great vulgar Effects to smash the lies of the Technocracy. Their egotism stems from their unshakeable belief that they are right and *any* who buy into the lie are wrong. While their ways seem chaotic, they do in fact have a cause — the destruction of the Technocratic paradigm. *Specialty Sphere: Forces*

Kahin: These mages rely more heavily on the mystical and esoteric. They tend to concentrate on divinations, healing and curses. Where the Zaotar are loud, the Kahin are contemplative. The Kahin concentrate most of their research on studies of fate, life and death; here, they believe, await the greatest truths. This is not to say that the Kahin do not use flashy, explosively vulgar Effects — they simply do not use them as often, because they're more likely to be found studying than blowing everything up around them.

License to . . . (1-5 Trait Merit)

This merit allows the type of licenses that allow you to kill, break laws, etc., as well as the more mundane types of civil permits. Depending on the cost of the Merit, you can:

One Trait	Own and operate specialized vehicles (limousines, trucks, planes, helicopters)
Two Traits	Practice medicine, law (lawyer, paramedic, doctor)
Three Traits	Uphold the law (police officer, government agent, detective)
Four Traits	Own/operate military hardware (heavy weapons, milspec vehicles, explosives)
Five Traits	Break the law in the course of duty (diplomat, secret agent — and yes, this level includes killing people)

The level of license you take requires certain responsibilities — typically a job, membership in certain groups/agencies/etc. There are also *always* consequences to abusing the license — a secret agent who kills four or five people a session is going to get called on by his superiors to find out why, possibly even having his license revoked. The Storyteller is completely within his rights to take this merit away from you if you abuse it.

Confidence (2 point Merit)

While the Technocracy may be "The Man," you are definitely "Da Man!" and you know it. You have an overwhelming self-confidence in your abilities, perhaps to the point of hubris, but you are sure of yourself — and others notice too.

This Merit grants you a two-Trait bonus for resolution of all *Leadership* and *Intimidation* challenges.

Officially Dead (2 Trait Merit)

According to all government records and documents, you are dead. Any attempts to locate official records of documents reflect this status — tracking you via official means is very difficult. All attempts to use *Bureaucracy* Influences directly against you fail. The Storyteller may give other Influences similar modifications at his discretion.

(Typically, going to see old family and friends who knew you from before is a good way to lose this Merit — enough "Elvis"-type sightings by old acquaintances, and someone will discover that you are not dead. This may cause you to lose the Merit, or, more likely, to actually be killed to make sure your secret is not exposed.)

Poker Face (2 Trait Merit)

You have the ultimate poker face — no sign of emotion ever crosses your face. You have one free defensive Social retest per night, as others always have trouble figuring you out.

(Note — you should have something on your person indicating that your face never shows any emotion; you may flinch, but your NWO agent won't. The Storyteller will tell you if and when you do show emotion.)

Iron Will (3 Trait Merit)

This Merit gives you a resistance to all mental magics and powers, such as the *Mind* Sphere and the vampiric *Dominate* Discipline. You receive a one-Trait bonus for resolution of challenges involving such powers being used against you. Further, if affected with such a power, you may expend a Willpower Trait to retest the effect. If you win, the effect is negated and you receive a five-minute immunity to further use of such powers upon you. This Merit only works in regards to mind-affecting powers, not to spirit charms or similar effects.

True Faith and Templars

While the Templars are truly faithful in the power and existence of their God, few Templar mages show signs of having True Faith. It is thought by some theologians and researchers, who know of this paradox, that Templars may not truly be mages in the strictest definition. The theory goes that their Avatars are Awakened by their faith, and their True Faith shows itself through their magic.

Perfect Liar (3 Trait Merit)

You are the ultimate silver-tongued devil. You receive a two-Trait bonus for resolution of all *Subterfuge* challenges, and for *Empathy* tests used against you. This bonus will also work against mundane means of veracity testing, such as a lie detector. It has no impact on any magic used to determine your emotions.

Master of Red Tape (4 Trait Merit)

You are an unparalleled master of red tape. You may use your *Bureaucracy* Influence twice as often as normally allowed, and in parallel with any other Influence where you go through official channels as if it was an Influence of that type. However, make sure to cover your tracks, because you are still going to leave a trail — no one is that good.

Inner Knight (5 Trait Merit)

Your spirit was one of the original Daedaleans in the early days of the Order of Reason. While you don't necessarily believe this, dreams about your past inspire you.

Once per game session, you may call for a retest on any one failed test. Unlike normal tests, this one challenge is resolved using your maximum number of Traits, rather than your current total. You also receive a Two-trait bonus on this challenge. Also, once per session you can refresh all your Traits in one category without expending a willpower Trait.

Technobabbler (1 Trait Flaw)

When you discuss anything, you use advanced technological and sociological terms, Orwellian newspeak and the like. Very few people can understand you. You receive a one-Trait penalty in discussing *anything* with a non-Technocrat.

Bigot (2 Trait Flaw)

There is some group within the Technocracy you just don't like, be it cyborgs, constructs or just normal agents. Pick one such group within the Technocracy. You have a two-Trait penalty on all Social Challenges with that group. Any dealings with another Technocrat that does not share this viewpoint also incurs the same penalty.

As *Bigotry* is a decidedly unpleasant and very real-life concept, the Storyteller may disallow this Flaw. Even if it is allowed, the group disliked must some group or faction within the Technocracy, not a real-world group, race, creed, etc.

Construct (2 Trait Flaw)

You aren't human-born, and you look it. For whatever reason, when you were created, steps were not taken to make sure you looked like a normal human. For this reason, you suffer a one-Trait penalty dealing with non-Technocrats, may not take any Appearance-based Traits, and are likely to be chased down like Frankenstein's monster if you venture out into the everyday world.

Icy (2 Trait Flaw)

You are so cold and emotionless that even other Technocrats find you creepy. You must take at least one Negative Social Trait; it counts double to any non-Technocrats. Your comrades are a bit more accepting, but even *they* still glance at you sideways.

Rose-Colored Mirrorshades (2 Trait Flaw)

To you, technology is it — man's creations are great and can have no side-effects. Problem is, you cannot accept any downfalls in said technology/ideas. When confronted with major proof of technology's failings (such as major pollution, animal testing subjects, etc), you suffer a two-Trait penalty to all tests until out of the presence of this proof.

Faulty Enhancements (2-5 Trait Flaw)

"Better, stronger, faster" turned out to have the caveat "sometimes." When you received your enhancements, some of them didn't work correctly. This results in some serious side effects from being implanted. At the beginning of every game session, make a Simple Test. If you lose, you suffer a Trait penalty equal to the level of this Flaw. If you tie, the penalty is halved (round down). If you win, you suffer no side-effects. This Flaw can only be taken if you have some kind of enhancement, and cannot be removed unless that enhancement is also removed.

Example of Gifts of Feng-tu

Living Hair: The mage's hair acts as a separate limb that can be controlled like a third arm. The mage may pick things up and manipulate fine objects with the hair, but may not wield any weapons. In hand-to-hand combat, the mage may take one extra attack action using his hair immediately after making a normal attack. The *Living Hair* uses the mage's current Physical Traits and inflicts one bashing level.

Corpse Skin: The mage's skin becomes pale and cool, with a strangely soft, leathery feel — altogether, not unlike that of a corpse. The skin also becomes tougher than normal and gives the mage one extra Healthy health level.

Seductress' Eyes: The mage's irises take on an unusual color like ice blue, emerald green or violet. During conversation, he makes eye contact with his target and initiates a Social Challenge, which may be retested with *Seduction*. If the mage wins, his victim becomes enamoured of him and will do one thing for him that does not place her in immediate danger. After the target finishes the task, she remains enamored with the mage for the rest of the scene.

Talons of Feng-tu: The mage's nails grow longer, usually three to five inches, and become razor-sharp. A mage with this gift may inflict lethal damage in hand-to-hand combat.

Angelic Voice: The mage's singing voice becomes enchanting and melodic, draining his opponent of aggression and hate. When the mage sings, any person within earshot that wishes to harm him must first defeat him in a Social Challenge or be sapped of her will to fight and unable to attack the mage. The mage may do nothing but sing during a round because of the concentration needed.

Stress Atavism (3 Trait Flaw)

Most technocrats are the embodiment of calm. You are an agent of rage. When in combat, you become a mindless, berserk beast that attacks and kills everything in its way.

Once you have entered combat, make a Static Willpower Test (against eight Traits). Failing or tying means you have entered an animalistic state. You have three extra Bruised health levels and three bonus Traits (*Brutal* x 3, which can take you over your maximum). The downside is that all you can do is fight. You cannot use any weapon more advanced than a firearm, and you cannot concentrate enough to use any Procedure or *Device*. Tactics more involved than charge and kill everything are incomprehensible. Once in this state, you cannot leave the fight or exit this state until all opponents are dead. The Storyteller may also require you make a Static Mental Challenge (difficulty 10) to recognize and avoid attacking allies. Control will have you terminated when you finally go too far, by the way, so have fun while it lasts.

Demented Eidolon (3 Trait Flaw)

No one told your Genius it was supposed to be a guide to an Enlightened man. Instead, it fills your head with mystic ideas and images, and is wholly not in line with the paradigm. You see your Eidolon as others see their Avatar, and it often is at odds with your Technocratic allegiance. At some point, you will most likely go mad, or be forced to leave the Union (in which case the Flaw must be bought off). In the meantime, all Seekings are at a plus one-Trait difficulty.

Rotten Liar (3 Trait Flaw)

Some people can lie to their priests. You can't even lie your way into bed. Anytime you attempt to deceive, lie or disguise yourself, you suffer a two-Trait penalty.

Mr. Red Tape (4 Trait Flaw)

Somehow, you always seem to get put at the bottom of the stack in any bureaucracy. Double the time and effort needed for all *Bureaucracy* Influence uses (for instance, faking a death certificate has a cost of six levels), as well as other influences (such as *Health*, *University*, *Police*) when they involve using official channels and/or paperwork.

Rogue (4 Trait Flaw)

You are on your own. You may still be a member of the Technocracy, but if you are, it's only because they haven't killed you yet. This Flaw indicates that you have had your status in the Union changed. One option is that you are out and set for destruction. Otherwise, you are still in the Union, but with no ability to requisition or receive aid, and are constantly sent on suicide missions. Enjoy the ride.

Fifth Degree (5 Trait Flaw)

This Flaw indicates you are in big trouble with the Union. You are under constant watch by your superiors in the Union, and feel their weight upon you. You suffer a three-Trait penalty to all Social tests with other Technocrats. The higher-ups still consider you a member of the

Union, so you will still get missions and assignments, though they are the worse sort. Further, your coworkers are under no orders to help you out, though the reverse is not true. You very rarely get support, and your requisitions are frequently lost. Double all internal *Requisitions* and Influence costs for use within the Technocracy.

Tradition Merits and Flaws

The following Merits and Flaws, translated from the **Guide to the Traditions**, are particularly appropriate for high-magic games. They may not be appropriate for all venues. Storytellers, remember that Merits and Flaws are optional — these even more so.

Physical Enhancement (3+ Trait Merit)

You have some sort of obvious physical enhancement that sets you apart from human — and probably makes you look decidedly demonic. This could be claws, horns, fangs, hooves or a tail with a barb or stinger. These might look mystical, or they could be somewhat mundane (such as surgically implanted spikes in your head). One such enhancement costs three Traits. Each additional one costs two Traits. Making a tail prehensile costs three Traits. One Trait raises the size to a fairly large version, and two Traits increases to a huge set of horns, claws or whatnot. One Trait also can make such a feature retractable. Each such feature grants you an extra Trait in physical combat (two if it's large, three if it's huge). On the flip side, you're likely to be noticed.

So long as you're playing in a private area, you should go out of your way to use makeup or prosthetics to represent this Trait. Storytellers should feel free to dock experience from players who demand huge horns for goring their enemies and then just wear a cheesy card taped to the forehead.

Anachronism (1 to 3 Trait Flaw)

You're from out of time — literally. You're not familiar with the ways of the current century. For one Trait, you're more familiar with the ways of a decade from the previous or next century (maybe you were raised in a Technocratic Horizon Construct, or you came from the past). For two Traits, raise this to two or three centuries away; for three Traits, it's further than that. You may require Mental Challenges to use simple tools and concepts; a 12th-century freeman probably doesn't understand democracy, and a phone is too primitive for a 24th-century man to use.

Failure to roleplay this Flaw and its consequences may result in the Storyteller docking experience to buy it off.

Personal Talisman (1 Trait Merit or Flaw)

While you're not a master mage yet, you managed to secure help from one long enough to make a personal Talisman for yourself. This minor Talisman has a Trait of your Willpower, so you have one extra Willpower as long as you hold it. It's also an arcane connection to you. In conjunction with Backgrounds, it might be a useful *Wonder*.

If you take this as a Merit, you still own the item. As a Flaw, it's in someone else's hands.

Nine Lives (6 Trait Merit)

For some reason, you have the luck of a cat. Anytime you fail a challenge that would result in your death or incapacitation, you gain an immediate retest. You can only do this nine times ever, and only once on any given challenge.

Resistant Pattern (7 Trait Merit)

Your Pattern is particularly stalwart and doesn't suffer damage easily. All aggravated damage is treated as lethal damage to you.

Immunity (Variable Trait Merit)

You have complete *Immunity* to one or more substances or attack forms that would normally injure or kill you. The power of your *Immunity* varies with the cost.

Two Traits	Immune to one very minor nuisance or rare threat: The bite of a chimera or sunburn.
Four Traits	A major or uncommon threat: poisons, diseases, death magic.
Six Traits	Terminal or common threats: Fire, drowning.
Eight Traits	Invulnerable to all physical harm, but with one large weak spot or vulnerability to one common item (vulnerable in the chest or to fire, for instance).
10 Traits	Invulnerabule with one small weak spot (the heel); or, one rare bane (mistletoe dagger); or, one common bane in a large spot (fire in the chest); or, immune to all but aggravated damage, or to damage inflicted by a specific condition (by your own body, with your *Phylactery*).
12 Traits	Immune to all but one very rare bane (radiation, specific spell); or one rare bane in specific circum stances (mistletoe dagger wielded by a woman)

14 Traits	Immune to all but one very rare bane in specific circumstance (mistletoe dagger wielded by a red-headed woman on the night of the full moon)
16 Traits	Immune to all but one unique, specific bane (A Tradition Blade, Excalibur, etc.)

For half cost, you take only half damage from the subject of the specified immunity.

Cast No Shadow or Reflection (1 Trait Flaw)

You do not show up in mirrors or other silvered reflective surfaces. You can still be caught on digital camera and color film, but you don't show up on the emulsion for black and white film.

Touch of Frost (1 Trait Flaw)

Your touch is *cold*, and transmits that cold. When you touch living people, they shiver; make your touch known. When you touch animals, they flee. Plants shrivel and die.

Vulnerability (1 to 7 Trait Flaw)

This is the reverse of *Immunity*. Some common substance does grievous harm to you.

Two Traits	One unique item can fatally injure you (The Heel of St. Vitus)
Three Traits	Something very rare can fatally injure you (rose petals blessed by the Pope)
Four Traits	Something moderately common can injure you (iron, sunlight)
Five Traits	Something very common can injure you (water, air)

You take one health level of aggravated damage per turn in contact with your *Vulnerability*. For an extra Trait, you die instantly if contacted by the substance. For another Trait, being in the same room as the Flaw causes you damage. For one less Trait, you must actually be struck by the substance as if it were used as a weapon.

Beast Within (5 Trait Flaw)

You're prone to violent fits of rage and berserk anger. When injured or humiliated, make a test of your number of Dynamic Resonance Traits against a difficulty of four Traits. If you *win*, you go *Berserk* (as the Merit of that name). If you lose, you retain control of yourself.

Bedeviled (6 Trait Flaw)

The devil — or some sort of powerful supernatural entity — is out to get you. You don't know what it is, but something wretched always happens to you at the last minute. Once per game the Storyteller may intervene and negate any one success you make completely; no test is required.

Disparates

The Traditions and Technocrats aren't the only players in the battle for enlightenment. Hidden in the sidelines and among the cracks are the Disparates — small Crafts of independent mages who refuse to take sides and practice separate cultural magics.

Ahl-i-Batin

"Inscrutable" and "confusing" are two words frequently used to describe the Ahl-i-Batin. Ever since they first revealed themselves to other mages, they have always been a mysterious group. Their views on unity and faith have carried them through the ages, even when most thought they had died out.

During the formation of the Council of Nine, the Ahl-i-Batin were instrumental in contacting mages all over the world and bringing them together so they might share ideas and debate philosophies. Underlying the Batini's desire to bring the disparate groups together, though, was their belief that the true path to enlightenment was through the unity of thought and belief. They believed that unity, cemented with faith, would result in a greater good that would bring all Mankind to Ascension.

Shortly after the forming of the Council of Nine and the events of the First Cabal, the Batini dropped from sight, leaving the Seat of *Correspondence* empty until the Virtual Adepts defected from the Technocracy. Many believed the Technocracy exterminated the Batini when they made a push into the Middle East, but over the centuries, Tradition mages spoke of seeing strange mages using Arabic trappings. Their purpose and goals were unknown; all that could be guessed was that they fought the Technocracy as the Traditions did.

In truth the Ahl-i-Batin have always been here — they just chose to remain secret. The Ahl-i-Batin had discovered many secrets, and had made just as many enemies, and it was safer for them to "disappear" from the world. Yet, even while hidden, they altered and manipulated from the shadows. Quietly they sought to maneuver the Sleepers toward

Ascension, and they remain a considerable power in their homelands of the Middle East, even with the incursions of the Technocracy.

Roleplaying Hints: The Batini are called the Subtle Ones for a reasons. The Batini do not isolate themselves to remain hidden, though — instead, they integrate themselves wholly. From their hidden positions among the Sleepers, the Batini may manipulate Sleepers and mages alike. Just as they are able to seamlessly integrate themselves as sleepers, however, they can also drop whatever role they play and pick up another just as easily — one day a healer, the next a beggar, the next a taxi driver. The Batini are masters of hiding in plain sight. Many Batini count themselves among the faithful of Islamic religions.

Specialty Sphere: *Correspondence*

Common Foci: Prayer, meditation, music, dancing, pen and ink

Advantage: The Subtle Ways

The subtlety of the Ahl-i-Batin has been enforced so strongly by the mages themselves and all who know of them that all Batini start the game with an extra Trait of *Arcane*. New Batini characters may start the game with up to six Arcane traits. Furthermore, the Subtle Ones may enact the **Rite of Occultation** (see **Hidden Paths**, page xx) upon themselves and increase their Arcane Traits up to a maximum of 10. Only Batini may uses the **Rite of Occultation**; it simply does not work on mages of other Traditions for reasons that have never been explained.

Disadvantage: Removed From Fate

Due to what some believe to be a Euthanatos curse, or maybe as a side-effect of their natural subtlety and seeming invisibility, Batini seem to be cut off from the control of Fate, which seems a paradox for the most subtle of all mages to be unable to effect the subtlest of all arts. Batini are unable start with or learn *Entropy*, ever. They essentially are all *Sphere Inept* at *Entropy*. This Disadvantage may never be bought off like the Flaw.

Sisters of Hippolyta

The Sisters of Hippolyta are an extended, entirely female family of Awakened willworkers and Enlightened Sleepers. Their historical roots lie with the ancient Amazons, but the Sisters of today have little in common with their violent, man-hating ancestors. The Sisters live most of their lives in isolated communities called conclaves; in the conclaves, they work together to produce food and commodities, engage in shared governance, and nurture each other's spiritual growth.

Some Sisters spend considerable time away from their conclaves, working in the outside world and helping the needy, then bringing back skills and tools to the community. Among the Sisters can be found physicians, computer programmers, teachers, accountants, farmers and chefs — any woman who professes her belief in the Sisters' communal lifestyle (with its joys of sisterhood and its isolation from the outside world) is welcome. For all their other duties, the Sisters do not neglect the magical arts. Skilled healers of mind and body, and intuitive diviners of time and nature, these mystics conduct their arts as rituals and celebrations of family ties. Their magic glorifies the unique nature of women, their voices, their inner strength, their connection to the earth and their ability to create life. Each Sister is a power unto herself, but with in the framework of communal magic, the group becomes mightier than the individual.

The near-fanatical devotion to the group over the individual is the thorn of this paradise, though. Those who forsake the community and return to the outside world are commonly cast from the Craft completely. Whether the Sister leaves due to love, familial duty or because of a disagreement is immaterial. While the Craft sanctions temporary sojourns, the Sisters consider each member who leaves permanently to be like a thread pulled from the tapestry of the community. In the Sisters' minds, those who depart and don't return have joined the enemy, and their relatives and companions share the blame for their defection.

Roleplaying Hints: Yes, they are *all* women. There are no men in the Sisterhood. Period. The Sisters are not man-haters, though — they simply do not believe they can exercise the power of their womanhood in the outside world. If a Sister was in a position to help a man in need, she would — not doing so would deny the nurturing nature of a woman's heart and lessen the Sisterhood as a whole. The Sisters believe strongly in the cycles of birth, life, death and rebirth. They see their ability to create and bear children as a metaphor for their spirituality which gives them a mystical tie to the power of creation.

Specialty Sphere: *Life*

Common Foci: Dance, poetry, song, meditation, massage, technological devices, sex, childbirth

Advantage: Sister's Synchronization

Since its creation, the Sisterhood has approached everything as a team effort. They do not concentrate on the group and the things the group can accomplish as a one. Because of this, Sisters are very skilled in leading and directing people in team efforts, from planting a field, to finding a lost child, to dealing with a wife-beater. In any mass or mob challenge where the Sister is the leader, she has a two-Trait competency bonus, and any member of her group may spend an Ability retest for the group, even if she is not the leader. Only one member of the group may make an Ability retest per challenge.

Disadvantage: Samantha's Tears

Women who live and learn under the Sisters become very used to their acceptance in the conclave, and when they are in the normal world, they find themselves pining for it. This is not to say the Sisters are weak; they just become so used to the environment of the conclave that they suffer an erosion of their morale. To represent this, Sisters regain Willpower at half the normal rate of other mages. If the game replenishes willpower at the beginning of each session for easier bookkeeping, then Sisterhood characters must spend one extra Willpower whenever they spend Willpower. This Disadvantage is negated if the Sister is at one of the few conclaves that the Sisterhood runs away from society.

Taftani

In Arabic mythology, there are stories of magi who bound and commanded djinn, rode on flying carpets, and laid curses that make even the most malicious Verbena blush. These are the Taftani, born from the cradle of civilization when Babylon was at its height. These willworkers are thought by some to be the bravest of all mages; others see them as the most absurd.

The Taftani worship the ideal of a world of truth and order, and fight against the forces of deceit and chaos, which they believe are embodied in the Technocracy. The Taftani believe the world as we know it is created by the friction between Asha (the force of truth and order) and Druj (the force of chaos and deceit). And the truth is that they have been gifted their power by the ancient gods to shape reality. This entitlement from the gods does not give them the right to do magic, though. It requires them to perform magic as a show of their faith and belief in their gods and paradigm. Taftani culture dictates that they must inflict their wills on reality to fight the forces of Druj.

The Taftani also represent throwbacks to older times — their magics are based on the beliefs and practices of ancient Babylon. Their fabled King Suleiman the Wise granted them some of their most valued lore, especially the Solomonic Code, the mysterious rules of order that all djinn must follow. The Craft's adherence to the old ways has been a constant stumbling block to the Technocracy's attempts to wipe out the Traditions in the Middle East. How does a Technocratic agent convince a populace that magic is not real and can be explained away with science and logic, when there is a madman on the mountain who can summon djinn and bend them to his will? The Taftani pay dearly for their fidelity to Asha and the gods, however. Most end up dying by their own hand due to an overabundance of Paradox. They accept this as part of the war that they must wage against the Technocracy's paradigm. Remarkably enough, the Taftani's constant use of obvious and memorable vulgar Effects has been able to jam a wedge in the Technocratic paradigm and halt or push back its advance. The Taftani also have an abhorrence for coincidental Effects, as they see such as giving in to the lies of the Technocracy. It is only through fighting for what they believe to be the truth and retaining their freedom to act in any way that they like that the Taftani have managed to survive.

Roleplaying Hints: Taftani take a rather arrogant view of their position in the world. They do believe that they have the right to do magic any way they like and everybody else be damned. They carry this attitude into everything that they do, and consequently, they do not present themselves as the most sociable of mages, even among each other. Taftani hate being limited, even by their own failings; they believe that the only way to remain free is to keep one's options open. Because of this, they try to be prepared for *anything* that might happen and learn a very broad array of skills so they can meet any situation prepared and ready to act. Many apprentices are required by their masters to show aptitude in many different skills before they are taught anything of magic. This has a secondary effect, though — because these mages concentrate so much on mastering their mundane abilities, they need not use their devastating and vulgar magics until they are more than ready.

Specialty Sphere: *Spirit*

Common Foci: Poetry, art, crafting, swords, bottles and other vessels, prayer

Advantage: Code of Solomon

Taftani apprentices are taught early on about the Solomonic Code, how it applies to the beings of the Invisible World, and the rules that all spirits must follow. By applying their knowledge, Taftani are able to manipulate certain spirits much easier than most other mages. In all dealings with djinn, Banes and elementals, Taftani have a two-Trait competency bonus to any Social Challenges with those spirits.

The Taftani do not attempt to hide their Resonance, and see it as a badge of identity and honor. A Taftani with little Resonance is obviously not trying to reawaken the magic in the world like his brethren, and is likely to be snubbed by them. Further, suppressing one's Resonance is seen as suppressing the truth of oneself and a mortal affront to the gods from whom magic springs. A Taftani who has very pronounced Resonance displays it proudly, and is respected and revered by his fellows. Because of the feeling of self-worth that this high Resonance gives, a Taftani with a combined number of Entropic and/or Dynamic Resonance Traits equaling five receives a bonus Social Trait of *Confident*. A combined number of Entropic and Dynamic Traits equaling 10 grants a second *Confident* Trait.

Disadvantage: Accepting the Lie

The Taftani abhor coincidental magic because they feel it only strengthens the structure of the Technocracy. Only by resisting what they perceive as the problem can they defeat the lie that permeates reality. Because of these strong beliefs, a Taftani must spend a Willpower Trait in order to accept the lie for one round and perform a coincidental Effect. This penalty does not apply if they are creating an Effect in an area where their paradigm is supported, such as their *Sanctum* or an Umbral Realm.

Templars

Most people have heard the history of the Templars, an order of knights founded in 1119 to protect pilgrims on the roads to Jerusalem. During the Crusades, they were regarded as some of the most brave and valiant warriors; they were the first into battle and the last to retreat (in fact, one of their tenets forbade retreat). The Templars not only became militarily successful but economically powerful, and this led to many rumors. After the fall of Jerusalem to the Muslims, the rumors became accusations, and in 1307 King Philip the Fair of France ordered all Templar Knights arrested on charges of heresy. Most of the knights recanted their "heresy" and joined other orders as penance, except for Jacques de Molay, the Grand Master of the order. He claimed that there was no heresy among the Knights Templar, and before his execution he stated that Philip the Fair and the Pope would stand with him before God's Throne in judgment before the end of the year; both of them died in that same year.

This is the history that the Sleepers know. In actuality, the Knights Templar were allied with the Cabal of Pure Thought, a member of the Order of Reason, and when the accusations of heresy were handed down, the remaining Templars went underground and joined the Cabal's membership. From their shelter, the Templars shepherded Christendom while remaining out of sight. During the turbulent years of the Reformation, the Templars grew to see *all* of Christendom as their charge, and began to limit their foes to the supernatural enemies of Christ. In 1837, the Order of Reason came to the conclusion that religion and faith were superstitious tripe to be expunged from Consensual reality, and any who strengthened religion needed to be removed. The Order attacked the Templars and killed many of them, but those who retreated and survived went even deeper underground.

The Templars exist today as a secret magical order that follows four major tenets, known as the Edicts of the Just — 1) Strive to create a new Christendom that is not created in the image of the Order of Reason; 2) Defend the innocent from the horrors of the supernatural and infernal; 3) Defeat the Order of Reason and gain justice for their betrayal and their promulgation of irreligion; and 4) Preserve the Order itself, with secrecy being the paramount directive. Over the past 150 years, the Order of Knights Templar have persevered, never surrendering, knowing that their mission to shepherd and protect the innocent in the name of God is what has brought them through all their past difficulties.

Roleplaying Hints: The Knights Templar are not all Catholic as they used to be and now encompass all of Christendom. They just require that their Knights agree on the primacy of the Gospel, and doctrinal argument within the Order is forbidden; theological debate is best left to theologians not warriors. And Templars do not fight for the ascension of mankind, they instead work to restore Christendom to what it was in ancient and believe that when this is done shall herald for the Reconciliation of God and the Salvation of the entire world. But it is very hard to do this with sword and shield; they now fight these battles with words in court rooms, universities, and parliaments; quietly they manipulate man and shepherd him into the loving arms of Christ.

Specialty Sphere: *Forces*

Common Foci: Bibles, altars, Eucharist, hymnal, crosses or crucifixes, flagellation, guns, knightly mantle, shields, sword, prayer

Advantage: Apocalyptic Destiny

The Templar knights do not merely believe they are the chosen warriors of Christendom — they *know* they are such. They know that they are the guardians of the innocent in the coming Apocalypse, and are prepared to face their destiny head on. Because of this knowledge, Templars get an extra number of traits of *Destiny* equal to their Arete rating (up to a maximum of five). These are bonus *Destiny* Traits and add on to any *Destiny* Traits bought at character creation. As the character increases his Arete rating, his *Destiny* also increases with it. A Templar character may have greater than five *Destiny* because of his bonus Traits, but still is limited to a *Destiny* x 5 when buying the Traits at character creation. Also the bonus *Destiny* of the Templar character cannot be removed by the Storyteller until — well, until the Storyteller happens to run the Apocalypse, and then the bonus *Destiny* is gone because it has been fulfilled.

Disadvantage: Scourge of God

Part of the oath of becoming a Templar is to be humble in the eyes of God and to accept His judgment above all others. Templars believe that Paradox is God showing His disfavor over something that the Templar has done. Because of this, Templars believe that they must take the judgment of God immediately because to make God wait is the highest form of hubris. Whenever a Templar spends a Willpower Trait in order to hold off a Paradox Flaw or backlash, he is at a Trait penalty equal to the number of accumulated Paradox on all magical Effect tests. This penalty immediately goes away after the Paradox has been allowed to dissipate.

Wu Keng

The Wu Keng did not start off as a Craft unto themselves. Originally, they were disparate shamans who tended to the spiritual matters of their home villages. They were brought together when their practices were outlawed by the secular Chou dynasty around 1000 BC. Many of the Wu avoided death by pursuing scholarly endeavors, while others maintained their shamanistic practices. Of the few who remained in their ancestors' villages, tending to the spirits for the villagers, some wished to restore the greatness of the past. Banding together, these shamans and scholars formed the Wu Keng, and they guarded the secrets of the spirit world preparing for a time when their lore would be necessary. To insure their success they made a deal with the ancient spirits of Feng-tu, the land of the dead. These spirits promised that after three millennia of devout service, they would renew the power and authority of the Wu Keng over the affairs of man. There was a catch, though — the magi would have to remain hidden and stay behind the scenes of the civilized world, using their magics only in the subtlest ways; and any who they taught would also become servants of the spirits.

Though the Wu Keng survived, they suffered greatly at the hands of their masters. During their most grueling trial, the entire Craft was captured and imprisoned by the cruel First Emperor Qin Shihuang and tortured mercilessly. The Feng-tu masters of the Wu Keng came to their rescue, but exacted payment for their assistance. The spirits ordered the Wu Keng to dress and act as women for the remainder of their service — the Yin energy of doing so would balance the aggressive Yang energy and make them subtler. As part of this punishment, and as a reminder of the shame of being captured, all Wu Keng had to bind their feet in the traditional Chinese way, resulting in slender mutilated feet that forced them to take mincing (and painful) steps. Further, they could not alleviate the pain by any means.

Now, with the third millennia of their service just past, the Wu Keng find that their founders, the Chou-an, have betrayed them. The Chou-an were the six remaining shamans from the Chou dynasty, and, according to the spirits of Feng-tu, betrayed the pact by teaching their arts to others who were not made servants of the spirits. Because of this, the spirits of Feng-tu have extended the deal for another millennia, and added another clause to it: The Wu Keng are to find all the Chou-an and their pupils and destroy them. This has a new catch, however — the spirits of Feng-tu will not let the Wu Keng teach any new mages, unless it is a replacement for one who has died. The oldest of the Wu Keng continually plead to the spirits to let them swell their ranks to fight this war in which they are finding they are outnumbered, but their pleas always fall on deaf ears.

Roleplaying Hints: Yes, the Wu Keng are all cross-dressing male mages; this means that players should either dress themselves as women or be women. Yes, they serve otherworldly masters. The Wu Keng do not think too much about their pact with the spirits of Feng-tu, and instead busy themselves with doing their masters' bidding, because tarrying on a task brings quick and painful punishment. Wu Keng tend to act like traditional Chinese women, quiet and humble, their feet bound, in remembrance of their shame. The Wu Keng do not actively hunt their wayward brethren, mainly because the spirits of Feng-tu keep them busy on other tasks, but they will attempt to destroy anythey find.

The Wu Keng see their service, however embarrassing, as a small price to pay if it resurrects their ancient culture.

Specialty Sphere: *Forces*

Common Foci: Painting, calligraphy, poetry, language, wood carving, sewing

Advantage: Wedding Gift of Feng-Tu

During character creation, the player may choose an Effect up to Disciple level to have as a permanent Effect (subject to Storyteller approval). These "gifts" are given to the mage by his Feng-tu "mate" and master as rewards for faithful service. These gifts are not truly magical, do not garner Paradox, and are not eroded by disbelief. The gift chosen may not be a *Spirit* or *Time* Effect, and may not be a conjunctional Sphere Effect. The Effect may not have any extra grades of success. With Storyteller permission, a mage may take an extra gift, but the character also receives five Traits in Flaws of the Storyteller's choosing.

Disadvantage: Mandates of Feng-tu

All Wu Keng are forced to dress and live like traditional Chinese women, to counteract the Yang of their male natures and bring them more into balance. Because of this, they receive the Negative Social Trait: *Passive*. The Wu Keng are also forced to bind their feet in the traditional way, a practice that is painful and crippling. They receive the Negative Physical Trait: *Lame* from this.

The Feng-tu spirits do not approve of their "wives" practicing the arts of *Spirit* or *Time* magic. Therefore, the Wu Keng are forbidden to learn or use either any way. In game terms, Wu Keng characters may never learn any levels of the *Spirit* or *Time* Spheres. If a Wu Keng uses a *Device* or *Wonder* that works with *Time* or *Spirit* magic, he gains Paradox equal to the *Wonder's* level, as he has angered his master and is punished harshly.

Wu Nung

A group of mysterious old women are the founders of this Craft, teaching the young to dance in the halls of the gods and speak with the dead as the old shamans of China once did before the Chou Dynasty outlawed such practices. These six women traveled throughout eastern and southeastern Asia in search of potential students. They sought those who could still touch the spirits of their loved ones, and they sought the malformed and misbegotten whose physical infirmity gave them a special link to the spirit world. They gathered their students into circles, teaching them the old ways and showing them the silvery paths to the halls of the gods. Each circle was taught quickly, then a new circle of pupils was gathered. Over a two-year period, the little group of subtle ladies created a formidable number of shamans.

The mysterious teachers taught their pupils, called the Wu Nung, two things. The first lesson was the ways to woo and flatter the gods and the etiquette required to gain their favor. The second lesson was on the ways of demons, specifically how to fight them effectively. The Wu Nung returned to their communities, from squalid inner cities to far-flung farming villages, and took up the mantle as spiritual guides of their communities. They rebuilt belief and respect for the spirits and old gods, slowly bringing back the culture of old China. In many places, the Shamans are still persecuted by the secular state, but they are usually hidden and supported by their faithful communities.

The numbers of the Wu Nung grew by leaps and bounds. The groups taught by the beneficial old ladies spread and took on more apprentices and taught them the ways of the gods. Then, almost overnight, things changed for the worse. Early in 2001, the beneficial ladies, who were the most learned among them, disappeared and have not been seen since. Soon after, there were reports of groups of Shamans being attacked by ladies like their original teachers. Many of their number have died at the hands of this mysterious new threat that they do not fully understand. Rumors claim that these are old students of the beneficial ladies who have somehow fallen from the grace of the gods. The Wu Nung now build their number in preparation for what they see as a coming war.

Roleplaying Hints: The Wu Nung's magic comes from their consorting with the old Chinese gods and spirits of the dead. They write poetry to these gods to gain their favor and attention, but there are very strict protocols that must be observed with each god to keep from angering them. The Shamans commonly go through many steps in the creation of a single Effect, and even after the Effect has been done, they make sure that the gods are sufficiently appeased. These practices become part of their daily lives; for example, they pray over a meal to three different gods in thanks for the meal itself, the fire that cooked it, and the spirits of the animals and plants that gave of themselves for it. A peasant Shaman is likely to be considered a superstitious person who does odd things at odd times in appeasement for different spirits and gods. Usually they are small acts of supplication and thanks, but they become far more elaborate rituals to court the spirits' affections and attention in the workings of something major.

Specialty Sphere: *Spirit*

Common Foci: Painting, calligraphy, poetry, language, wood carving, sewing, flower arranging, *feng shui*

Advantage: Oni Slayer

The mysterious mentors of the Wu Nung hinted that they had served demonic masters in the past, and had recorded the weaknesses, strengths, needs and desires of their masters during that service. They taught this knowledge to the Wu Nung, impressing on them the necessity of fighting fire with fire. This training gives Shamans an advantage when fighting demons and Banes. The Wu Nung receives a one-Trait training bonus to any challenge when in combat against a demon or Bane. This bonus applies if the mage is initiating or defending against a challenge with a demon or Bane, or if she attempts to perform an Effect against such a beast.

Disadvantage: Loss of the A-ma

About a year ago, the mentors of the Shamans disappeared. It is believed by some that they are in hiding and will come to the aid of the Shamans when they need it. Others believe some evil force discovered that they were teaching the lost ways and destroyed them. All that is known is that the mentors of the Shamans are gone, and the Wu Nung must now teach themselves how to carry on the mission. In game terms a Shaman cannot start with the *Mentor* or *Library* Backgrounds, and any Spheres above Disciple level must be taught to them by a mage of another Tradition.

The Orphans

Some people are raised in certain paradigms, then learn about others, and grow to combine the beliefs, fears and differing aspects of reality into one cohesive worldview. Everybody does this — it is a natural way of life and a way of evolving with the changing times and the shrinking of the world. We are born into one culture, but have easy exposure to other cultures and tend to take parts of those cultures into our own. We accept their art, their stories and even parts of their language without too much thought. Because the culture we live in changes, the world culture globalizes. But this mixing of paradigms and beliefs has a very profound effect on the World of Darkness.

Each culture is built on certain mythic threads, bits of mythology and belief that endure even in the Technocratic society of today. These threads are the reason why some things can be done with magic and some things cannot. Certain mythic threads are more powerful in some places than others because the culture supports them in one place and does not in another. For instance, in Ireland the mythic thread of "the little people," the fae and the spirits of the land is still very strong. People report seeing evidence of a brownie or a selkie, and they warn their children away from certain moors saying they are haunted by the *bane-sidhe*. Verbena and their magic find few challenges to certain Effects in this region because of the strength of those particular mythic threads. Were that same Verbena to visit midwestern America and attempt the same feats, she'd get a rude surprise because the mythic threads have changed. In the Midwest, the mythic thread speaks of cattle mutilations and crop circles caused by strange little gray men. Both beliefs are of the same mythic thread — the wild things from parts unknown with mysterious powers — but viewed through different lenses.

These mythic threads are important to mages because it is through these that they form their own magical paradigms. Some leniency is expected in the way that individual members within a Tradition view mythic threads, but for the most part all the mages of that Tradition believe in and follow those threads. What can happen is that sometimes these mixing and clashing cultures can create a confusing welter of mythic threads within an individual. While this is usually not a problem, sometimes these people come to an epiphany and Awaken. Usually it is quite sudden, and goes unnoticed by other mages in the area. Some of these are later discovered by a Tradition or the Hollow Ones and taught to control their powers; others destroy themselves accidentally with a vulgar Effect. Still others simply wander about, lost in a world they no longer understand. It is a rare Orphan who is able to teach himself how to control his own power and avoid killing himself in the process. Those who are discovered by a Tradition rarely become productive members of their adoptive Tradition. These lost mages tend to move from Tradition to Tradition looking for bits and pieces of information that sound like truth to them, learning what they can here and there but never quite grasping hold of one paradigm completely.

Orphans are commonly taken in by the Hollow Ones, who see kindred spirits in those who have been so royally screwed by the magical world. This feeling of being of kindred may be quite true as the Hollow Ones rarely fit into any one grouping of mystical ideas, like the Orphans. And like the Orphans, the Hollow Ones are not usually respected by the established Traditions and Conventions because their belief structure does not match that of the more established groups. Here is where the similarities end, though. Orphans tend to be their own people and do not necessarily buy into the Hollower idea that the world is doomed to decay and destruction. The Orphans are also not counterculture revolutionaries as many of the Hollow Ones claim to be. They are in fact the most extreme of individualists, creating their own individual paradigms that may be bits and pieces of others meshed together but in the end something that is wholly unique to the Orphan.

Optional Rules for Orphans

So, if Orphans hold this special place in Limbo when it comes to other mages, then how do they do certain things like learn rotes and Spheres? Must they teach themselves everything from the ground up? Mostly, they *do* have to teach themselves everything. A Storyteller may want to include one some, or all of the optional rules below to flesh out the special lifestyle that Orphans must lead in the World of Darkness.

Mixed Paradigm Flaws (Optional Rule)

Sometimes an Orphan exhibits traits of more than one Tradition. Orphans in this situation usually start by learning with one Tradition and then moving on to learn with another one when the original Tradition does not fit in with the rest of their beliefs. With the Storyteller's approval, the Orphan may take the specialty Sphere of one Tradition and take the other Tradition's specialty Sphere as a faction Sphere. The Orphan also takes the Tradition Flaw from the Tradition his specialty Sphere comes from and the Tradition Advantage from the Tradition his faction Sphere comes from. The only exception to this is that no Orphan may have the Order of Hermes Tradition Advantage, as it is completely dependant on the clout and backing of the Order of Hermes. The Orphan would not be able to use that Advantage unless he trained with and became accepted as a member of the Order of Hermes, which is *highly* unlikely.

Avatar Filter (Optional Rule)

Some Orphans are born with Avatars that are, for lack of a better term, confused. Such Avatars force these mages to become Orphans because they are nothing but chaotic whirlwinds of paradigms and ideas. An Orphan with a chaotic Avatar must learn everything on her own because her Avatar, which ultimately determines the mage's ability to use magic, is continually shifting the paradigm. Orphans so cursed require twice as long to learn any new Spheres or rotes — they are spending all that time in guesswork and experimentation as they fumble their way through creating Effects.

On the plus side, these mages' Avatars also result in very flexible paradigms, and every new discovery that the mages make in their Sphere also gives them new ways to focus their magic. It gives them a little more insight into the natures of their unique Avatars, and a little more choice in how they wield their magic. In game terms, every time an Orphan increases his level in a Sphere, he may choose a new specialty focus for that Sphere or make a specific item used as a focus a unique focus.

Do-It-Yourself Paradigm (Optional Rule)

Your average Orphan Awakens with his own preconceived notions of the world and the way reality works. Orphans do not have a society of mages to guide them and teach them about the magic, so they tend to create their own magical paradigms as both a mental defense for the shock of Awakening, and to be able to actually manipulate their newly discovered power. Because they start with no Traditions to guide them, they do not start with the Advantages of any of the Traditions, but likewise they do not start with the Weaknesses.

The player should create a paradigm for the character, and choose between five and 10 common foci that the character would use to manipulate magical energies. The player also starts with no specialty Sphere. The Orphan starts as a *tabula rasa* as mages go and forges her own paradigm in the magical World of Darkness.

In addition to the rotes and Wonders sampled in **Laws of Ascension**, a near-infinite variety of other magical happenings is possible. In order to broaden mage options (especially in games that don't use dynamic magic) and simply to offer examples of *what mages do* with magic from day to day, this chapter includes a lengthy listing of rotes, *Wonders* and other magics that you can try out for your games.

Archimage Spheres (Optional Rule)

This rule only works if you're ready to have tremendously powerful mages in a long-running chronicle.

As chronicles advance and characters become more powerful, there may come a point when a character is able learn Spheres above the Master level, by Mastering a given Sphere and raising Arete above five Traits. This optional rule facilitates the use of Spheres above the Master level.

The additional levels of magic beyond Advanced level are Superior, Exceptional, Ascendant and Transcendent, all of which are classed as Archmaster-rank Spheres. Higher levels of Spheres grant a mage much greater efficiency in all magical workings with that Sphere. Furthermore, they provide benefits in concrete, physical terms, allowing a mage to expand slightly beyond human limitations. Each level of a Sphere beyond the Master level allows the mage to gain (with experience) one additional Attribute Trait above and beyond all other capabilities, according to the Sphere's association: *Life*, *Matter* and *Forces* to Physical;

Entropy, *Spirit* and *Prime* to Social; *Mind*, *Correspondence* and *Time* to Mental. Archmages thus can have *very* high Trait maximums, if the "Beyond Human Limits" optional rule is in effect (see **Laws of Ascension** p. 123).

Gaining an archmage Sphere grants a sixth Reputation Trait. No further Reputation is earned for levels beyond this.

When an archmage performs an Effect that uses one of his Archmaster Spheres, he automatically gains an additional number of grades of success equal to his levels exceeding Master. Thus, using Archmaster (Superior) *Forces* grants one extra grade of success on any *Forces* Effect. Invoking this bonus costs one Quintessence Trait, but that single Trait is sufficient to grant all applicable levels. A conjunctional Effect gains bonuses only according to the single highest Sphere knowledge used (so the Archmaster will often be tempted to build new rotes using his Archmaster Sphere, in order to gain the bonus successes — which is one reason that Archmasters often become known for having a favorite Sphere).

Learning Archmaster-level Spheres takes twice as long as usual (four sessions per Sphere level, or two for a specialty Sphere). The Superior level costs 16 experience, Exceptional costs 20 experience, Ascendant costs 24 experience and Transcendent costs 28 experience Traits as a specialty Sphere. For a non-specialty Sphere, the cost is 20/25/30/35.

The Contested Effect Rule (Optional Rule)

This rule only works if you believe strongly that no magical Effect should be a sure thing.

Some rotes or Effects might not always list a need for a challenge. Even if not listed, assume that a challenge is always required for an Effect that has an immediate, direct effect on a character — whether it means dropping a conjured piano on someone or striking with a curse that causes infertility 10 years later. The caster, after performing the Effect, must make a follow-up challenge against the target. The Traits used depend upon the spell: aiming the conjured piano mentioned above would pit the caster's Mental Traits against the target's Physical Traits. In general, attacks on the body use Physical, mental and occult attacks use Mental, and spiritual or emotional attacks use Social.

Grades of Power (Optional Rule)

This rule only works if you want mages to risk casting more powerful spells in order to have a stronger chance at affecting their targets, especially for mages with high Arete and Sphere levels.

The "grades of power" rule assumes that, when a mage generates grades of success for a spell, these could potentially be used to make the spell more powerful in its targeting, instead of increasing its duration or area. A caster may trade one grade of success for two additional Traits in any follow-up challenge resolution, such as the test to strike an enemy with a conjured lightning bolt or to penetrate a mind shield. This could even precipitate an overbid. Remember, though, that no amount of modifiers can raise a character's Trait total for a challenge above double the character's normal number of unaided Traits in a given Attribute (that is, a mage who normally has seven Physical Traits can never bid more than 14 Physical Traits in a challenge, regardless of aids and bonuses).

Two months	One grade
Three months	One grade
Six months	One grade
12 months	One grades
Two years	Two grades
Three years	Two grades
Five years	Two grades
10 years	Three grades
25 years	Three grades
50 years	Four grades
One century	Five grades

Extended Grades of Duration (Optional Rule)

This rule only works if you feel the need for a much larger scope of lasting Effects in your game, beyond the grades presented in the core rules.

Sometimes a player is going to want to create an Effect that he wants to last for much longer than the basic rules allow. It is suggested that no Effect should be created to last for more than one month, but depending on how you wish to run your game and the scope of the game that you are playing, having Effect durations longer than a month may be needed. Set out below is a quick chart for the grades of duration beyond one month.

For these Effects, the character is going to have expend more than the normal amount of energy to extend the duration to the levels listed below. The reason this extra energy has to be expended is because the

Effect has to stand up to the erosive effects of consensual reality. Even long-lasting coincidental Effects will eventually be worn away. To simulate this, beside each grade of success is a listing for any extra grades of success that have to be expended past the normal grades of success for extra grades of duration. For example, if Gary wants to increase the duration of an Effect that has a standard duration of one month to two years, then he would have to spend 11 grades of success — five for each grade of duration as listed below, plus six more for the extra cost (one for two months, three months, six months and 12 months; and two more for two years).

Shapechanging

Shapechanging is one of those sticky areas in a LARP because it takes the greatest amount of suspension of disbelief of all the players to be able to roleplay with it properly. For this reason you may want to limit how you allow mages to use shapechanging Effects. Listed below are some examples of ways to deal with shapechanging rotes and a few examples of such rotes that may show up in your game.

Appearance Changes

These changes are done to conceal a character's appearance either for stealth or subterfuge. When a mage is concealing her features in this way, the player should either hold her chin with her hand, or hold her hand in front of her face, to represent that she does not look the way that other characters would recognize her. If necessary the player should announce to people out of character what she looks like when she does that. Listed below are three variations on disguising effects.

Hello, my name is...: Adept *Mind.* This rote, created by a rather resourceful Hollow One, has been adopted by other Traditions in differing forms. The Hollower would take a "Hello, my name is..." sticker and write on it the name of what she wanted to look like. Doing this took advantage of the fact that most people took things they saw for granted. Whatever she wrote on the tag and stuck on herself was what people saw — she drew a small badge, and people saw a cop; she wrote "Bob Dole" and looked like an impotent presidential candidate. The Effect does not allow the mage to look inhuman or inanimate. Any person who is interacting with the mage under this Effect, and has some form of heightened sensory perception, may make a Mental Challenge against three times the mage's Arete Traits to notice there is something wrong with what he is seeing. Technological devices are not fooled by this Effect. The Effect lasts for one minute/conflict. *Grades of Success:* Increase the grade of duration.

Camouflage Field Generator: Disciple *Forces*. This rote, created by the Sons of Ether, uses etheric manipulation to form a pattern of light around the user so he appears as another person. Etherites commonly use this Effect to make their robotic minions look like regular people as they are walking around in public. The field can make the affected target look like anything that is the same general shape and size of the target. Sometimes, though, the field does not show the proper interaction with exterior stimuli — for instance, the image's hair might stay perfect in a stiff breeze. Any person who is interacting with the mage under this Effect may make a Mental Challenge against the caster to notice that there is something wrong with what she is seeing. Technological devices are just as fooled as anybody else by this Effect. The Effect lasts for one minute/conflict. *Grades of Success:* Increase the grade of duration.

Butcher's Disguise: Disciple *Life*. Some of the more pain-oriented Cultists use this rote to help disguise themselves or to change their faces dramatically. The mage uses a razor blade to cut his face and molds it into the appearance that he wants to have. The new face lasts for one minute/conflict. When he is done, the mage looks different than when he began. The process is quite painful and causes two lethal wounds that cannot be healed for as long as the Effect's duration. When the duration ends, the mage heals the damage and his face returns to its original shape. The mage has two choices when doing this Effect: he may make himself look like a different person, or he may increase his Social Traits temporarily. If the mage makes himself look like a different person, there is no real way for anybody to see what is really underneath since the mage is changed physically. A character who knows the person being imitiated might use an *Investigation* Social Challenge to realize that the mage isn't who he appears to be. If the mage changes his Social Traits, he may add three Traits relating to Appearance or intimidation. *Grades of Success:* Increase the grade of duration.

Animal Forms

There are two rotes in the main book dealing with taking on animal forms: *Mutate Form* (Adept *Life*) and *Perfect Metamorphosis* (Master *Life*). Both of these create their own minor problems in game when the player needs to make a representation of herself as said animal. Some suggestions are for the player to crawl around on all fours, like an animal, or to wear a mask of the animal in question. An equally good option for those players who are not spryly built or are poor is to hold your hands up at about shoulder height right up against the body with the palms facing away from you.

Animal Form Knowledge (Optional Rule)

This rule only works if you want a little more "realism" in your shapeshifting at the expense of more complexity.

Realistically, if you were suddenly changed into a bird, would you know exactly how to flap your wings to be able to take flight? If you were to shape-change into a wolf, would you be able to decipher the sudden increase in your range of olfactory senses and deal with the fact that your sight was now only black and white? You probably would be caught off guard while in your new form, and so it would be with your character. It would take practice for you to actually use this new form to its fullest extent. To simulate this difficulty with the new form, a character must bid an additional Trait to enter any challenge as an unfamiliar shape penalty. With practice, the shapeshifting mage could become used to the new senses and body and eliminate the penalty. This knowledge may be either bought with experience, or a magnanimous Storyteller might grant the knowledge with the appropriate amount of practice (one month is usually good). Each *Knowledge* Ability is specifically tailored to one animal form and one alone. For instance, Bob is playing a Dreamspeaker named Wind Walker who has *Animal Knowledge: Eagles*. Wind Walker enjoys soaring in the clouds and watching the earth below. Today, though, he needs stealth, not soaring ability, so he changes himself into an owl; he suffers the unfamiliar shape penalty. He sees what he needs to see, and changes into a human form, but not his own; since he has been a human his entire life, he suffers no penalty from this form. He then decides to change shape one more time into a hawk. This time, he receives no penalty, because a hawk and an eagle have the same general body form.

Bestial Forms

Eventually you are going to have a character who researches or creates a rote that changes him into something that is neither animal nor human but some type of amalgam between the two. These Effects are almost universally Paradoxical — how do you explain to reality that it's perfectly acceptable for you to be 20-foot-tall, half-man, donkey-creature with lobster claws? The most difficult part about these shape-changes is representing them in play without Tom Savini or Ray Harryhausen doing your props for you. A suggestion is to have the players hold their hands above their head with their fingers out stretched.

A couple examples of bestial forms are below, but your players will undoubtedly think up even more bizarre creations than these.

Iron Avatar: Disciple *Life*, Disciple *Matter*, Initiate *Mind*, Initiate *Prime*. By attuning herself to the essence of Kali, a Euthanatos may take on the guise of goddess (male members of the Tradition channel the form of Shiva). Iron daggers appear in the mage's hands, and six arms sprout from her shoulders. The mage also grows to a height of 10 feet, and her skin turns black as night. While in this form, the mage gains three extra Physical Traits from the extra arms and blades, and gains an extra attack each turn immediately after her initial attack for the turn. The transformation lasts for one combat round, after which the mage is exhausted and may not initiate any further challenges for the session. *Grades of Success:* One grade gives the mage an extra Healthy health level per grade spent. One grade of success increases the grade of duration per grade of success spent up to a maximum of one scene/hour. One grade of success increases the bonus Physical Traits by three.

Avatar Form: Disciple *Life*, Disciple *Mind*, Disciple *Prime*. By bringing mind, body and soul into alignment, an Akashic Brother may project his Avatar's form through his own physical body. The mage's skin turns blue and becomes as tough as wood. He also sprouts four extra arms that can be controlled as normal, because the *Mind* part of the Effect divides the mind in the ways necessary for controlling the extra arms naturally. The mage's hands glow with a white-blue light of Prime energy. While in this form, the mage gains one extra Healthy health level, and his Do attacks cause aggravated damage. The transformation lasts for only one turn. The mage's Avatar rating is reduced to zero, and he loses all Quintessence stored in his Pattern. When the session ends, his Avatar rating returns to normal and he may store Quintessence in his Pattern again. *Grades of Success:* One grade of success increases the grade of duration by one per grade spent on it, up to a maximum of one scene/ hour. One grade gives the mage an extra action that occurs immediately after the character's initial attack for the turn; one extra attack is gained for each grade of success spent in this way. One grade of success gives the mage an extra Healthy health level.

Wonders

Wonders come in all shapes and sizes, of course; the trick lies in determining the *Wonder*'s capabilities and in assigning it an appropriate value. The sample *Wonders* here serve not only as potential additions to a game, but also as guidelines for the capabilities of other *Wonders*.

The broad, separate classifications for *Wonders* are:

Artifact — An Artifact is a *Wonder* with some sort of invoked or continuous mystical power. Body armor enhanced by Technocratic material science is an Artifact, because it relies on physically enhanced properties outside the bounds of normal science. An Artifact costs one Trait per level of the Sphere magic involved. Thus, if an item has a *Disciple*-level Effect, it is a three-Trait *Wonder*. An Artifact's Effect typically has only the base success for the rote or Sphere in question. At the Storyteller's discretion, an Artifact might have extra grades of success built in for extra Traits (typically on a one-for-one basis).

Charm — A Charm is a small, single-use, disposable item, such as a magic potion or candle. Once it's used, its effect takes place, but the item is gone. A Charm generally works just like an Artifact. It costs one less Trait, however, and counts as a set of 10. Therefore, a set of 10 Charms that invoke a *Disciple*-level Sphere would cost two Traits. All Charms in a set have the same power.

Fetish — Spirits bound into material objects can grant their powers as a type of *Wonder*. Generally, equate the spirit's power to a rote of the same type; the cost equals a number of Traits equal to the Sphere levels involved. Since spirit powers aren't Paradoxical and just about anyone can use them, Fetishes have great advantages. On the downside, the spirit might come loose or run out of Power, or simply refuse to work for some users. In some cases, a mage must best the spirit in a psychic contest (a continuous series of Mental Challenges, with the loser losing one Willpower Trait each time until a victor emerges) or else grant it Power (through Quintessence, typically one Trait each time the user invokes the Fetish).

Periapt — A Periapt is a power source. Every Trait invested in a Periapt grants it five Quintessence of storage space. A Periapt typically comes charged, but the mage must see to recharging it with *Prime* after using its power. Like a battery, the Periapt's Quintessence may be spent and then restored.

Talisman — Rare Talismans hold a small piece of the creator's will. A Talisman typically has a single Trait of Arete, at a cost of one Trait. This allows the Talisman to invoke Spheres invested into it at the same cost as an Artifact. Since the Talisman performs the work, it's usable even by a Sleeper, and it gains any Paradox from the effect. Paradox backlashes that do damage reduce the item's bonus Traits or health levels until none are left, at which point the Talisman is broken. On the up side, this means that the user didn't suffer the Paradox effect, so these *Wonders* are popular among mages for working vulgar effects.

A *Wonder* can contain multiple powers for the appropriate costs added together.

Wonders and Drama

As rare items of magical mystery, *Wonders* can add a great deal of drama. They're wonderful McGuffins — quest items and gewgaws for mages to seek. Unfortunately, too many *Wonders* in the hands of the players can cause a mess. Mages may fall back on the magic item of the week, or a few players might hoard all of the *Wonders* and thereby gain disproportionate power.

It's possible to create *Wonders* with phenomenal powers, beyond the usual five-Trait system. Such *Wonders* won't start out in the hands of players' characters, though. Rather, they tend to be the focus of story arcs, often with careful caveats as to why they can't solve all problems — narrow set of highly efficient powers, severe drawbacks, have owners looking for them, etc. Each and every *Wonder* should have some story behind it and some purpose in the game.

Speaking of drawbacks, a *Wonder*'s powers can have limits or problems. Such drawbacks mitigate the cost of the *Wonder*. Typically, apply a Flaw as a limit or hindrance, and lower the *Wonder*'s cost by that number of Traits. For instance, a *Wonder* that causes its holder to suffer a minor *Vulnerability* (as the two-Trait version of that Flaw) would knock two Traits from its cost, potentially allowing more powers along with the problems. A *Wonder* might have conditional magic — it might not work during the day, or on women, or in other strange circumstances. Just remember, when players purchase *Wonders* on starting characters, any disadvantage clearly mitigated by the character's innate capabilities (such as the aforementioned *Vulnerability* granting *Wonder* held by a character with a specific *Invulnerability*) gains no bonus points for those non-drawbacks.

Ultimately, the Storyteller should shift the values of *Wonders* as necessary to comfortably integrate them into the game. Some games will want to make *Wonders* very rare and thus will raise their Trait value. Others will encourage the use of minor *Wonders* and thus make them very cheap.

Fuel Pellets

One-Trait Charm

Shaped like small red plastic balls, these spheres are placed in a quantity of water of no more than eight gallons. The water must then be agitated for 15 minutes in a *very* careful manner away from any open flames. At the end of 15 minutes, the water is changed into eight gallons of high-octane gasoline.

Intuitive Medicine Bag

One-Trait Artifact

This Wonder is usually shaped like a doctor's bag, but has been known to look like a stethoscope or scalpel. With it, the user of the bag can intuitively sense the ailments and injuries of a person he tries to treat. As long as the user has at least one level of the *Medicine* Ability, he will be up two extra Traits on all *Medicine* challenges used on a patient.

Mata Hari's Bobby Pin

One-Trait Artifact

This *Wonder* is usually a hairpin or some small piece of wire. It is very small and easy to conceal, and its actual use is hard to determine. The pin grants two extra Traits whenever trying to pick a mechanical lock. The *Wonder* unfortunately does not give any kind of bonus against electronic locks like keypads or magnetic card locks.

Motion Sensor

One-Trait Artifact

A small hand-held device with a display that shows the location of all moving objects in a 180-degree arc in front of the holder of the device, up to a range of 10 paces. The display can show movement on the other side of walls and can show invisible objects, by winning a Mental Challenge against the invisible object, as long as the invisibility is not created using any *Correspondence* or *Mind* Effect. The sensor cannot display anything other than the size of the moving object and its relative speed and direction, making it impossible to tell if the big, slow blip is Bob or some hungry alien coming to eat you.

Night Vision Bifocals

One-Trait Artifact

These bifocal lenses use an *Apprentice*-level *Forces* effect to allow the wearer to see into the infrared and ultraviolet spectrum. The wearer suffers no ill effects from darkness while wearing these glasses.

Baby's New Shoes Dice

Two-Trait Artifact

This *Wonder* is usually shaped like a pair of dice, but has also been shaped like a deck of cards. The user of the dice can choose to roll them again if the first roll is not what was wanted, and he can then choose the preferred roll. To activate the dice he simply needs to blow on them, or say, "Baby needs a new pair of shoes", or some other appropriate ritual for luck. The user receives the bonus of the *Games of Luck* (Initiate *Entropy)* Effect, when using this *Wonder* and only in use of this *Wonder*.

Bob's Pipe

Two-Trait Artifact/ Periapt, holds five Quintessence

This rather ordinary-looking pipe tends to be overlooked, sometimes even used without the smoker even realizing its power, for it functions like a normal pipe. The pipe is activated when held firmly between the teeth on the right side of the mouth and puffed on once — which expends one of its points of Quintessence. When the pipe is activated the user wins all ties on the next Mental Challenge dealing specifically and solely with knowledge or *Lore*.

Mercury Sword

Two-Trait Artifact

This silvery blade is usually attached to a hilt common to most short swords. The blade of the sword can be in almost any form imaginable. Each sword has a name that it responds to, and when this name is chanted to it, the wielder of the blade may shape the blade with his hands. Successfully shaping the blade requires a *Crafts* challenge against seven traits and at least a minute of work. The blade may take the shape and Traits of a dagger, a rapier or a short sword; it will keep this shape until the wielder attempts to reshape it again. When in one of these three forms, it assumes all the bonus Traits, Negative Traits, damage and abilities of the weapon it is shaped like.

Force Shield

Three-Trait Artifact/ Periapt, holds five Quintessence

This *Wonder* is shaped like a rather bulky belt, looking a little like a comic book hero's utility belt. It is impossible to conceal under clothing, and if it is hidden, it is unable to function. The force shield creates a small shield of tangible energy around the wearer that can stop one level of damage at the cost of one Quintessence. Any single attack that does more than one level of damage is only reduced by a single level, with the rest of the damage being applied to the mage. The type of damage blocked does not matter — it can be bashing, lethal or aggravated and the force shield will stop it. The person inside the force shield may attack people as normal as the shield only stops incoming energy.

Magic Eight Ball

Two-Trait Artifact

A recent means of divination that has gained popularity. The holder of the eight ball asks it a question, and it returns an answer. Though usually this is a confusing answer, sometimes these things can be frighteningly accurate. The player should ask a Narrator the question and the Narrator should choose one of the following answers (at least mostly true): Outlook Good, Outlook Not So Good, My Reply Is No, Don't Count On It, You May Rely On It, Most Likely, Cannot Predict Now, Yes, Yes Definitely, It Is Certain, Very Doubtful, It Is Decidedly So, Signs Point to Yes, My Sources Say No, Without a Doubt.

Carte Blanche

Three-Trait Artifact

The carte blanche looks like a simple magnetic strip card with no markings on it, but it imitates a legitimate card of a needed type. It can be placed in an ATM and allow the mage to withdraw up to $100 a day, and it can also be used as a credit card for the same amount. If used on a card reading security system, and the owner wins a Static Mental Challenge against a difficulty based on the complexity of the security system, the card is accepted and whatever was locked now opens. These cards tend to gain the attention of the Syndicate, and overusing one can cause the Syndicate to liquidate your assets. Furthermore, Technocratically enhanced security stations tend to be immune to this card's blandishments.

Efreet Bottle

Three-Trait Artifact

These talismans are commonly shaped like small glass or clay bottles, sometimes boxes. They are created to trap Umbral beings. By pointing the uncorked bottle at the target spirit and beating the spirit in an opposed Willpower Challenge, the holder causes the spirit to be sucked into the bottle, whereupon the mage may the cork the bottle and trap the spirit. This Effect only works on Umbral creatures such as Umbrood, demons and spirits. Entities like shapechangers, Bygones and Umbral traveling mages are not truly spiritual creatures and have a physical form. A spirit trapped in the bottle may not use a Charm to reform outside the bottle, and may not affect anything outside the bottle. Only one spirit may inhabit one bottle at a time. A spirit may escape the bottle if the bottle is destroyed, uncorked or if the spirit wins a Static Willpower Challenge against 10 Traits (the spirit must spend five Power to do this). After the spirit escapes, the bottle becomes inert, and appears to be cracked or the cork has fallen out. Spirits of exceeding power, like Celestines and Incarna, may either test to escape every turn at no cost or automatically escape at the Narrator's discretion. Spirits trapped in this way tend to become *very* angry and will seek the destruction of the one who trapped them if they escape. These bottles are in no way related to the objects created by the Taftani to trap and bind djinn; they are in fact cheap knock-offs of the same.

Mr. Fusion's Atomic Sleep-Enhancing Mask

Three-Trait Artifact

These odd, somewhat uncomfortable sleeping masks are rarely found these days, though they were all the rage some 50 years ago; most of them now collect dust in curio shops and grandmothers' attics, their magic long vanished. The mask itself is made of "space age polymers" that affect the way a wearer sleeps, altering brain waves to give the wearer a restful night's sleep. In game terms, these little *Wonders* make any dream-affecting Effects used upon the wearer three Traits more difficult while the mask is worn and the wearer is asleep.

Sabot of Lud

Three-Trait Artifact

This *Wonder* is a wooden shoe that would fit the average woman's foot. The shoe appears somewhat aged, possibly even petrified, but is lightweight and easily carried, though not at all comfortable to wear. Now other than shodding a person's foot, this *Wonder* has another rather impressive effect. If placed on a mechanical or electronic device that is as technologically advanced as a steam engine or better, the device takes one level of damage, or loses one bonus Trait, for every minute that the sabot is in contact with the device. The damage appears to be caused by normal wear and tear on the parts.

Universal Cookbook

Three-Trait Artifact

This red and white checkered tome contains recipes for anything that you may want to eat, even if it might not usually be edible. The owner of the cookbook simply needs some raw material, a modestly outfitted kitchen and one hour to work. After an hour in the kitchen, the mage has enough nutritious food to feed four people. The food will not be a great culinary delight; in fact the best way to describe it would be tasteless — but when all you have is crap to eat, tasteless crap is preferable to the alternative.

Vorpal Letter Opener

Three-Trait Artifact

This letter opener was created by a very old archmage who had a palsy problem and tended to cut himself whenever he was opening a letter with his letter opener. He created this in replacement, one that could cut through anything that he needed — paper, bread, wood, steel, diamonds, etc. The one thing it would not cut was living matter. It is not a quick cutter, though, because it is a dull blade, and takes a turn for the letter opener to cut six inches.

One of the other things that this handy little knife does is allow any cut that it makes to be reversed, causing the cut to reseal itself as the blade is drawn back. It also takes a turn to reseal a cut six inches. The knife can cut any material unless it is created by an *Adept*-level *Matter* Effect or higher.

The vorpal letter opener cannot automatically cut through certain magic-resistant materials, such as Primium. Since it can't injure living things, it's not very useful as a weapon. A clever mage can still find all manner of uses for it, though.

Weapon of the Psyche

Three-Trait Artifact

This small piece of jewelry, which looks like a miniature melee weapon worn around the neck or wrist, is actually a type of psychic image that forges a structure within the wearer's psyche. This structure is always present in the wearer's subconscious and is used to defend against psychic intrusion. In mindscapes and dreams, the character is immediately armed with a weapon like the charm, and may use Physical or Mental Traits to attack beings encountered in the dream or mental realm. The weapon itself gives three extra Traits and causes one lethal wound when it strikes successfully, no matter the type of weapon that the charm is shaped like. If the wearer of the charm becomes aware of a being that has forged a mental link with her, she may attack the linking mind by engaging in a Mental Challenge. With success, she inflicts one lethal wound on the invader and may choose to eject him.

Wild Certamen Card

Three-Trait Artifact/ Periapt, holds five Quintessence

The last time a mage was caught using one of these it was shaped as a simple playing card — the Jack of Spades, to be precise. This *Wonder* has been around for centuries in many different forms, but it always has the same use: to allow the user an unfair advantage in certamen matches. The first way it allows the magician to cheat is an Initiate *Prime* Effect that weakens incoming attacks, giving the user a one-Trait bonus to defense during the match. The second way is that it conceals a pool of three Quintessence that the user can access at any point during the match. The certamen referee must make an *Awareness* test as a Mental Challenge if either of the *Wonder's* abilities are used during the match; the referee only gets one chance to see this, as the *Wonder* is very subtle.

Ebony Horse

Four-Trait Artifact

A life-size horse statue made of ebony, with a single ivory knob in place of the pommel. The knob is turned as the rider thinks about a place within the present realm (Umbra, Horizon Realm, etc) that she's been to previously and knows fairly well. The statue turns into a horse that gallops off at an incredible pace. Ten minutes later, the horse and rider appear near the destination, the horse gallops up to the destination and turns back into a statue. The horse is unaffected by physical harm, and travels through obstacles by moving through them with rider through the use of co-location. These horses are rarely seen these days because their effect is very Paradoxical, but are useful as quick means of transportation in some Horizon Realms and even in the Umbra. Note that the horse does not actually become a real, living horse; rather, it animates through the use of *Matter* and phases (with rider) through solid objects as it gallops.

Kali's Tongue

Four-Trait Artifact

A punch dagger with a wave-shaped blade, the metal of the blade is usually stained red or green. The dagger, when successfully used in an attack, activates an *Adept*-level *Life* Effect to harm the victim severely. The blade never actually pierces the flesh of the victim, though. The attack inflicts two lethal wounds to the victim, but on examination these wounds appear to be perfectly natural breakdowns of the internal organs. A stab in the gut might appear as a ruptured spleen, a stab in the leg might appear as a compounded fracture of the tibia, and a stab in the chest might appear as a heart attack.

Lightning Gun

Four-Trait Artifact/ Periapt, holds five Quintessence

This *Wonder*, commonly shaped like a '50s-style plastic toy laser gun, is not a toy at all. It is, in fact, a very dangerous weapon. The gun emits a low-powered laser beam at its intended target. This beam ionizes the air between the shooter and the target, which creates a perfect pathway for the arc of electricity that is released by a very powerful capacitor — at least, this is the mundane explanation for what would usually be a very Paradoxical effect. The shooter uses a standard energy weapons test to hit his intended target, and if he hits, the shot scores two levels of aggravated damage. Since this weapon inflicts aggravated wounds, each shot uses one charge of Quintessence.

Questor's Map

Four-Trait Artifact

These maps — also known as pathway guides, hyperdimensional pathway maps, and treasure maps — have appeared in a multitude of different forms from ratty vellum maps to hand-held GPS maps, but their use is always the same. The map shows a rough picture of the Gauntlet and Near Umbra in a one square mile area around the mage. The rating of the Gauntlet is seen as a topographical map with high elevations representing high Gauntlet ratings and low areas showing low Gauntlet ratings. Also shown are Shallowings and Airts, though the destinations of these Airts is rarely clear and the Shallowings tend to appear as rather indistinct markings on the map, marking general areas where Shallowing may lie but no details on how to activate the Shallowing.

Extra-Dimensional Backpack

Five-Trait Artifact

The extra-dimensional backpack is created to fold and spatially mutate any thing placed within it so that it fits. As long as the object can fit into the opening of the backpack, the backpack will be able to hold the object. The weight of the object does not change, though. So, even though you can place an I-beam into the backpack, you are not going to be able to move once you do. It takes time to place anything into the backpack, usually a turn or more depending on the size. Living things cannot enter the backpack.

Folk Ward

One-Trait Charm

These wards tend to take many different shapes and forms depending on the paradigm and culture of their mage creators. These small wards and charms act as single-use anti-magic talismans, designed to counter specific Spheres or types of magic. To be used, the Charm must be in plain sight and easily identifiable. Whenever an Effect is done with the holder of the Charm named as the target of the Effect, and the Effect is of the category of the Charm, then the Effect is resolved at a one-Trait penalty (as if a Trait of Quintessence had been used for anti-magic). At this point the Charm becomes inert and cannot be reimbued for the same purpose. These Charms must have types of spells specified as what they guard against. For instance curses, lightning and teleportation are acceptable; damage-causing effects are not, as the category is too broad. These Charms may only be used one per effect. Even if you have a Folk Ward against fire spells and curses, and somebody creates an Effect cursing you with flaming urine, only one of the talismans will activate, although you may choose which. Common Folk Wards are things like four-leaf clovers that ward against bad luck, blue ribbons around the neck that ward against the evil eye (curses), and handfuls of posies to ward off disease.

Ninja Smoke Bomb

Two-Trait Charm

These small clay balls, when broken open, cause the surrounding area to become filled with choking, irritating, obscuring smoke. Only the activator of the talisman is unaffected by the smoke. The smoke cloud created by the Charm is six paces wide and 10 feet tall. Anyone in the cloud (except the activator) loses all ties in Physical Challenges because of blindness. The choking effect of the cloud causes anyone within to suffer a two-Trait penalty on all challenges. The smoke cloud lasts for two rounds or until a strong wind causes the smoke to dissipate. Note that use of appropriate Abilities (*Blind-Fighting*) and effects (*Correspondence* or other sensory Effects) can negate the penalties.

Tornado in a Can

Three-Trait Charm

This is a one-use Charm that is thrown at a target using normal physical ranged attack rules. If the attack is successful, a spinning kinetic force erupts from the can and holds the victim in place for three turns. The spinning vortex makes the victim unable to initiate any challenges and impervious to personal-scale physical attack but not to damage. So, if the victim is shot at, he will be unaffected by the attack, but if a building falls on him, he will most likely die. (Treat this as an Intermediate *Forces* Effect that attempts to negate kinetic energy and hold the victim in place.)

Spirit Rattle

Two-Trait Fetish

These rattles — sometimes made of dried gourds, or from the tails of rattlesnakes — are made to ward off spirits by making the area uncomfortable for them. When the spirit rattle is rattled purposefully, all spiritual beings in the area suffer a two-Trait penalty for all actions. This penalty applies not only to spirits, but also to any being that is in the Umbra, because the rattle sounds like thunder in the Umbra when it is shaken. For as long as the rattle is shaken, the penalty persists; the shaker of the rattle may do nothing except shake the rattle to get the effect of the *Wonder*. A spirit that is materialized suffers the same penalty as if it were in the Umbra.

Dragon Pearl

Five-Trait Talisman

These perfectly formed pearls, each about the size of a large marble, could easily fetch $1000 a piece, but mages who know their true nature would never sell them for such a paltry sum. The pearls are always slightly warm to the touch and in near darkness they seem to reflect back more light than what strikes them. If a person swallows one of these pearls he must first win a static Physical Challenge against eight traits or take two aggravated wounds as the pearl releases its powerful magic with in the body. Over the next turn the character may do nothing as his body transforms into a 10-foot-long, serpentlike Eastern dragon. When the transformation is done, the mage receives six extra Physical Traits (*Ferocious* x 2, *Enduring* x 2, *Lithe* x 2), two extra Healthy health levels, his brawl attacks inflict lethal damage, and he can take six steps for movement instead of three. The transformation lasts for a single combat or one minute, whichever comes first. While in the dragon form you may still talk and do magical effects if you were able to do so before, but you may not use any tools or weapons as the dragon form does not have opposable thumbs. After the effect wears off any damage done to you is applied to your normal health levels — if you took six wounds while in the dragon form, when you transform back, the six wounds applied to your normal health levels. A dragon pearl typically works only once, releasing all of its stored power as it transforms the user.

Translating *Wonders*

Not all *Wonders* from other **Mage** supplements translate easily into the live-action format. Due to the differences in pricing for live-action

Wonders as compared to their tabletop cousins, some *Wonders* might be out of reach of live-action characters, while others might be a little cheaper.

The recommended solution is to translate all *Wonders* according to the pricing guidelines for **Laws of Ascension**. Those guidelines are balanced for the live-action game, which has slightly different scales of power than the tabletop **Mage**. Figure the Trait value of a *Wonder* based upon its powers, and assign it a new value for live-action play.

In some cases the Storyteller may wish to make an exception for a *Wonder* that has Effects particularly difficult for a live-action game or especially useless for a given venue; this can adjust the value up or down. The important part of the estimate is to recalculate from the live-action perspective rather than being wedded to the tabletop numbers, since live-action items may have different scope, smaller Effect and different numbers of effective Traits. A *Wonder* that grants a bonus Trait, for instance, is probably not as powerful in live-action play as a *Wonder* that grants a –1 difficulty in tabletop play, because the Traits can often spread beyond a 1-10 range while difficulties rarely reflect a spread beyond 2-10.

Technocratic Enhancements

Because they're placed inside the body and attached to a mage's Pattern, Technocratic *Enhancements* don't quite follow the same rules as other *Wonders*. See the Background on p. XX for information. The samples listed below only scratch the surface of potential *Enhancements* for your operatives. In general, an *Enhancement*'s value should be roughly similar to that of a *Wonder* (Artifact). The *Enhancement* has the advantage that it can't be lost, but the disadvantage that it causes Paradox.

Extrasensory Access Device

One-Trait Enhancement

Your field agent has some sort of extra device or sense — either an engineered organ or implanted bionic piece — that permits a range of sensation beyond the human norms. In game terms, your character benefits from one *Apprentice*-level Sphere sensory Effect at all times. To your character, it's as normal as seeing and hearing.

Night Vision

One-Trait Enhancement

Biological modifications to include higher densities of the right rods and cones, or completely re-engineered bionic eyes, allow the operative to see in near darkness. Your character can see in anything but total darkness with no penalties.

Skeletal Enhancement

One-Trait Enhancement

Internal bracings or specially engineered spiral bone structure grants a superstrong skeleton and better muscular attachment points. Your agent can mount heavy hardware such as energy weapons along these bracings. You also gain one extra Bruised health level.

Claws

Two-Trait Enhancement

Claws — either bony or metallic — extend on command and allow you to rake your opponents for lethal damage. The claws grant you a one-Trait bonus in hand combat and in climbing.

Computer Coprocessor

Two-Trait Enhancement

You have a computer chip tied into your brain — or a part of your brain is so finely wired that it functions just as well as a computer. You gain all the benefits of permanent mental enhancement: Incredible math skills, ability to record reams of raw text data, even the potential to process other information if (say) you have some cybernetic recording device and a means to tie it into the computer headware. With an output port or a dermal interface, you can output your computer's information to another system or upload new programs.

Environmental Adaptability

Three-Trait Enhancement

Improved filters, gills, pressure compensators and similar redundancies enable your operative to function underwater, in intense heat or perhaps even in a vacuum. Choose one type of high-threat environment, such as high heat, radioactivity or space. Your character suffers neither damage nor Trait penalties in that environment, even without any protections. Note that fiery and freezing substances can still cause damage — just because you're engineered to work near the heart of a volcano doesn't mean you'll survive a dip in the lava.

Rotes

The sample rotes here run a wide gamut. Some are highly useful to politically or militarily active mages; others tie in specifically to everyday life. Many are conjunctional. Again, like the sample *Wonders* presented previously, these pieces provide examples, not concrete guidelines for all situations. From these rotes can spring inspiration for other magical Effects and ideas. Just as important as the powers of the rotes is their intended use. Remember that mages can and do make magical Effects for things that some people might consider trivial, and not all spells are designed for battle, curses or defenses.

Access This: Initiate *Forces*, Initiate *Correspondence*. This rote, primarily used by the Virtual Adepts, forges a link between two electronic devices, allowing one to control/access another within visual sight. The control that the casting mage has is limited by the mechanics of the device that he uses to access the other device. For instance, a mage using a Game Boy to access a computer may only be able access the monitor through his LCD and move the mouse around; by using a palmtop computer, he would be able to access the computer much more effectively. For one hour/scene, the mage may use the accessed device. If there is any type of security on the device being accessed, the mage must win a Mental Challenge using the *Computer* Ability against a number of Traits determined by a Narrator. *Grades of Success:* None.

Activate Next Clone: Master *Life*, Adept *Time*, Master *Mind*, Adept *Spirit*, Adept *Prime*, Disciple *Correspondence*. This incredibly powerful Effect done through a conjunctional effort by multiple arms of the Conventions is reserved for only their most highly ranked members. A clone is created of the caster, then placed in a stasis chamber. A piece of cyberware is then implanted in the mage that monitors physical status and transfers his consciousness when he is at risk of being killed. When the monitor detects that the mage is at Incapacitated or worse, his consciousness is instantly downloaded into the clone that wakes up 10 minutes later exactly as the mage was before, except with no damage. The shock of the transfer and the near-death experience has a profound effect on the mage, as he loses a permanent Trait of Willpower and gains a derangement. If the mage was at worse than Mortally Wounded when this occurred, then the toll is doubled (loss of two permanent Willpower and gaining two derangements). The stasis chamber is only able to keep the clone viable for one month. After one month, the Effect wears off and the mage simply dies as normal. If the mage is killed while his consciousness is outside of his body, the transfer fails and the mage dies. If there is another consciousness in the body when it dies, that consciousness is transferred to the new clone with all the penalties imposed from the transfer. If the mage's consciousness and another consciousness are in the body when it dies, the transfer takes place and the transfer device tries to make as close an approximation as it can — the final result is the clone having both wills with in it fighting for control (winner of a Mental Challenge has control for a scene/hour). *Grades of Success:* Increase the grade of duration of the stasis field.

Akashic Cliff Notes: Apprentice *Mind*. This rote has been quietly passed from apprentice to apprentice over the years among the Akashic Brotherhood. Through meditation the apprentice is better able to concentrate and understand the koans and proverbs his sensei is trying to teach. In game terms, the mage receives a one-Trait bonus on any *Enigmas* challenges. *Grades of Success:* None.

Ball of Abysmal Flame: Master *Forces*, Master *Prime*, Adept *Time*, Disciple *Matter*. This is the most powerful destructive spell known to exist in the lone mage's repertoire. It has been used few times, and only in the direst of circumstances, as it is highly dangerous to perform and the results can be devastating. To cast this spell, the mage draws a pentagram that points south. During the first turn of casting, a little bit of Quintessence is drawn from everything in the surrounding area (an effect that can be detected with a Static *Awareness* Mental Challenge against 12 Traits). The second turn of casting transmutes this Quintessence into heat and fire that is bound within the confines of the pentagram. At this point it looks like a short column of roiling flames. During the third turn, the caster must hold the Effect in place long enough for him to get away from the blast area. The first parts of the spell are easy compared to the timing element, and this is the part that tends to break down (and this is when the actual casting test is made). The Effect requires three turns to gather the necessary energy. On detonating, it inflicts four aggravated wounds to everything with half a mile of the pentagram. If the casting test fails, the effect goes off immediately, but the blast radius is only about 100 yards. In conjunction with *Correspondence*, the mage can selectively target areas, using grades of success to eliminate certain people or objects from the blast. This spell is, in many ways, the mage's version of a bomb, and Storytellers should treat it as such. It's not a cheap way to destabilize a game, but a powerful and dangerous tool for a story that demands a tremendous overhaul. *Grades of Success:* Increases the damage by one aggravated wound per grade.

Battery Man: Adept *Life*, Initiate *Forces*. Created at first as a practical joke by a less-than-humorous Son of Ether, it changes the caster's body to act as a wet cell battery and able to store enough electricity to inflict a serious shock. The mage can store up to two charges that each inflict one lethal wound; these charges must be discharged one at a time. The charges can be discharged against any person or metal object that is touching the ground and touching the caster. The caster may also power anything that can be powered with electricity, up to a car battery, for one minute per charge. The Effect lasts for one hour, and if there are any charges left after that hour, they all ground out through the caster causing the damage to him. *Grades of Success:* Each grade increases the number of charges by two.

Bean: Apprentice *Mind.* A Virtual Adept who was a bit of Frank Herbert freak created this rote so that he could stay awake longer. The mage chews on a single coffee bean and chants the mantra: "It is through will alone I set my mind in motion, through the juice of the coffee bean the thoughts acquire speed, the hands acquire shakes, the shakes become a warning. It is through will alone I set my mind in motion." The Virtual Adept may now remain awake for a full 24 hours longer than normal without incurring any penalties. When the duration ends, he sleeps for twice as long as he forced himself to stay wakeful. *Grades of Success:* None.

Be Cool: Initiate *Mind.* A Hollow One rote to make the caster more socially accepted wherever she is. When the Effect is done, it makes everybody who interacts with the mage feel like she belongs there and whatever she says is socially acceptable. For one scene, the mage receives a bonus Social Trait of *Charming. Grades of Success:* One grade increases the bonus Trait by one, to a maximum of three, or increases the duration by one grade.

Bending Willow: Adept *Correspondence*. The Akashic Brotherhood has used this rote to make entire groups of thugs obliterate each other without the mage striking a single one. Through the use of Do, the Brother bends space around himself to cause attacks that would have hit him to strike other attackers. The opponents he is affecting must be within arm's reach of him. For the one-turn duration of the Effect, a single attack that has hit the mage strikes a different opponent of the mage's choice. Only non-magical physical attacks directed against the caster may be redirected with this rote. *Grades of Success:* One grade increases the grade of duration (to a maximum of one scene/hour); one grade of success redirects an extra attack per turn.

Call the Tempest: Disciple *Entropy*, Adept *Forces*, Disciple *Spirit*. This rote is attributed to the weather witches of the Verbena, and has rarely been seen to be used in any form by any other Tradition. They would seem to be the only ones who either understand nature enough to use the rote, or the only ones mad enough to unleash this level of uncontrolled energy. Typically this Effect is done beside a seething cauldron with many unmentionable ingredients thrown into it, along with a lot of dancing and chanting. The culmination of the Effect releases a violent squall of wind, rain and lightning that is nominally under the mage's control. After the Effect is finished, it takes one hour for the storm to gather — over that hour, the clouds become more and more threatening, the wind picks up, and rain starts to fall. After the storm has formed, the violent center lasts for an hour over the area where the Effect was done. Everything within a mile of the center of the storm is buffeted by high winds, hail and rain. Any character who is unprotected in this weather must win a Static Physical Challenge against eight Traits every 10 minutes or take one level of bashing damage from flying debris and hail. The caster is unaffected by his own storm. For the duration of the storm, the caster may focus the storm against a single target. He may only do this once and must win a magical attack test against the target. If the mage succeeds, he may hit the target with a wind attack that inflicts two bashing levels and knocks her down, or with a lightning strike that inflicts two aggravated levels of damage. *Grades of Success:* One grade of success for one extra attack by the storm per grade; these grades cannot be done in the same turn.

Change the Flow of the Masses: Adept *Entropy*, Initiate *Correspondence*, Apprentice *Time*. Crowds of moving people actually emulate the flow of viscous fluids, simulating compression waves, tremors and flows. Because of this, the movement of the people is predictable and can be altered in minute ways. This rote does just that: it allows the prediction and control of large groups of people to either increase or decrease a person's movement through the crowd. It can be used in traffic jams to always be in the lane that is moving. It can be used on a bank teller line, so that the line you choose moves fastest. It can be used to remain untrampled while people are panicked and running for the emergency exits.

But just as it can be used to speed movement though crowds, it can also be used slow movement through the same crowded sidewalk, rush-hour traffic jam or bank teller line. The mage selects if he will speed or slow movement when he casts. If the mage chooses to increase speed, then the target may take one extra step through the crowd of people; choosing to slow decreases the target's steps by one. *Grades of Success:* None.

Circle Ward: Initiate *Spirit*, Apprentice *Mind*, Initiate *Prime*. This rote is used primarily by Verbena to protect them from hostile magic. It is cast by creating a circle and making an offering to the elements or some spirits to protect the caster and the circle. The mage then stays in the circle and chants, meditates or dances. As long as the caster stays with in the circle, which may be no more than three feet wide, the caster has a one-Trait bonus on all countermagic against any Effect directed against anything within the circle from anything outside the circle. The circle lasts for one hour or one scene, whichever comes first; when the mage leaves the circle; or when he makes any action other than concentrating on maintaining the circle. The mage can do nothing during the duration except maintain the spell; if he is disrupted, he must win a Static Mental Challenge against five Traits (plus one Trait per grade of success). *Grades of Success:* One grade increases the diameter of the circle by three feet, one grade increases the Trait bonus by one Trait, one grade increases the grade of duration.

Cleansing Penance: Disciple *Prime*, Disciple *Entropy*, Disciple *Life*. This dangerous rote allows a Chorister to attempt to cleanse a penitent person of something that is tainting her soul. Usually this requires both the Chorister and the tainted subject to undergo a strenuous and painful ordeal. In the process, the Chorister takes on some of the taint from the subject and cleanses it from himself, making the suffering less upon the subject so that she does not kill herself in the process. Each hour during the process, the Chorister and the subject must win Static Physical Challenges against three times the subject's Entropy Traits, or take three aggravated wounds from the cleansing of the Entropic energy that is flowing through them. The process can be stopped at any time, but the subject only loses as many Entropy Resonance Traits as she has gone through tests. For example: Bill the Chorister has met a repentant Hollow One who has racked up four Traits of Entropy and wants to get rid of them. They start the ritual and go through two hours and two Static Challenges, but Bill has been having a bad time of it and ends the ritual with six aggravated wounds. The Hollow One has two Entropic Traits removed of her four. The nature of this rote makes it so that an Avatar will only allow this process to be done once per incarnation — any other attempts to cleanse the same person will fail automatically. Also, there are some souls that are too far gone to be affected by this rote. People who have gone through the Cauls and become Nephandi cannot be helped by this rote, and any creature born of Entropic Resonance are unaffected by this rote. People who have made demonic pacts are beyond the help of this rote; and Euthanatos who have five Entropic Resonance Traits cannot be helped. This rote can never reduce a mage to less than one Trait of Entropic Resonance. *Grades of Success:* None.

Code: FIDA: Master *Spirit*, Disciple *Correspondence*, Disciple *Life*, Adept *Mind*. When the rest of the Conventions cannot deal with a particularly difficult Reality Deviant, they call in the Marines — namely the Void Engineer Marines. The Engineers set up a portable dimensional rift teleportation generator at a point in the near Umbra. The equipment generates a shell of reality around them that is friendly to the Technocratic paradigm. They focus on their intended target and open a dimensional rift, which sucks in the intended victim and transports the hapless target to the Engineers' location where there are usually 10 to 20 well-armed and -armored Marines awaiting them. The *Mind* portion of the Effect keeps bystanders from noticing what happened or that the victim was even there. The rift only stays open long enough for the victim to be pulled through; there is not enough time for anybody to jump into the rift as well. The transportation to the prepared site is instantaneous, and the victim does take damage from the Avatar Storm if that is applicable. This rote is unfortunately very Paradoxical, and the Void Engineers have become loath to risk their resources on what they usually see as other people's problems. *Grades of Success:* None.

Command the Summoned Beast: Master *Entropy*, Initiate *Spirit*. This important rote gives a Hermetic mage a way to create binding agreements with summoned beings. Most summoned beings feel no need to keep their agreements with mortals, even with mortals who are magically adept. This rote makes sure the spirit will hold to a bargained agreement. The rote does not actually command the spirit to do anything — because it can say no — but once it makes an agreement to perform a task, the spirit is bound to carry out the task to its completion. Along the same lines, though, if the mage agrees to do something in exchange for service done by the spirit, the Effect compels the mage to keep up his part of the bargain. *Grades of Success:* None.

Commune: Initiate *Spirit*, Initiate *Time*, Initiate *Mind*, Initiate *Prime*. There is nothing as beautiful as watching the sun rise over a hill, to see all the world come to life as the rays of the sun strike each blade of grass and each leaf on a tree. The world changes in that instant from night to day. Ecstatic mages hunger for these moments in order to commune with spirits of nature. When they are able to find one of these moments, they may extend the time when they remain in that moment of ecstasy for up to an hour/scene. During this time, they are a little distracted and suffer a two-Trait penalty on all actions for the duration of the Effect. They may also use this extended feeling as a focus, but once they do so, the Effect ends after the next Effect is done. *Grades of Success:* Increase in the grade of duration.

Cracks in the Conscience: Apprentice *Entropy*, Initiate *Mind*. By watching the Dharma of a subject and sensing the subconscious mind, an initiate Euthanatos senses pangs of guilt and the deviation from a subject's past path, and know when the victim lies. For the one scene/hour duration of the Effect, the mage engage the subject in a Social Challenge to judge if the last statement was a lie. *Grades of Success:* One grade of success detects one derangement of the subject's choosing.

Curse of Luck: Adept *Entropy*, Adept *Mind*. This rote, created ages ago, has remained pretty much the same over the centuries, altering slightly from culture to culture. It requires a small object with some connection to the potential victim and a statement to the effect of "May all that you do come to naught." The victim is then cursed to be unsuccessful in almost every task he attempts, even the simplest ones, and worse, his mental faculties may be dulled to the point that he does not realize what is happening to him. In game turns, for the one-turn duration of the spell, the victim loses on all ties in all challenges as fate works against him. The *Mind* component causes his mental faculties to dull, making any learned Abilities nearly useless. *Grades of Success:* Increase the grade of duration.

Decrypt Thoughts: Disciple *Mind*, Disciple *Entropy*. A Virtual Adept named C.H. Modroot created this as a means to mess with people who always kept their thoughts encrypted. The rote probes the person's mind and uses complex algorithms to decipher a target's mind, using cues from the victim's own id, and giving the caster of the rote the keyword to gain access whenever desired. The caster engages the protected mage in a Mental Challenge. If the caster wins, he gets the keyword; if he loses, he doesn't. The target of the spell may attempt an *Awareness* Mental Challenge against the caster to see if he realizes what occurred. Ever since this rote started becoming common, many paranoid Virtual Adepts have created increasingly complex and secure rotes to protect their thoughts. *Grades of Success:* None.

Discordant Sanctum: Initiate *Correspondence*, Initiate *Mind*. Used to halt intruders, the **Discordant Sanctum** causes the mage's home or *Sanctum* to become confusing and disorienting to invaders. The victim sees the room as constantly shifting and chaotic, lights will flicker for him and concentration on anything becomes difficult. The victim suffers a one-Trait penalty on all actions. The spell lasts for as long as the victim remains in the affected room or building. Typically, the subject must lose a Static Mental Challenge (difficulty of the casting mage's Mental Traits) at the time of the rote's casting. This makes the rote particularly formidable if the mage uses enhancements to gain temporary Mental Traits and then invokes this protection. *Grade of Success:* Each of grade of success increases the penalty by one Trait or affects one additional victim.

Duct Tape and WD-40: Apprentice *Matter*, Apprentice *Entropy*. This rote allows a machine to function for just a little bit longer. The mage casts the spell after checking for weak points in a machine and applying copious amounts of duct tape and WD-40. With success, the machine gains one extra health level for one scene/hour. *Grades of Success:* None.

Encrypt Thoughts: Apprentice *Mind*, Apprentice *Life*, Initiate *Prime*. A very paranoid Virtual Adept who was always afraid somebody was trying to read his mind created this rote. The rote gives the protected mage a free retest on any attempts to read his mind. This includes magical lie detection and telepathy. The mage must select an encryption keyword at the casting of the spell (this keyword should be written on a card). He may tell people the keyword so that they may freely gain access. Any of these people may spread the keyword to anybody else; any who have the keyword get a free retest when trying to access the protected mage's mind. The *Life* and *Mind* magic affects both the physical brain and the mental projection, so that all forms of reading have to penetrate the encryption, while the *Prime* magic actually overlays the encryption on the Pattern level. The effect lasts one scene or one hour, whichever comes first. *Grades of Success:* Increase the grade of duration.

Fall Upon Thy Knees: Adept *Mind* or Disciple *Forces*, Initiate *Prime*. This rote used by the Celestial Chorus reveals the awesome power of the One and forces a target to a kneeling position unable to move or act. The *Mind* version of this places the subject in a state of awe that makes him incapable of initiating any Physical Challenges as he falls upon his knees from the overwhelming emotion. The *Forces* version creates physical pressure upon the target and forces him to his knees, unable to initiate any Physical Challenges. The victim must win a Static Physical Challenge against three times the mage's Arete to stand. *Grades of Success:* None.

Faux Curse: Initiate *Mind*. This insidious rote was created by the Verbena, but has seen variations in many different paradigms. The effect is done by verbally chanting a curse at a target where he can hear, usually accompanied with a brew or hand gesture of some sort and a Mental Challenge. If the Effect succeeds, the target is struck with a sense of foreboding that he is cursed. This uneasy feeling causes the victim to be one Trait down on all challenges due to his fear. After the one minute/conflict duration is complete, the victim may attempt to win a Static Mental Challenge against a number of Traits equal to the mage's Arete times three. If the victim fails, he still believes himself to be cursed and still has the penalty because his mind has fooled itself into believing the curse to be true. The victim sees any small misfortune as a sign that the curse still hounds him. The victim may only shake the curse if he convinces the mage to "remove" it, or if he spends a Willpower Trait and wins the Static Mental Challenge. *Grades of Success:* None.

Feng Shui: Disciple *Correspondence*, Disciple *Prime*. By taking one hour and rearranging the furniture, and thereby encouraging the flow of chi in the room to collect in one place, the mage may gather bits of excess energy and gain one Quintessence Trait. After this is done, it may not be done in the same building again for one month. *Grades of Success:* Each grade channels one extra Quintessence Trait.

Find Reality Flaws: Apprentice *Prime*, Apprentice *Entropy*. By examining the faults and damage to the Tapestry, the mage can better judge how to cast an Effect without causing as much damage to reality. The mage discovers the level of the Domino Effect and the direction of the ebb and flow of Paradox. As long as the mage is the next person to cast a coincidental Effect, he will feel no penalties from the Domino Effect when casting that single spell. No other mage can take advantage of this bonus, and while neither spell is penalized by the Domino Effect, they do add to the tally. The bonus from **Find Reality Flaws** will not work if the penalty from the Domino Effect has reached three Traits, because at that point all Effects are vulgar. Because this rote was created only to look at the state of reality, it is not penalized by the Domino Effect. *Grades of Success:* None.

Got a Hunch: Initiate *Correspondence*, Initiate *Spirit*, Initiate *Time*, Apprentice *Mind*. This rote has gone through many incarnations and names, but an Orphan who worked as a private investigator coined its most recent one. The rote gives the mage the ability to look at multiple aspects of an area where she is standing and correlate all that information to give her some intuitive ideas of what is going on. When cast, the mage may ask a Narrator one question of the area, such as "Has the Nephandus been through here?" The Narrator need only give one answer to one question (i.e., a two-part question will only get one part answered — Narrator's choice regarding which part). Note that the answer does not have to be specific or detailed: "You see some Morley Cigarette butts," while not directly an answer, would be a significant clue. *Grades of Success:* None.

Gremlins: Disciple *Spirit*. This rote, first created by a Dreamspeaker who was angered by the Industrial Revolution, has seen many versions and incarnations over time. The rote awakens the spirit residing in a machine and imbues it with a malevolent personality. The machine becomes "temperamental," usually refusing to work correctly, sometimes even making attacks against its owner. For one hour/scene (whichever comes first), any challenges made with the machine will be at a one-Trait penalty. For example, a computer with a gremlin loosed in it will cause all *Computer* challenges performed with it to be at a one-Trait penalty. If an object has bonus Traits that are reduced to zero, the object simply refuses to work for the duration. *Grades of Success:* One grade of success increases the grade of duration. One grade of success increases the Trait penalty by one. Three grades of success gives the object some anthropomorphism and lets the object make physical attacks against anybody in contact with it every turn. The object has six Physical Traits and the type of damage should be appropriate for what the object may be able to physically do. For instance, a computer may shock a victim for lethal damage, an oven may shoot flames for aggravated damage, and so on.

Guilty Whispers: Adept *Mind*, Initiate *Entropy*, Initiate *Prime*. This rote, used by some inquisitors of the Celestial Chorus, feeds energy to the conscience of a subject, summoning up a whispering voice in the back of the person's mind that hounds her about her misdeeds and sins. No matter what the morals of the target may be, for the duration of the Effect, her whispering conscience has the moral beliefs of the mage. The affected character should roleplay having these voices in her head, and they are quite persistent, becoming louder when she is asked about one of her misdeeds. In game terms, for the one hour/scene duration, the character feels compelled to admit to any misdeed that she has committed when she are asked about it. The character may opt to spend a

Willpower rather than spill the beans. Once the affected character has admitted to a misdeed that he is asked about, the voice calms down and returns to sleep, having been sated. Striking with **Guilty Whispers** generally involves a Mental Challenge between the caster and victim. *Grades of Success:* None.

Head of a Pin: Initiate *Prime*. How many angels can dance on the head of a pin? How many drops of water are there in a drop of water? According to most paradigms, there is only one angel on the pin, and there is only one drop of water, but the Chorus sees the infinity of reality and sees that the drop of water can be separated into an infinite number of drops of water, and that an infinite number of angels can dance on the impossibly small head of a pin. Because of this, the Chorus is able to concentrate Tass to hold multiple Traits of Quintessence. After this is done, though, it becomes impossible for any but a Chorister to access all the Quintessence within the Tass. A Chorister with some of this treated Tass can access all the Quintessence within it all at once. For instance, an Ecstatic has a mushroom that is a piece of Tass — he eats the mushroom and gets a Trait of Quintessence. A Chorister has some holy water with eight Traits of Quintessence — he anoints himself with the holy water and may choose to either access all eight Traits or only one at that instant. The Chorister needs to have a single source of Tass to start with; through prayer and ritual, he then concentrates other Traits of Quintessence (either from his Pattern or from other sources of Tass) into the initial source of Tass. He may place one extra Trait of Quintessence into the source of Tass; it will remain there until removed. *Grades of Success:* One grade of success allows for an extra Trait of Quintessence to be stored.

Historic Editing: Master *Entropy* or Adept *Time*. This tool of the New World Order has allowed them to destroy or alter almost every historical event to their favor and to reflect their paradigm. The Effect is set into motion by historical studies and media coverage of "newly discovered facts." These facts then disseminate through the populace and alter the Consensus' perception of the events. Any person trying to find out atrue facts about an event in the past that has been changed by this Effect must win a Static Mental Challenge against three times the Arete of the mage who made the edit. A mage using *Time* magic to look back at the event must make the same Mental Challenge in order to see the true history. *Grades of Success:* None.

Hungarian Phrase Book: Master *Entropy*. This amusing yet dangerous curse causes everything the victim says to sound like nonsensical (sometimes silly) words. If cast properly, the victim can say nothing correctly — he should use the wrong nouns and verbs and be unable to be understood at all verbally. The victim does not realize he is speaking gibberish, and will likely become quite frustrated and confused. Anyone who wants to understand the victim must win a Static Mental Challenge against three times the caster's Arete Traits. This spell lasts for one hour or one scene, whichever comes first. *Grades of Success:* Increase the grade of duration.

Imbue the Living Vessel: Disciple *Prime*, Disciple *Life*. The mage can store Quintessence in another person. This rote takes advantage of the fact that even the unAwakened have Patterns that can hold Quintessence, and temporarily makes a person into walking, talking Tass. This is commonly used by Verbena on their followers before rituals to have extra Quintessence on hand for magical works. It is commonly cast by using sex, drugs or ordeals. During the casting, the mage transfers some Quintessence from himself or from some Tass into the target. There is an added side-effect to this rote — the target feels a great rush of energy that tends to bring on a strong sense of euphoria. In the case of some types of Tass, it may bring on feelings of depression or intense focus. This side-effect fades within an hour, and the Tass takes on a Resonance appropriate to the target's emotional state when the Quintessence is drawn from her. The rote stores one Quintessence for one day. After a day, any unused Quintessence leaks out of the target's Pattern at the rate of one per day. The caster of the rote can draw upon the Tass at any time while the Quintessence is still in the Pattern. *Grades of Success:* Increase the number of Quintessence stored by one per grade.

Information Glut: Initiate *Correspondence*, Disciple *Mind*, Initiate *Time*. The mage gains the Mental Trait: *Observant* and sees and hear things at longer distances than would normally be possible. The mage may also take in a glut of confusing information and sort through the data, getting what he wants without being confused by the overload or missing necessary details. The duration of the Effect is one scene or one hour, whichever comes first. *Grades of Success:* Increase the grade of duration per success. Two grades of success adds an extra observer for the duration.

Instant Karma: Disciple *Correspondence*, Adept *Entropy*. This rote is a kind of curse employed recently by some Euthanatos, but has been used in different forms by the Celestial Chorus and the Verbena. It uses the interconnections of all things in the universe and the inexorable cascade of events to cause a victim to feel immediate consequences for his actions. When cast, the Euthanatos must choose an action that the victim should not do and then choose a consequence of that action. The banned action must be something that the victim would have to willfully do as an immoral action and cannot be an action necessary for normal survival. For example, you cannot ban the victim from breathing, eating or pissing; but you could ban them from killing, stealing or even using foul language. Placing a ban against killing on a person also counts if that person accidentally kills a person in self-defense, because the desire causes the action and this brings about the karmic justice. The consequence of the action is chosen by the mage when the Effect is done, and may either cause a wound (up to aggravated), or give the victim a Negative Trait. After the Effect is cast, the victim becomes aware that his actions cause immediate consequence, and knows what those consequences will be. The Effect lasts for one day. For example: Bob the Euthanatos knows a man named Jim. Jim is at a crossroads in his destiny — on one path, he could become a great and benevolent leader; on the other he could become a thief who would prey on the weak and cause the further decay of the world. So Bob places a ban on Jim, causing Jim to suffer one lethal wound every time he steals something. Jim ignores his conscience and steals an old lady's purse, only to feel a stabbing pain in his hand. By this, Bob quietly guides Jim onto the preferred path. Casting this unusual curse on someone requires besting the subject in a Social Challenge. *Grades of Success:* Increase the duration by a grade of duration.

Knock Out: Disciple *Mind*, Initiate *Prime*. Invented by a Son of Ether who hated killing, this rote effectively incapacitates a target without causing any serious harm. The caster must succeed in a magical attack against the intended target. If successful, the target is stunned and unable to initiate any challenges or move. This stun status is canceled if any aggressive damage-causing action is directed at the stunned character (this includes indirect sources of damage like hand grenades and burning buildings). The target is only stunned for one turn, so it is best that the mage move quickly after doing this. *Grades of Success:* Increase the grade of duration.

Know the Leper's Mind: Initiate *Mind*, Disciple *Spirit*. A Dreamspeaker created this rote centuries ago when he tended a small colony of lepers. The rote summons a spirit of hatred and binds it to a single victim to follow and torment him. This spirit inspires hatred and disgust in every person who comes into contact with the victim. While under the effect of the spell, the victim is unable to initiate any Social Challenges except for intimidation; the victim also loses all ties in all Social Challenges. The victim should inform everybody that he interacts with of the aura of hatred, and encourage roleplaying appropriately. The casting mage must best the target in a Social Challenge, to bind the spirit to the intended victim. The effect last for one scene. *Grades of Success:* Increase the grade of duration.

Manna from Heaven: Initiate *Matter*, Initiate *Prime*. This simple rote created by the Celestial Chorus gives them the ability to change air into bread, cheese or water. It creates enough food for one person to survive on for one day, or enough water for one person to survive on for one day. The mage must choose what she wishes to create at the time of casting. *Grades of Success:* Creates additional foodstuffs for one additional person per grade.

Masochism Tango: Disciple *Life*, Apprentice *Mind*. This rote used by the Hollow Ones and some Cultists allows them to sustain incredible amounts of punishment without being crippled by pain. It shuts off some of the nerve ending in the skin and places the mind in a state where it recognizes pain but does not report it as such. While under the effect of this rote, the mage has the Negative Physical Trait of *Clumsy* because of a slightly reduced tactile sense, but also receives no wound penalties. Of course when the mage reaches Mortally Wounded, he falls down, stops moving, and begins dying. The Effect lasts for one minute or conflict. At the end of the duration, the mage suffers *all* of the effects of any damage he has taken. *Grades of Success:* None.

Mimir's Head: Adept *Spirit* or Master *Mind*. Mimir was said to be the wisest of all creatures that protected the Well of Knowledge, and even after his death, his severed head remained aware and communicative. This Effect, used by the Verbena, requires them to take the head from a recently (no more than a day) dead person. After being treated with unguents and oils, the head can answer questions pertaining to its past life and its knowledge. The Effect lasts for one day, and in that day, questions may be asked of the talking head about one subject pertaining to its life or a *Lore* that it had. Only one subject may be covered in a single day — the dead speak slowly. If the talking head would not have asnwered what it is being asked, then the querent must win a Static Social Challenge against the original Social Traits of the previous owner of the head. The mage may learn the answer to a single question about a *Lore* that the head knew in life, or ask a single question about its living days. Spheres, rotes and Abilities may not be learned from the enchanted head, and it only speaks when alone with the caster. *Grades of Success:* Increase the grade of duration.

Mind GREP: Disciple *Mind*. By attaching a computer to a victim's head with a SQUID helmet, a Virtual Adept may use GREP searches to find information from a victim's brain. For one minute/conflict, the mage may ask one question of the victim, which he must answer truthfully (if the mage wins a Mental Challenge). *Grades of Success:* Each grade of success allows the mage to ask one more question of the victim.

Moment of Inspiration: Apprentice *Time*, Apprentice *Spirit*. Many initiates of the Cult of Ecstasy are artists of some type, and they come to realize that the Muses of old are still present, but they now speak to artists infrequently and tease with fleeting glimpses of inspiration. Apprentices use this rote to concentrate on these brief moments and hold onto them for as long as possible. With this they gain a one-Trait bonus on any challenge dealing with artistic ability or creativity (*Crafts*, *Performance*, *Expression*, etc.) *Grades of Success:* None.

Mr. Fusion's Clean Burning Fuel Fabrication Formula: Disciple *Matter*. This formula created by the mad Mr. Fusion changes an amount of non-living inorganic matter into an equal volume of methane. While most people don't see much use for this rote, Mr. Fusion thought it was just keen and was planning on making loads of money when he started selling his kerosene-burning line of cars. *Grades of Success:* None.

Murder of Crows: Disciple *Life*, Initiate *Mind*. This rote, first created by the Verbena, has been adopted in different forms by other Traditions and changed to match their paradigm and the animals available. The Effect summons a group of a specific type of animal that does the mage's bidding. It takes one full turn for the swarm to arrive. Since this is not a natural action it takes a bit of concentration from the user to keep them on track. Other actions may be performed, but attempting to summon another swarm of animals causes both swarms to dissipate and go back to what they were interrupted. The swarm has seven Physical Traits and four Healthy health levels; it inflicts lethal damage when it hits and may only attack one target at a time. The swarm remains around the caster for one scene/hour (whichever comes first). If its four health levels are removed, the swarm dissipates, as instinct overcomes the magical compulsion. *Grades of Success:* Increase the Physical Traits of the swarm by one, or increase the health levels of the swarm by one Healthy health level.

My God Can Beat Up Your God: Disciple *Spirit*, Disciple *Prime*. In the past, the Choristers have crushed cults to dangerous Umbroods and demons with this rote. The rote summons a spirit, which usually appears as an angel, that does battle with another spirit in the area that threatens the Chorister or is an enemy of the Chorister. The "angel" does retain free will, and will refuse to attack a spirit without good reason, and will never attack a non-spiritual creature (but it will attack a materialized spirit). The angel summoned with this particular Effect has eight Traits in Rage and Gnosis, 20 Power, and has the Charms *Airt Sense* and *Flames of Purification*. During the battle, the mage may spend his Quintessence to increase the Power of the spirit at a one-to one rate. The mage may spend his own Ability Traits to give the angel retests, and the mage may take on damage for the spirit. *Grades of Success:* None.

Mystic Tag: Initiate *Spirit*, Initiate *Prime*. This rote, created by a Hollow One, is used as a clandestine means of communications. A Hollow One writes a stylized tag (a picture or a nickname usually written with a Sharpee permanent marker, for those unfamiliar with tagging) on something out in the open that can be easily seen. As she is writing the tag, she also writes a small message on the webs of the structure she is tagging. Any person with Apprentice *Spirit* can immediately see the message contained in the tag. The message may be up to five words long, and is usually used to warn other Hollow Ones of dangers in an area or to point "newbies" toward gathering places. The message lasts as long as the tag remains visible on the structure. *Grades of Success:* Increase the size of the hidden message by five words.

Nice Boots, Wanna Fuck?: Disciple *Life*, Disciple *Mind*. This Hollow Ones rote starts by increasing a few hormones in the target's body to make him more "aroused." The *Mind* part of the rote gives the mage information on the right things to say to her target. As a consequence, the target becomes more open to carnal suggestions, and the mage receives two bonus Traits of *Seductive* against the person she targets with the Effect. (As a side note, just because *your character* is able to seduce another character does not mean *you* the player can get frisky with the player of that character. We really should not have to mention this, but we will, because inevitably there will be somebody who tries to use this rote as a kind of LARPer mating ritual. Remember, *No Touching.*) *Grades of Success:* None.

Parma Magica: Disciple *Prime*. The famed **Parma Magica**, created by House Bonisagus of the Order of Hermes, is one of the catalysts of the organized Traditions as they are today. It is cast on a small object — usually something with some importance to the caster, and many times is fashioned to look like a shield. The newly empowered object then acts as a store for Quintessence that is instantly accessible in any amount to be used for countermagic. For Sphere countermagic, it makes the shielded mage's difficulty one less per Quintessence used. The Talisman can hold two Quintessence, and is unique to the caster and cannot be used by anybody else. The mage must still have the Quintessence to place in the object, of course. *Grades of Success:* One grade increases the held Quintessence by two.

Place in the Dance: Apprentice *Correspondence*. The Dreamspeakers have a slightly different view of the *Correspondence* Sphere. They do not see it as a Sphere of space and distance, but as the Sphere of interconnectedness, in which all beings are part of the Great Dance and what they do affects everything else in the dance. This rote, taught to young students of this Sphere among the Dreamspeakers, gives the mage a vision of where a subject belongs in the Great Dance. In game terms, the player may ask one question about the subject's geographic background — i.e., what culture is she from, where was she born/ created, what area does she live in, etc. The question may also be about connection the subject may have, such as is she married, is she a sibling, who she is owned by. Unwilling victims can resist with a Social Challenge. *Grades of Success:* Each grade gives an extra question.

Plastic Body: Disciple *Life*, Adept *Correspondence*. The mage can contort and stretch his body in unbelievable ways. He may contract parts of his body as small as three inches or stretch an appendage up to a length of six feet (including his torso). Making a change of shape takes one turn of concentration to complete and is very uncomfortable, causing one level of bashing damage. The duration of the Effect is one round, and the mage's body returns to its original shape immediately at the end of the duration, even if the mage does not fit his present confinements. The Storyteller should assign damage he sees fit for such an unfortunate occurrence. *Grades of Success:* Increase the grade of duration.

Portal's Herald: Initiate *Correspondence*, Apprentice *Life*; with Initiate *Mind* and Initiate *Prime*, or Disciple *Spirit*. When cast on a door, the **Portal's Herald** immediately alerts the casting mage when a living being crosses through the threshold. The base duration of the rote is one night. *Grades of Success:* Increase the grade of duration.

Praise Asphalta: Disciple *Correspondence*, Initiate *Spirit*. This odd Verbena rote asks Asphalta, the goddess of parking lots and parking spaces, for assistance in finding a place to park a vehicle. After paying homage to Asphalta, a parking space is found immediately, and it is always near the place the mage wanted to go in the first place — usually less than 10 steps, and it isn't even a handicapped spot. *Grades of Success:* None.

Precipitate the Summoned Form: Adept *Life*, Disciple *Spirit*, Initiate *Prime* or Adept *Matter*, Disciple *Spirit*, Initiate *Prime*. By preparing a body for a spirit, a Hermetic may force a summoned spirit into a physical form. Some spirits will be more than happy about this, while others may become quite violent. While the spirit is in the physical form, the mage holds no control over it except the threat of physical harm. Older and more powerful spirits are not likely to feel threatened by physical harm, as they know that the destruction of the form will not destroy them. The form is temporary, and is destroyed after one hour or scene, whichever comes first. The new form has six Physical Traits, and its Mental/ Social Traits are based on the spirit's Gnosis; the form also starts with the normal number of health levels. *Grades of Success:* Increase the grade of duration, or increase the Physical Traits of the form by two Traits, or give the form an extra Healthy health level.

Pyro Manos: Initiate *Forces*. With this rote, taught to most new members of House Flambeau, the initiate lights a small chunk of sulphur and throws it at a target. A magical attack (typically a Physical Challenge) must be made to hit. If the mage succeeds in the challenge against the target, the chunk of sulphur explodes, causing one aggravated wound to the intended target. *Grades of Success:* None.

Red Ones Go Faster: Initiate *Forces*. This odd little rote uses a little-known theory that says different wavelengths of light move faster than others in certain situations. Mages use this rote to make things move just a little bit faster than everything else by painting them red, as it is the lowest wavelength of visible of light, and therefore will reflect the slowest wavelength of red while absorbing the faster wavelengths. Hence the red object is given a little extra energy from all the other more energetic wavelengths being absorbed. Anything that the Sons of Ether use this rote on and paint completely red gains one extra step in movement when in combat, and vehicles this rote is used on will move 10 percent faster than normal. Sadly, the Effect is only temporary as the paint quickly becomes saturated with energetic light, so the Effect only lasts for one hour/scene. *Grades of Success:* None.

Release the Red Death: Adept *Life*, Disciple *Spirit*. This deadly rote is cast very rarely by the Verbena because of its indifference toward innocent bystanders. The Effect summons a spirit of disease; the disease is different each time, but always fatal. The spirit infects all living beings within a single building with a wasting disease. Each half-hour, the victims lose one Physical Trait. Once they are out of Physical Traits, they fall into a coma and suffer one level of lethal damage each half-hour. A Static *Medicine* Mental Challenge against three times the mage's Arete Traits is required to find a cure for the disease; magical Effects may also be used to find a cure. The disease usually manifests as something familiar, but in a highly resistant form. The disease is not communicable, because it is caused by the presence of the spirit, which is only present long enough to infect everybody in its target building. *Grades of Success*: None.

Re-live Experience: Disciple *Time*, Apprentice *Mind*. The Cult of Ecstasy is always looking for new experiences and new sensations. A lot of times they simply stare off into space and remember an experience from the past. This rote allows a Cultist to initiate a full recall of an experience by doing something that emulates a sensation from the moment in time she wishes to recall. If the Effect succeeds, the Cultist can recall any detail from the experience vividly, and may make any appropriate *Investigation*, *Alertness* or other challenges to see if she can recognize something from the scene that her subconscious picked up before. The mage only has a minute to do this before the flash of experience will fade. *Grades of Success:* None.

Reveal the Holy Path: Disciple *Correspondence*, Apprentice *Prime*. By making a prayer to the One and asking it to show the mage the path to the divine, the mage sees a glowing path before him that leads him to the closest source of Tass. Sometimes this leads the Chorister to creatures or places that are not exactly holy.... This Effect will not detect Quintessence within Avatars, but it will detect Nodes and Tass that a mage may be carrying. Typical range starts at sight. *Grades of Success:* Each grade of success extends the range by one *Correspondence* range block.

Remove Divine Favor: Disciple *Prime*. This rote of the Celestial Chorus is one of their more devastating weapons in war. With it the mage can cause the extra Quintessence within a Pattern to be expelled. The effect causes one Trait of Quintessence to evaporate from a Pattern that contains more Quintessence than is normal, such as Tass or a mage with more Quintessence than his Avatar rating. The effect can only remove Quintessence from one pattern. Typically this requires a Social Challenge between the attacker and target. *Grades of Success:* Removes one extra Quintessence per grade of success.

Ringing Strike: Disciple *Matter*. This technique is used by the Akashic Brotherhood to damage inanimate objects. It has been used by Doists to break swords with their bare hands, shatter stone columns with a single kick, or destroy an opponent's helmet with a head butt. The rote allows the mage to shatter *Matter* Patterns; it is either done with a weapon or a Do strike. The mage must make a magical attack challenge against the inanimate object. If the object being worn or held by another character, then he must make the magical attack challenge against the holder. This Effect can damage any non-magical material, but cannot damage the Pattern of *Wonders* or of materials made with *Master*-level *Matter* like Primium. Magically altered materials may be damaged as normal. If the magical attack test is successful, the object instantly takes one health level of aggravated damage. If an object has no health levels, reduce any bonus Traits it gives, destroying the object when it is reduced to zero Traits. *Grades of Success:* Each grade of success causes an extra health level of damage to the object or removes one bonus Trait.

Sanctify Sacred Relic: Initiate *Prime*, Apprentice *Matter*. Initiate Choristers preparing foci for larger ceremonies use this rote. Through various cleansing and purifying rituals, they prepare the focus. The next spell cast using this focus is at one difficulty less. This Effect may not be combined with any other Effects that reduce the difficulty of creating magical Effects. *Grades of Success*: None.

Sanctum's Sense (also known as "Where are my Keys"): Initiate *Correspondence*; with Apprentice *Matter* or Apprentice *Life*. This rote is cast in a place familiar to the mage, usually with his *Sanctum* or home. It allows the mage to locate any one thing he is looking for — his keys, his wallet, a handy gun or maybe a bug. The *Life* variation of this rote allows the caster to locate interlopers. Use the *Correspondence* ranges for location range. *Grades of Success:* Grades increase the range as for *Correspondence* Effects.

See the Tainted Soul: Apprentice *Prime*, Apprentice *Spirit*, Apprentice *Entropy*. The Choristers learned this long ago from a mysterious race of half-men, half-angels who claimed to battle the evil of the world. With proper cleansing rituals, the mage may see stains on another's soul that are sometimes left by exposure to Nephandi, some demons and even by Jhor. By winning an *Awareness* Social Challenge against a target, the mage can discover how many traits of Entropic

Resonance the target holds. Though this is not always a sure sign of the subject being evil and a force of destruction, it does identify potential problems. *Grades of Success:* None.

Semi-Auto Cad-Cam: Disciple *Matter*, Master *Correspondence*. The rote allows the mage to combine two guns into a single weapon that has Traits from both weapons. The combined weapon looks like a patchwork gun with parts of both, and looks like no other weapon in existence. During the combination, the mage must choose two attributes from one weapon and two attributes from the other; the Negative Traits of both weapons are combined. For instance, Eddie wants to take his shotgun and combine it with his pistol. He takes the bonus Traits from the shotgun (three); the concealability of the pistol (Pocket); the damage of the pistol (two lethal wounds); and lastly the Special Abilities of the shotgun (spray and mass trauma); the Negative Traits of this weapon are *Loud* x 2. What he gets is a really small, really loud shotgun with a pearl-handled pistol grip. The Effect lasts for one turn, and the weapon falls back into the two original guns. With sufficient duration, it might be possible to combine **Semi-Auto Cad-Cam** on multiple objects in a series. *Grades of Success:* Each grade of success increases the grade of duration.

Sense the Fleeting Moment: Apprentice *Time*. Through the use of astrology, a Verbena may figure out the exact moment to act on something so that the action has a better chance of succeeding. In game terms, the mage may choose one non-magical Ability and on the next use of that Ability, receive a one-Trait bonus to that one challenge. *Grades of Success:* Increase the Trait bonus by one per grade of success.

Sharing the Experience: Disciple *Mind*, Initiate *Correspondence*, Disciple *Time*. This rote allows a Cultist of Ecstasy to share experiences and messages in instantaneous flashes of thought that are usually seen by most around them as only a lingering meeting of the eyes. Where telepathy among other Traditions takes just as much time as talking does, this rote flashes meaningful experiences and visions between the Cultists that they can easily interpret into conversation. The two mages in the conversation may ask for a one-minute time-stop to discuss whatever they wish to discuss privately. This minute should be timed by a Narrator and kept strictly down to a single minute to keep from interfering with the game flow too much. Nothing other than communication can be done over this fleeting connection, and this communication can only be understood by other Cultists. Other Traditions receiving the visions are not able to process them properly and simply become confused by them. *Grades of Success:* None.

Solomon's Binding: Disciple *Spirit*, Disciple *Correspondence*. To start this Effect, the Hermetic mage must create a seal of Solomon upon the ground surrounded by a ring of salt. The ring of salt need not be completed until a spirit is summoned. Upon the summoning, the ring of salt is completed and the spirit is trapped within the circle. The spirit may try to force its way out by winning a Static Physical Challenge against three times the mage's Arete; if it is unable to win the initial Static Challenge, it cannot try to force its way out again for 24 hours. The spirit may not affect anything outside the circle; if anything were break into the circle, it would break the binding and the spirit would be free to leave any time thereafter. The spirit may be held in the binding for as long as the physical circle of salt exists around the seal, or until the spirit is able to force its way out. The spirit held by this binding is in no way under the mage's control. *Grades of Success:* None.

Spirit Cloak: Initiate *Mind*, Initiate *Spirit*. This important rote is taught to many Dreamspeakers early in their lives to give them a small edge in the spirit world. The denizens that call it home often take an unhealthy interest in a mage walking along the spirit paths, so to protect themselves, Dreamspeakers create this Effect to dim their presence to otherworldly eyes. In game terms, this Effect makes it more difficult for spirits to notice the mage, giving her a one-Trait bonus on any *Stealth* and *Subterfuge* tests for one hour/scene. *Grades of Success:* Increase the grade if duration, or increase the bonus by one Trait.

Spoliatio Posterus ad Pensio Nam Nunc: Apprentice *Correspondence*, Apprentice *Prime*, Initiate *Time*. An apprentice Hermetic named Stephanie Russel created this rote when her Chantry was in a pinch and needed some quick Tass for a major Effect. It is done by measuring all the possible factors that affect the strength of a Node — the timing, ley lines and the flow of *Prime* energy. After calculating all of these variables, the mage discovers the ideal place and time to gather Tass at that Node, and gathers one extra Tass than usual. In game terms, the *Node* Background is increased by one for the session. This rote can only be performed once a month on a Node, and after it is performed, the Node produces one *less* Tass in the next month — i.e., the *Node* Background is reduced by one for the next month. *Grades of Success:* None.

Surprise, You're Dead!: Master *Entropy*. The Syndicate is interested in keeping everybody in the system, but sometimes a Deviant becomes such a problem that the Syndicate needs to remove her so she cannot further affect the Technocracy's delicate machinery of economics and influence. To do this, the Syndicate employs this insidious rote. It starts with an obituary that declares the Deviant as dead. All the proper paperwork is processed, including coroner's report, burial schedules and account closings. The victim's worldly ties slowly begin to disappear as her accounts are closed and turned over to the state. Contacts and Sleeper associates also begin to believe the Deviant is dead, remembering to have witnessed her funeral, and may believe she is actually an imposter. In game terms, each month the victim loses the top level of each of her Influences, *Allies*, *Contacts* and *Resources*. The degradation continues until all of those Backgrounds go to nothing or the mage figures out a way to stop the Effect. Any new Backgrounds bought while the Effect is working are lost as well. *Grades of Success:* None — ain't it bad enough already?

Taliesin's Song: Disciple *Matter*, Disciple *Spirit*, Initiate *Prime*. In the times when the world was young and the material and the spiritual were one, it is said that the wizard-bard Taliesin could sing new things into existence. Though the world has changed, parts of that original shaping song still remain. The mage begins this Effect by singing about the object he wants to create as he mimes shaping it with his hands. He needs no tools to craft the object, though an appropriate *Crafts* Ability may be necessary. The rote draws ephemera from the Umbra and solidifies it into a material object. The finished object may be made of any normal substance and may be any non-technological/mechanical object that the mage desires. The object must be no larger than the mage's closed fist. Objects created this way sometimes suffer from Unbelief, especially if conjured in front of Sleepers. Paradox from this rote tends to unravel the item in question. Objects that don't degrade thusly still have a basic duration of only 10 minutes/ conflict. *Grades of Success:* Each grade expands the maximum object size by one handspan, or one grade can extend the duration by a grade.

Trick Shot: Apprentice *Correspondence*, Apprentice *Forces*, Apprentice *Time*, Apprentice *Entropy*. The **Trick Shot** rote gives the mage a better understanding of the forces, timing and distances involved in firing a gun. In game terms, it gives the mage a one-Trait bonus on the next firearms attack. *Grades of Success:* One grade allows the mage to ricochet the shot off one object with no penalty. One more allows the ricochet to hit a target that is behind full cover with no penalty. (The firer must still win an attack challenge.)

Trippy Light Show: Adept *Mind* or Initiate *Forces*. This Hollow One rote requires that the area being affected have multiple, different colored lights illuminating it. The Effect causes a single person to be confused and dazzled by the lights in an area, leaving him distracted. The victim of the Effect receives the Negative Mental Trait: *Oblivious* for the one scene/hour duration. *Grades of Success:* One grade allows the Effect to be extended to one more victim, or one grade gives the victim one more Negative Trait up to a maximum of three.

Undying Endurance: Disciple *Life*. The Cult of Ecstasy has used this rote for more than a few millennia. Usually the Effect is activated by enchanting a garlic bulb — or, more recently, a ginseng root — and then the enchanted item is eaten by the person who needs the **Undying Endurance**. From that point, for the rest of the session, that character may expend any of his Physical Traits as if they are Stamina-related Traits. At the end of the session, the character is exhausted and unable to initiate any Physical Challenges for the rest of the day. *Grades of Success:* For one grade of success, the mage may add the option of letting the character take levels of lethal damage and replenish three Physical Traits; damage taken in this way does not adversely affect the character unless he takes damage from any other source, then all penalties of his current health status will take effect. A character reaching Mortally Wounded while under this Effect can still function unless he has taken damage from another source. Once the Effect ends, whatever damage he has taken hits him all at once, so it's entirely possible for a mage to kill himself doing this.

Void Strike: Adept *Spirit*, Initiate *Correspondence*. This rote was created recently by a Dreamspeaker ecoterrorist. He first created this to push enemies into the Umbra where he was much more skilled and would have the upper hand. After the appearance of the Avatar Storm, he found a new use for it. He discovered that the same rote could be used on mages to force them into the Umbra and therefore into the Avatar Storm. In game terms, when the Effect is peformed, a rift opens in the Gauntlet to the Umbra. The attacker must win a magical attack challenge (Social, if it's done solely with *Correspondence* manipulation; Physical, if the attacker physically pushes) against the intended victim. If he wins, the victim is unceremoniously dumped into the near Umbra; if the victim is a mage, she takes the damage from the Avatar Storm. *Grades of Success:* None.

Ward the Inner Sanctum: Disciple *Correspondence*; Disciple *Life*, *Prime*, or *Spirit*. This rote is made to create specific bans on an area to limit access according to the caster's needs. The *Life* version creates a ban (per the ward effect of the Initiate *Correspondence*) against a specific person or type of creature, or to allow only a specific person or creature to enter. For a violator to cross into the banned area, she must win a Static Physical Challenge against three times the caster's Arete Traits. The *Spirit* version acts the same as the *Life* version, except the invading spirit must win a Static Willpower Challenge against two times the caster's Traits. The *Prime* version acts as a standing anti-magic shell around the banned area; any spell that is cast at anything inside the banned area has its casting difficulty increased by the warding mage's Arete Traits. As with other wards and bans, the base duration is one hour or one scene, whichever comes first, and can protect an area of 15 paces in diameter, plus three paces per Arete Trait. *Grades of Success*: Each grade of success doubles the area diameter or increase the grade of duration.

Woad Warrior: Disciple *Life*, Initiate *Mind*. The warriors of the ancient Picts used to paint themselves in blue woad before battle, believing it would protect them. Roman soldiers were rarely prepared for the sight of the howling, blue-painted boogeymen. The Verbena recently rediscovered the rote used by the druids of the time to protect their warriors from the spears and swords of Roman soldiers. The Verbena creates a paste from a mix of herbs and clay and paints it in curling knots and whorls on the person he wishes to enchant. If the Effect test is successful, the affected character receives no penalties from wounds and has one extra Healthy health level when he activates the woad patterns by spending a Willpower Trait. The activated woad sends the character into a berserker frenzy bent on destruction. While the woad is active, the affected character may initiate only Physical Challenges. Physical attacks that may be performed as Mental Challenges (such as *Firearms*) must bid Physical Traits. The Effect lasts for the rest of the session, or until the enchanted character spending a Willpower activates it. Once activated, the Effect lasts for one combat or one minute, whichever comes first. *Grades of Success:* One grade gives the character one extra Healthy health level per grade, or one grade of success gives the effected character three extra Physical Traits.

Work or Else: Disciple *Spirit*, Disciple *Matter*. Supposedly a Son of Ether got the idea for this Effect from a Hermetic scholar who was researching old magics of the Babylonians. The mage makes a vague threat toward one of his technological foci to make it work more effectively. The next Effect cast with that focus has its casting difficulty reduced by one Trait. Foci under this Effect may be used together, but no more than a one-Trait bonus may be gained. Similar rotes, which reduce the difficulty of magical effects, cannot be stacked with this rote. *Grades of Success:* None.

Chapter Five: Addenda

Rules help a game to flow smoothly — at least, ideally. All too often, however, rules also become the focus of endless debate and argument. For a live-action game, that's a problem; the game must run quickly and seamlessly, so that a dozen players don't wind up standing around completely bored for an hour while the Storyteller and Narrators have it out with a couple of recalcitrant players.

To that end, all of the rules in **Laws of Ascension** are designed to be as streamlined and simple as possible. Inevitably, issues will crop up, regardless of the attention paid to detail. Therefore, the updates here ultimately should *only* be used as a way to try to *help* a game, not simply to add more complexity.

Right after "Have fun," and just after the rules of safe play, the next most important rule is:

The Storyteller is always right.

Some players make a habit of arguing the rules in hopes of garnering special privileges or pulling out weird benefits for their characters. These players often consider rules a challenge in engineering, a way to work "the system" in order to maximize the benefits for themselves. They also tend to see the game as an antagonistic affair, with their characters pitted against all of the other characters and up against anything the Storyteller can throw at them.

The previous approach is fundamentally flawed. Live-action games, by their nature, often have large player bases. For everyone to have fun, everyone must have a chance to participate. It's not about centering on one person as the protagonist to everyone else's expense. It's not about "beating the system" to force a Storyteller to comply with some absurd notion supported by a convoluted interpretation of the rules. It's about having a good time in a social setting with a shared story.

The result of this is: No amount of rules-lawyering or arguing can save you from the Storyteller. It doesn't matter that page XX of some random sourcebook says "You can blow up another character's head with this Effect without making a test." If the Storyteller says it doesn't fly, it doesn't happen. This may be for any number of reasons. It's a mistake to assume that the Storyteller does this just to screw with a character. Storytellers also juggle huge games; it's possible that something isn't working as expected due to some unknown background condition that the Storyteller's aware of but isn't sharing. Perhaps the Storyteller has a character with certain exceptions to the rules. If the Storyteller makes a call, it's done.

This means that the player's responsibility is to accept a Storyteller or Narrator's ruling with good grace and allow the game to move on. Stopping the game to argue an obscure point of rules over what is ultimately an imaginary character is not only missing the point, it's *selfish*. It's demanding that the game come to a screeching halt so that *your* character can have some perceived challenge to the Natural Order as represented by the Storyteller. The worst is taking advantage of a player who doesn't *know* the rules well in order to destroy that player's enjoyment of the game. Such antisocial behavior has no place in a community-driven social activity. Characters can and will come to blows, but that doesn't mean that it's OK to have a character whose sole purpose is to exploit a rules loophole in order to blow up less rules-proficient players' characters. Know when to step aside so that *everybody* may participate.

All of this, of course, must still bow to the most important rule: **Have fun**. Sometimes Storytellers *do* make mistakes; they're only human. Pointing out that something is potentially a mistake is no crime. Once the Storyteller says "No, this is deliberate," it's time to drop the issue and proceed with the game. Similarly, the Storyteller's task is to provide a fun and compelling environment for many characters to interact, not just to throw antagonists at the players' characters. A Storyteller isn't there to show off how he can make powerful critters that can crush any player, or solve any plot problem with his pet Narrator character. Once the Storyteller's rulings push the game out of the players' hands and turn them into passive observers, they're watching a (probably tragic) play, not participating in a game.

Once again, to quote a prodigious writer of game material, "Rules are nothing. Story is everything. Obey your Storyteller."

Live-action games aren't contests or fights. They're social activities for everyone's enjoyment.

With all that out of the way, here are some more ideas for speeding your game along.

No Instant Kills (Optional Rule)

This rule only works if you're willing to suspend a little disbelief in order to prohibit some characters from exploiting super-powerful attack combinations.

It's never very fun to have an unbeatable antagonist, which is what happens when someone's rote performs instant-kill effects. Some rotes can be powered-up with grades of success, potentially to the level of whacking a character instantly.

When in doubt, assume that it's not possible to instantly kill a healthy character with a single strike (whether from a spell or weapon or whatever). No Effect may kill a character who isn't already at the Mortally Wounded health level (or equivalent, for non-humans). Thus, if you hit a perfectly healthy (or even Bruised, Wounded or Incapacitated) character with an Effect that somehow inflicts 10 levels of damage, all this does is bring the character to the Mortally Wounded health level. This may not make sense in some cases; if you drop someone into a volcano, hit a character with a Quintessence-charged Buick or otherwise perform a spectacular damaging feat, you'd expect the victim to vaporize instantly. This rule simply keeps some players from charging around with super-spells ready to vaporize anyone in their way. It also means that a character must deliberately take an action to kill a downed opponent — something the Storyteller should play up for the full realization of the literally murderous act about to be committed.

The Half-Dead Rule (Optional Rule)

This rule only works if your combat-heavy chronicle has people dropping like flies, and needs to insure that everyone gains a little breathing room and at least a chance to retaliate in battle.

Occasionally, even with the No Instant Kills rule (above), wandering hit squads will jump characters and make short work of them in a single turn. Actually, it's pretty common. To mitigate this, you might make combat a more protracted and risky affair by making it harder to kill people with large attacks. Under this system, no attack, regardless of grades of success or magnitude, can inflict more than three health levels. Thus, several turns are necessary to pull apart a victim character, unless the attackers come up with a complex plan (and somehow manage to avoid using a mob challenge, which should happen automatically if they gang up, so that each can do damage separately).

Final Retribution (Optional Rule)

This rule only works if you feel the need for victims to have a last-ditch bit of justice so that no fight is a "sure thing."

When the brute squad rolls up on a hapless foe and has a cunning plan in mind, sometimes the victim pretty much folds up and dies at once without a chance to do anything. This isn't very sporting, and if there's absolutely no risk to the attackers, it's very one-sided — and also tends to generate more such brute squads, as people gang up to form cabals specifically designed to take out their enemies without ever having to risk a counter-attack.

With this rule, a character who's about to die — that is, just suffered an attack that would Incapacitate the individual or worse— may spend one Willpower Trait and immediately perform *one* action at *full, normal Attribute Trait values*. Thus, even if the brute squad busts out on a hapless soul and pounds the victim into the ground, removing all Traits and kicking the sod into the Dead health level, the victim can spend that last ounce of Willpower to make a single action as if *none* of those Attribute Traits were lost. (The character must still apply penalties for being Bruised and Wounded, unless another Willpower Trait is spent or other magic supersedes this. Incapacitation and worse don't apply to this action.) The victim isn't guaranteed a win and doesn't get back any lost Quintessence, Willpower or Abilities, but at least has one chance to make the attackers hurt.

Immediately after Final Retribution is done, the character becomes comatose or expires, at the discretion of the attackers. (You can't use this rule to get in a final shot *and* deliberately avoid capture by killing yourself.)

You may only use Final Retribution once in any fight. Seesawing back and forth around the Incapacitated health level with healing magic doesn't mean that you can do this many times.

Combat Mobility (Optional Rule)

This rule only works if you want to represent the benefits of flexibility in combat response situations.

As per **Laws of Ascension**, p. 193, a typical character can move up to three normal-sized paces in a single action.

Characters with enhanced speed can take multiple movement actions: A mage with two actions can thus move six paces.

Characters with special Devices or Effects might be able to fly or move with incredible speed. Typically, this allows the character to disengage by Fair Escape if the opponent has no plausible way of stopping the target. For instance, a character with a jet pack fighting a group of club-wielding thugs can, as an action, declare Fair Escape by flying up and away. If one of the thugs pulls out a gun, though, the combat must continue until the flying character manages to escape or is shot down.

A character who has higher ground, partial cover or enhanced mobility — such as the aforementioned jet-pack wearing trooper, or someone fighting from the top of stairs with a sword, or from behind a car door — gains a one-Trait bonus due to beneficial circumstances.

Managing the Mob: Mob Challenges

Mob challenges are some of the worst nightmares for Storytellers; they're slow and some people don't quite "get it," which can make them easily exploited. Keep the following things in mind with a mob challenge, and you'll be OK.

1. No talking. Players who're waiting for their turn tend to kibitz among themselves. This disrupts the game and slowly escalates the volume. If you catch people stepping out of character to chit-chat while waiting, give one warning; after that, pull the player from the scene and assign an appropriate penalty. ("Oh, you decided to chit-chat with your friends so I'd pull you from the scene and you'd 'escape'? Gotcha. Mortally Wounded. Enjoy.")

2. No arguing. This goes hand-in-hand with "The Storyteller is always right." Every player should have *one* appeal for any given ruling, just to point out if something might be a mistake. But nobody else butts in, and if the player insists on arguing, pull the player out of the scene. It's not fair or fun for all of the other players to wait on one arguing antagonist's rules cheese.

3. No more than five people per physical mob against a normal opponent. A normal, human-size opponent can suffer a mob challenge physically from five, normal human-size enemies. Any more than that and they have to stand back and wait. You can't fire through such a crowd without potentially hitting the people in the way, too. Thus, for physical mob challenges, limit it to five people. The Storyteller and Narrators decide who's close enough and who waits.

Red Joker — Paradox Realm.

Black Joker — Paradox Spirit.

Ace — Paradox hangs; character holds the Paradox points until next backlash.

Number Card — Regular Paradox backlash; the character simply suffers damage.

Face Card — Lasting Paradox effect; the character garners a troublesome Flaw, of a type determined by the suit (see below).

Clubs — Physical effect. The Paradox has a physical backlash: The character might suffer from static build-up, muscle spasms, appearance change, bad body odor, changes to clothes, appearance of strange items, changing certain items (like all milk products becoming rancid within 10 paces, all clocks running backward when touched) or other manifestations on physical, material processes.

Diamonds — Mental effect. The Paradox has a mental backlash: The character has trouble translating short-term memory to long-term memory, can only speak in quotes, can't add, can't read, causes dementia in nearby people, suffers sudden bouts of derangements, causes all redheads to suffer mild headaches, turns signs into jumbled-up nonsense or otherwise undergoes some mental change.

Hearts — Emotional effect. The Paradox has a social backlash: The character suffers radical mood changes, gives off emotional states to others, causes animals to behave strangely, colors all interactions with some emotional by-product (like all liquids taking on a color according to the character's emotions), or otherwise has Social-related Attributes played out.

Spades — Spiritual effect. The Paradox has some sort of supernatural backlash: The character leaves a smoke trail in the Umbra, nearby ghosts become translucently visible, normal people have flashes of their past lives when touching the character, or otherwise strange supernatural phenomena go on.

4. If multiple people assault someone using similar attack forms, they *must* mob. You can't decide "not" to mob challenge an enemy just so that you and your friends can all potentially do three levels of damage in separate attacks and bypass some of the damage reducing optional rules previously listed. If you and your buddies gang up on an enemy with physical attacks, you *must* use the mob challenge rules, because you *are* a mob.

Limited Mobs (Optional Rule)

This rule only works if your game has an abundance of multiple mobs all challenging victims at once, and you want to stretch realism for playability.

Sometimes a mob challenge gets *way* out of hand, as a physical mob wades into combat while a couple of mental and social attack power mobs hang back and target the same individual. Once again, such beat squads have a tendency to wreck just about anything. You may *want* this to be the case in your game, so that nobody feels invincible; on the other hand, you might have a mob challenge on your hands with 50 people all attacking one or two victims (this happens a lot at large convention games).

For the sake of expedience, assume that no more than one mob of each attack type can assault a given victim. This means five physical attackers as one mob, five mental attackers as a second mob and five social attackers as a third mob. Anyone else must wait for an opening.

Paradox

Players naturally learn to dread the intervention of the Paradox Judge. This is in some ways as it should be: Mages should never just "shrug off" Paradox. It's a balancing force, and not always a fair one. Don't mistake this, however, for making the Paradox Judge out to be a bad guy. While the Paradox Judge may not be buddy-buddy with all of the players, the players also shouldn't have the impression that the Judge is someone to be hated or someone who's out to screw them over.

At the same time, Paradox itself is not always impartial or even-handed. Some players may feel they've gotten a raw deal with Paradox. This happens. They must learn to live with it. It's one of the foibles of **Mage**.

Paradox Playing Deck

If you don't have the time or inclination to build a custom Paradox deck out with 3" x 5" cards, you can always use a regular deck of playing cards for your Paradox effects. It's simple. Have a player draw a card whenever Paradox fires off. Reshuffle. Repeat *ad infinitum*. You might sometimes remove a card from the deck in order to keep people from suffering the same sorts of Paradoxes. If you don't want the headache of running Paradox spirits and realms, just remove the Jokers.

In order to spread out your probabilities, you can use the following layout of the cards:

If you really want to go all-out, you can customize your deck, so that each card indicates a specific Paradox problem. For instance, you might decide that you really want to emphasize Paradox Flaws; to do so, reverse the effects of face and numbered cards, thereby making backlash damage less common and Flaws more so. You could have a table that indicates a specific Paradox backlash for each card: the 10 of hearts might mean broadcasting melancholy while the nine of hearts indicates sudden bouts of rage. You'll want to change these from time to time just to keep players on their toes.

Reputation Systems

While mages can and do have a complex system of Reputation, it's sometimes a bear to track — especially for games networked across multiple chronicles, where characters might gain or lose Reputation according to different standards. For this reason, Storytellers need to be clear on having specific standards for Reputation. You may want to indulge in the following rules to clarify your Reputation system.

Slow Reputation Build (Optional Rule)

This rule only works if you want to limit Reputation to long-term works over the course of a potentially lengthy game.

No character can gain more than one Reputation Trait per session. If the character gains Reputation from improving a Sphere to a higher level (going from a Disciple to an Adept, for instance), that's the only Reputation the character gains in that session. The character wouldn't gain any Reputation for noteworthy deeds or chantry positions until a later session.

The order of precedence is Reputation for Sphere achievement, then positions, then notable deeds.

There's no limit to how much Reputation a character can lose in a game, though. The journey up is tough; the fall is fast and uncontrolled.

Staggered Reputation Build (Optional Rule)

This rule only works if you're having problems with people gaining Reputation every game by specifically doing one big thing each game and then sitting around.

Characters don't gain a Reputation just for one great deed. The Storyteller should track a character's noteworthy achievements — things that the Storyteller hears about after the game or witnesses in play. (If people don't see it or hear about it, you won't gain Reputation for it.) Each time a character does something noteworthy, this gains one point toward more Reputation. Each time the character does something dumb, this loses one such point. To gain a new Reputation Trait, the character must amass a number of partial points equal to the current number of Traits. So, an Apprentice with only one *Accepted* Reputation Trait would gain a deed-based Trait for a single noteworthy deed, while a Master would have to perform at least five, because people expect more from characters who already have a strong Reputation and a lot of skill.

Reputation Erosion (Optional Rule)

This rule only works if you're running a long-term game where the characters gain Reputation and then just sit on it.

Reputation is very much a "What have you done for me lately?" system. A character loses one deed-earned Reputation Trait every three game sessions. The character must constantly perform noteworthy deeds in order to keep a high Reputation.

Reputation Maximums (Optional Rule)

This rule only works if you want to make Reputation a more closed-in, challenging system, instead of an open-ended system of legendary social standing.

Some characters will do their best to gain Reputation at every turn, going to as many games as possible and being loud and flamboyant to draw notice. These characters may occasionally rocket up in Reputation to obscene heights — 12, 15, even 20 or more Reputation Traits. To limit this, allow no character to gain more Reputation than *double* the character's Rank, plus *Destiny*. Thus, an Apprentice (Rank 1) with *Destiny* x 4 could have a maximum of six Reputation Traits. People expect more from high-ranking characters or characters destined for great things, but will in return give them accolades when they achieve skillful things.

Negative Reputation (Optional Rule)

This system only works if you need a way to socially punish characters who constantly flout the Traditions and don't expect any sort of social consequences.

A character who repeatedly and demonstrably screws up in mage society not only risks the punishments of the Traditions, but could gain a nasty Reputation to boot. A character might potentially gain one negative Reputation Trait: *Witless*, *Tactless*, *Brash*, *Obnoxious*, *Pushy* and the like are all possibilities. A negative Reputation Trait can be assigned by a Storyteller or by any means that would be sufficient to strip Reputation Traits from a character. This Reputation Trait counts as a Negative Trait against the character and can be used as such, and the *Politics* Ability does allow opponents to know about it.

A character may have as many negative Reputation Traits as his or her maximum Reputation total (there might *be* no maximum, if you don't establish a top end). A character may have both positive and negative Reputation at the same time.

Crossovers

Crossover games, even moreso than mob challenges, present a host of nightmares for Storytellers. What power trumps what? Who has the upper hand? What the heck is the mood and theme of the game, anyway? Some stories, though, subsist on the collision of the very different natures of **World of Darkness** inhabitants.

It's impossible to present a totally comprehensive guide to all things crossover. There's too much to track and it would require that every game developer become totally enmeshed in the ongoing work of every game line. Storytellers will have to judge many cases for themselves, but the guidelines here may help at least a little.

Power Source Separation (Optional Rule)

This rule only works if you need to keep your players from being "buddy-buddy" between supernatural types and trying to share around their power sources.

Vitae is not Gnosis is not Quintessence. While mages can perform phenomenal transmutative feats, it's no simple matter to pull the mystic energy out of other supernatural creatures, and it's even harder to turn it into something else.

A supernatural creature's power reserve up to its Willpower rating is considered inviolable, just like a mage's Quintessence from the *Avatar* Background. Thus, a mage facing off against a vampire with three Willpower Traits cannot remove the power from the vampire's last three Blood Traits, short of actually cutting the vampire open and suctioning the blood out.

By the same token, a mage cannot simply remove magical energy from other creatures' power sources, or change power from one type into another. The mage must have specific *Lore* relating to the creature type and must build a rote that accounts for the shift. This requires at least *Prime* (for working with Quintessence) and usually two other Spheres as well (*Matter* and *Life* for vampires, *Spirit* and *Life* for shapeshifters, and so on as detailed in **Laws of Ascension** on pp. 266-271). The mage must also have extensive study with the power source. A mage doesn't just pick up some vampire blood and suck the magical potential out of it; the mage must fundamentally understand how and why vitae holds magical energy. Even if a mage has the know-how to do this, the energy *always* carries Resonance (generally Entropic for vampires and ghosts, Dynamic for shapeshifters and changelings). Trying to turn Quintessence without the right Resonance into a different supernatural power type is doomed to failure: You cannot, for instance, take Gnosis, turn it into Dynamic Quintessence, and then turn it into vitae, because vitae has Entropic Resonance, not Dynamic. Similarly, if your mage wants to conjure vampire blood, it must have Entropic Resonance.

A mage cannot simply inject Quintessence into a different supernatural creature's Pattern. The difference between mage and critter is too great. Therefore, a mage cannot (for example) cause a vampire to never need blood by just giving the vampire transmuted Quintessence; the vampire would still require blood. Similarly, a mage cannot easily restore a werewolf's Gnosis.

Just by way of keeping things from getting really out of hand, a Storyteller should probably *never* allow a mage to duplicate specific supernatural qualities of a power type. That is, a mage cannot simply conjure a sample of sixth-generation vampire blood and use it to make some seventh-generation vampires.

Vampires

Since vampires often permeate many levels of human society and try to move invisibly through supernatural circles, they're natural adversaries to mages. The book **Blood Treachery** even covers, in detail, some of the potential consequences of such a secret war. Both sides crave influence and hope to shape the future of human society. As a result, they'll almost inevitably butt heads.

Ideally, crossover interaction with vampires should come down mostly to Influence Backgrounds. The Technocracy doesn't crack down on vampires as much as it could, simply because it has less experience with vampire-hunting than with mage-hunting. Tradition mages trying to protect and promote specific social programs will often run afoul of the influence of conservative vampires who want to maintain the corrupt status quo. This can be a perfect game of dodging hidden bullets as each side slowly becomes aware of the other without resorting to physical combat.

More commonly, though, games will feature a cast of multitudes, wherein mages confront the undead directly or vice versa. There are several important points to keep in mind:

• A mage below Archmaster level cannot remove the Curse of Caine. Turning a vampire back into a mortal for more than a minute requires fighting a primal curse with tens of thousands of years of historical inertia behind it.

• By the same token, no rotes exist of "Transmute vampire to lawn chair." While this oft-discussed humorous sort of transmutation might be theoretically possible, remember that magic follows paradigm, and paradigm follows Tradition teachings. The Order of Hermes specifically forbids dealing with vampires. Verbena, Akashic Brothers and Euthanatos consider them unnatural, and avoid them. Other Traditions rarely encounter them. The upshot is that most Traditions don't have the knowledge of vampires necessary to make effects specifically to affect them in such gross ways. (As another writer said, "Okay, you transmute the vampire into a gingerbread man. It's now a six-foot-tall gingerbread man animated by the blood of Caine.")

• In brute-force contests, vampires tend to win. They're more resilient than mages, and their powers are slightly easier for them to learn. Conversely, mages with a lot of set-up time or an arcane connection can make unlife very difficult for the undead by using long-range attacks and things that vampires can't easily counter, like spirits.

Specific instances of stuff you might want to know can go like this.

• A vampire's *Obfuscate* Discipline is mental. Thus, it's resisted by a mage's *Mind* Sphere Effect of *Mind Shielding*. If a mage has *Mind Shielding*, use a standard Mental Challenge between the two to see if the vampire's unnoticed or not. Treat the mage's level of the *Mind* Sphere as equivalent to levels of *Auspex* for purposes of modifying the challenge difficulty. Conversely, a vampire can use *Auspex* to try to notice a mage who's invisible with *Forces*, *Mind* or *Life*, in each case contesting it just like it's *Obfuscate*.

• Mages will probably want to make their blood toxic or simply unpalatable to vampires. This is doable with a *Life* Effect to transmute personal Pattern (to make it valueless) and with *Prime* to make it a weapon (to make it toxic). Doing so will cause Pattern bleeding because it alters the nature of the mage's own blood.

• A vampire's *Chimerstry* works normally against mages, just like they're mortals. A mage can use *Mind* to contest it just like a vampire with *Auspex*.

• *Auspex* (*Telepathy*) and *Dominate* must penetrate a *Mind Shield* as well to have an effect on a mage. As a general rule of thumb, a *Mind Shield* created with *Mind* Sphere magic at least equal to the *Dominate* level (Basic *Mind* versus Basic *Dominate*, for instance) offers a special retest against the *Dominate*.

• Since *Presence* is a Social Discipline and works on spiritual ties as well as emotions, you might want to have mages defend against it with *Spirit* instead of *Mind* (especially for powers like *Summon* that clearly work over long distances according to supernatural ties). This functions just like a *Mind Shield*: A special retest against the power in question.

• *Necromancy*, *Spirit Manipulation* and *Spirit* Sphere all resolve by contesting between the opposing controllers (vampire's appropriate Attribute Traits versus mage's appropriate Attribute Traits), with a difference in levels granting a one-Trait up bonus (one Trait for having Intermediate power against an opponent's Basic, for example).

• Sunlight *Corresponded* from other parts of the world causes full damage to vampires. Sunlight created or transmuted must use *Prime* to be fully vibrant.

• The *Animalism* power *Quell the Beast* works on emotions like *Presence*, by contesting the vampire's Beast against the victim's instinct, so it's shielded against with *Spirit*.

• The *Spirit's Touch* power always picks up a mage's Resonance as part of any image that includes the mage in any way, unless the mage specifically used an effect to remove the Resonance from an area.

• A mage can invoke countermagic against vampiric *Thaumaturgy* using the normal countermagic rules. You might require a mage to have at least a modicum of *Vampire Lore* to do this, since *Thaumaturgy* isn't quite the same as Hermetic magic any more.

Shapeshifters

Some players assume that, since it's possible for mages to be Kinfolk and some mages (like Dreamspeakers and Verbena) have a respect for the natural world, that mages and shapeshifters can get along beautifully. This is a horribly mistaken notion. As the werewolves and other changers see it, mages perform feats that are fundamentally *wrong*; they invoke powers they shouldn't have, which is why Gaia punishes them (with Paradox). Worse still, mages and werewolves sometimes clash over places of natural power — the Garou caerns, which also sometimes serve as mage Nodes. These fights are no-holds-barred, as the Garou battle to protect their sacred areas.

Remember the following when dealing with mage-shapeshifter interaction:

• Even moreso than with vampires, mages are *flimsy* compared to shapeshifters. As normal humans, mages will tend to die in two turns (or less!) against even a single moderately experienced shifter.

• Mages don't have the ability to artificially change a Pattern from a human into a werewolf, or vice versa. You can't just reshape someone's Life/ Spirit Pattern into a werewolf. Attempting to do so tends to draw down the wrath of Gaia and the related spirits.

• Speaking of spirits, mages don't have any sort of Pact the way that Garou do. While spirits are inclined to at least talk to Garou and deal with them reasonably fairly, they have no compunctions about just killing or cheating mages out of hand. A mage cannot assume that just because he's a Garou ally he will gain any special favors from the Garou spirits. Hand-in-hand with this, mages can't necessarily guarantee that a given child will be a full-fledged Garou, although mages could barter with spirits for intercession in this matter and a Master of *Spirit* could probably compel a powerful spirit to "fudge things" (with severe consequences down the road for such arrogance, of course).

• Mages are immune to the Delirium, but this doesn't mean that a mage is stupidly oblivious in the face of a nine-foot-tall furry killing machine. Most sensible mages — especially those who know nothing about shapeshifters — will run like madmen without needing the Delirium as incentive.

Specific rules might go as follows:

• For powers that work with supernatural concealment, treat this much like the interaction of mages with vampiric *Obfuscate* or *Auspex*. Thus, a mage uses *Mind* to penetrate *Blissful Ignorance*.

• Powers that create social effects should be resisted with *Spirit* magic: If a Garou uses *Roll Over* to force subservience, for instance, the mage uses a *Spirit* shield to protect against this and gain a retest (assuming the mage already had such a shield in place).

• Powers that change speeds (like Rage or *Spirit of the Fray*) are, of course, countered with *Time* magic. A mage can use *Time* to try to cancel any of these powers, but requires a test against the Garou. For instance, canceling *Spirit of the Fray* requires the mage to make an Arete challenge for a *Time* Effect, then make a challenge against the Garou (Mental versus Physical in this case). If the mage wins, the *Spirit of the Fray* is retroactively removed in a sort of "time crunch," even though the Garou normally would've gone first. Otherwise, it's a fine red mist of mage.

• *No* Garou will allow mages into a caern. Period. Even Kinfolk. This is "allowing a caern to be violated," since mages are known caern-raiders. No amount of fast-talking will cover this. Spirits (who help track Garou Renown) will take note of this and punish Garou who violate this rule, if the other Garou don't get to them first.

• Mages can't perform shapeshifter rites. A mage can *simulate* a Garou rite with *Spirit* magic, but unless compelled or bartered with, spirits won't respond to the rites as they would to a shapeshifter.

Wraiths

Few mages want anything to do with the Shadowlands. The realms of the Dead are not a place for mortals to walk. Nonetheless, ghosts do haunt the living, and sometimes mages are the intermediaries for them.

Dealing with wraiths is somewhat troublesome; dealing with the Underworld itself is *exceedingly* dangerous. Keep the following caveats in mind:

• A mage uses *Spirit* magic on wraiths, as with other spirits; most compulsions require a Social Challenge. A wraith can spend a Pathos Trait for one retest on a *Spirit*-backed binding or compulsion.

• A mage must combine *Spirit* with *Mind* for any Effect that would try to penetrate wraith concealment or trickery on the other side of the Shroud — for instance, to look into the Shadowlands and see a wraith hidden with *Argos*. If the wraith manifests across the Shroud, on the other hand, *Spirit* isn't necessary except to smack the wraith directly. Thus, if a wraith tries to *Skinride* a mage, the mage can defend with *Mind* alone, but could only counterattack by adding *Spirit*.

• A mage's Pattern Effects go through incorporeal wraiths just like normal things — mage-created fire is no different from normal fire to an incorporeal wraith, and equally ineffective.

• Most mages won't understand the workings of the Shadow or Catharsis. Mages with a lot of study of wraiths might be able to tell the difference between the two states with *Mind* and *Spirit* magic.

Magic working in the Underworld itself is very, very dangerous.

• Crossing into the Underworld (without a Shallowing or like) does cross the Avatar Storm.

• Once in the Underworld, the mage is at grave risk. A failed attempt to return, or being "killed" in the Underworld, means that the mage dies and becomes a wraith there.

• Any Effect done in the Underworld automatically has extra Entropic Resonance.

• The necrotic effects of the Underworld leach away magical wards and creations, causing their durations to unravel with one less grade of duration. Thus the mage must generate more grades of success to keep protections and sensory Effects and conjurations running.

Changelings

The so-called Fair Folk would seem to have a lot of natural interaction with Tradition mages — both sides champion creativity, the magical world and mysticism. Indeed, the Verbena and the Order of Hermes explicitly consider faeries and changelings a necessary component of their magical worldview. Still, relations between changelings and mages have often been rocky, for many reasons. At least both sides are *usually* not actively hostile.

Changelings' biggest defense, the Mists, works equally well against mages as against anyone else. This means that mages often don't remember their interactions with changelings, chalk up changeling powers to coincidence and coincidental magic, and usually can't remember anything they learn from the fae. Changelings, on the other hand, may find some mages too banal to deal with.

As some rules of thumb, assume the following:

• Technocrats average Banality 9 or 10, because they're typically Conditioned, procedurally oriented and not given to a whole lot of fanciful imagination. Some rare theoretical or abstract scientists might have a lower Banality because of their sense of wonder and imagination about science, but even they don't believe in faeries and are thus poisonous to changelings.

• Tradition mages have wildly varying Banality ratings: stratified Traditions like the Order of Hermes and Technomantic Traditions like the Virtual Adepts tend to have Banality ratings of 7 or 8. Highly mystical and whimsical mages like Verbena and some immature Cultists of Ecstasy might go as low as 5. (A Cultist on a binge could temporarily dip to a 3 or 4.)

• Mages have no special capacity to see or interact with fae miens, although mages can be enchanted like anyone else.

• For a mage to figure out how to do "faerie magic" and see the Dreaming, the mage must have enough *Lore* to understand the workings of Glamour, changelings and the Dreaming, and *Mind* and *Spirit* magic. Unfortunately, since almost anything a mage learns disappears with the Mists, this means that very few mages will ever know enough to build such an Effect or remember how to do it later.

• A mage who scans through Mist-distorted memories with *Mind* may realize "Something has magically altered these memories," but won't necessarily understand what or how, or how to undo it, without appropriate *Lore*.

• A changeling may enact countermagic against a mage's Effect just like trying to cancel an opposing Glamour, but gains a Banality Trait for doing so.

• Mages can and do generate Glamour like regular mortals when they're inspired. Cultists of Ecstasy are the most likely to have friendly long-term relations with the fae, followed by the Verbena (who often see changelings as threatening) and then distantly by the Order of Hermes (who have a few members who specialize in faerie magic). "Making up rotes" doesn't count as artistic inspiration, though. The mage must do something of phenomenal breakthrough creativity, like developing an entirely new metaphysical theory.

In all cases of "appropriate *Lore*" for crossovers, the assumption is 4 or 5 levels — enough that the mage has been immersed in that subculture and fully understands that creature type's (un)life style and supernatural qualities.

Chapter Six: Places of Stories

Mages have, potentially, all the universe to explore. Unfortunately, the universe is a big place, which means that it can be a real headache for Storytellers! This is especially true for a game with a budget and limited available space.

How does one go about setting a story in many exotic sets without having the means to fly people out "on location?" A little preparation and a lot of imagination, of course. As usual, the key is early prep work — get to the site before hand and turn it into the type of site you want or need.

Many places make good settings for **Mage** games. Some can easily be dressed up into something phenomenal with just a little work. Of course, the Storyteller should be aware of the advantages and disadvantages of each site beforehand — hence, the ideas presented here.

Local Parks

Benefits: Usually have plenty of space, often free

Drawbacks: Very public, rarely have actual rooms

A local park often serves as one of the first meeting places for a brand-new game. It's generally cheap and spacious enough that everyone can fit in without worry to cost or elbow room. Mages among the Dreamspeakers and Verbena find these settings right at home, but often local parks are small enough and centrally located enough that other mages will find them easy to visit, too; this makes it convenient for everyone in the game to plausibly show up.

The largest problem with a local park is its very public venue. The troupe must take extreme care to avoid drawing too much attention from the local populace. While a little curiosity isn't bad, especially if it brings new players, a game with players running around screaming and pantomiming combat or massive magical Effects may draw lots of negative attention. There's also no easy way to dress up the park or separate it into rooms. Without multiple rooms, there's a tendency for the players to stick together in large clumps, which makes running storylines much more difficult. It's easier to run a plot with a small group to manage instead of trying to cover things for dozens of people at once.

Your best bet with a park is to have multiple Narrators on hand to split up the players into groups. Work out plotlines that cover different areas of the park, and fire them off simultaneously; this way, your players are forced to split into smaller groups. You don't have any way to easily represent exotic costuming or locations, so you'll have to rely on descriptions, but you can bring pictures or sketches to indicate special things.

A few parks have an entertainment center that you can use. If you can make arrangements ahead of time, you can often have access to a room or two at a minimal cost. This provides you with an opportunity to dress up a single area as an office, complex, part of a larger building or whatever you need on the spot.

Also, be careful of weather conditions. Character sheets and Paradox cards often don't survive well against sudden rain and wind.

State or National Parks

Benefits: Large; may have organized buildings for camping

Drawbacks: Usually cost money; sometimes too public; require upkeep from the rangers

For a large-scale game with a little money, a state or national park presents a special opportunity. Most troupes can't afford to host a game in an entire city block or apartment complex of their own. Renting out a campsite at a large park, though, provides just as much room.

Some parks are purely natural preserves, with simple benches, trails and the occasional pavilion. These parks run much like small local parks, above. The advantage lies in the ability to split people up along specific landmarks or areas of the park, since the park often has multiple small clearings with wooden furnishings — leftovers of public works improvements.

Camping sites offer the unique opportunity to spend the night in a game, if you don't mind shelling out money for rentals and organizing schedules ahead of time. This opens the door to a fully immersive game. You can often find sites that rent small cabins for the weekend, and use them as different locations. This even lets you set the game easily in the Umbra or in different times, since you can put special signs up on specific cabins or use different cabin blocs to represent different sites.

If you're not careful, though, you may find frequent interruptions a problem for your game. While state and national parks often have an abundance of back trails that allow for some privacy, there's also the constant chance of hikers or campers passing through. Your best bet is simply to suspend game play until they move on, or drop to soft roleplaying (no challenges) for the duration.

Furthermore, state and national parks abide by multiple special laws. Most of these won't be a problem — as long as you're following the basic **Mind's Eye Theatre** rules, and you eschew weapons, drinking, etc. at your games. Often, you'll have to entice your players to pitch in for clean-up, especially if you brought along foodstuffs for picnicking. Rangers can fine you if they don't like your treatment of the site, and may deny you later access.

Identifying Badges

Yes, you need stinkin' badges. In highly public venues, you don't want your players walking up to random people and initiating challenges. This draws all the *wrong* kinds of attention, when innocent bystanders find themselves dragged into the game without knowing what the heck is going on.

The simplest solution lies in handing out identifying badges to everyone in play. This way, everyone knows who's "safe" to talk to or challenge. Make sure that your badge is something small and non-intrusive — a symbol of some sort is a good choice; name-tags are a little too conspicuous. Everyone should use the same sort of badge, just to avoid confusion.

Amusement Parks

Benefits: Surreal; lots to do

Drawbacks: Expensive; very public; distracting

An unusual one-shot event might take place in an amusement park, such as Universal Studios. Generally, it's best to plan such an event as a special one — most games can't handle constant, monthly play in such an environment. On the flip side, it's a great departure from the routine and a way to have everyone enjoy themselves in the game as well as out of play.

An amusement park can make for a strange, *Prisoner*-esque episode to your chronicle. Technocrats may hide out in the bowels of the park, or perhaps they use it as a social experiment. Maybe some supernatural menace lurks in a back lot. Perhaps the sets themselves have a special Resonance, or a strange Node is hidden somewhere on the premises.

Of course, an amusement park is also *terribly* public. Such venues often become very crowded very quickly. This can be a special challenge to the players, who want to "blend in" and look like normal people. Make sure that everyone in your game wears some sort of identifying badge.

Also, be wary of distraction. Your players may wander off to experience the park itself. This is fine, but they should remain in character while they're going on the rides or watching the shows. Try to set up regular meeting times and places (every four hours or so is good) to make sure that you don't lose anybody, and so that you can run necessary follow-ups to long-range challenges and Effects.

Zoos and Animal Preserves

Benefits: Spacious; change of pace

Drawbacks: Public; limited venue; may be costly

Zoos and animal preserves have some of the advantages and many of the disadvantages afforded to amusement and local parks. While they're usually fairly large and thus offer a wide-ranging area in which to play, they're also public. They can be costly for entry and they risk distracting players.

That said, a zoo or animal preserve makes for a unique change of venue; few people consider using such a spot. It's a good showcase for Progenitor activities, or for urban Dreamspeakers and Verbena. Outside of these boundaries, a zoo is pretty limited in its capabilities. Since you probably won't have spaces to dress up as your own, you'll have to rely on the setting itself, and that means you may have difficulty getting across anything more than the location of the zoo.

Libraries and Museums

Benefits: Esoteric; often spacious; sometimes allow special groups

Drawbacks: Require quiet; public; may be costly

Studious mages make a habit of frequenting libraries and museums — so why shouldn't the games? The logistics of handling such venues can be touchy, but also rewarding.

With a few Narrator characters devoted to roles of your game world "museum staff," you can provide an academic experience that Hermetics, Virtual Adepts and similar characters will love. It's also a great way to show off some odd part of a storyline — say, by stationing a Narrator with special information as a character at a particular display that matches up with your current story arc.

Museums and libraries have all the drawbacks of other public locations, of course. Identifying tags are a must. More troublingly is the problem of quiet. Most museums and libraries demand silence from their patrons, so running a scene can become a chore, especially if overexcited players start shouting and running. It's best to lay out ground rules in advance: Anyone whose voice winds up carrying sits out of the rest of the scene. This will quickly pare down scenes to manageable levels if the players can't control themselves.

The Storyteller's Office

Unless your game takes place in a *very* small area, you should always set aside a small Storyteller's office. Have a Narrator or Storyteller on hand here at all times — or, at the very worst, check back every 15 minutes. Keep all of your papers, your computer, your Storyteller props and records here. This gives you a central planning location, so you don't risk accidentally dropping something off in some obscure corner and losing it. It also affords a place where the players can come and know that they'll shortly receive the attentions of a Storyteller.

Note also that some museums have entry fees. If you schedule things right, you can often get in for free on "founder's day," but these days are also packed with visitors.

Some libraries have back rooms that they'll open or rent to clubs by special arrangement. Such rooms offer a good opportunity to have a small space away from everything else, if necessary, and a place where you can make a little noise.

Nightclubs

Benefits: Atmospheric; often spacious

Drawbacks: Semi-public; may be costly

The nightclub is the venue *de rigeur* for the World of Darkness, and it seems that every game stops by one at some point or another. While it's not the perfect venue site, it has several advantages.

First, despite being a fairly public area, most nightclubs rely upon anonymity; few people will give trouble to a group of gamers who're going about their own business without bugging other people. Treat it as a live-action attempt to uphold the Rule of Shade.

Second, a nightclub practically demands atmosphere. It's a great way to encourage your players to dress up and partake of the World of Darkness mood. If you pick your club carefully, you can make sure it has a specific style and music that fit with what you want in your game.

Of course, all of your players will have to be able to pay cover, and make sure that you can all meet the dress code. Still, a punk, rave or Goth style club probably won't pay much attention to outlandish props and tchotchkes.

If you're fortunate enough to know the owner of a club, you might gain access to a back room, as well. You can use this for an off-stage location or just as a Storyteller's office.

Restaurants and Coffee Shops

Benefits: Good social atmosphere; wide varieties for cultural mood

Drawbacks: Public; may be costly

Unlike other denizens of the World of Darkness, mages can and do congregate in public places for social activities with each other and with normal people. Restaurants are key among these gatherings: Sharing a meal is a very sociable setting. Plus, the choice of restaurant can vastly influence the mood of the game. A Japanese steakhouse provides a pseudo-Asiatic influence and encourages socialization around the table, while a somber, Renaissance-recreation tavern won't blink an eye at a group of gamers, and a large pub may have a whole room to dedicate to the troupe.

The key to restauranteering is, like other public venues, to be aware of the surrounding people. If the group has enough players and calls ahead, most restaurants can make arrangements for a specific party room. This provides a great setting not only for socializing, but also for Tradition leaders to discuss business and for mages to ponder over clues or talk shop. If you're in a bar or other setting with lots of the public around, try to pick a specific corner or set of large tables and isolate your group, so that you don't risk accidentally shocking the folks just down the way.

Depending upon your venue, you may need to gather up a little extra money in advance. Sometimes players will be a little too poor for your choice of restaurant, or someone might accidentally stiff part of the bill or tip. It's usually best if the Storyteller takes on the responsibility for coordinating payment, sticks it all on one tab and gathers up money from the players at check-out.

Business Offices

Benefits: Good Technocratic setting; practically guarantees privacy

Drawbacks: May be hard to secure; can interfere with real-life job

If some of your players (or you!) work in big business, chances are that your company has a building with one or more meeting rooms. With the proper arrangements, many businesses may be happy to open these to the employees after hours, so long as there's no security issue. Playing in meeting rooms and offices gives the game a very Technocratic feel, so it's perfect for just that sort of venue.

On the down side, some managers and companies don't quite "get" the whole gaming thing. They may be less than pleased to learn that the after-hours club activity is actually some sort of strange organized theaterlike game. Furthermore, there's always the risk that, if some damage or theft occurs, the troupe could be blamed. You must be *extremely* careful to stress the consequences of players getting out of hand.

Malls and Commercial Districts

Benefits: Spacious, with many locations

Drawbacks: Public; limited hours

An unusual sort of game could take place in or near a mall, or along a series of commercial streets. The players have the opportunity to spread out among the many stores, restaurants and plazas. Meetings are easily disguised in the back of a café or at the edge of a plaza as just a bunch of friends chatting. As long as players avoid running, shouting and making a mess in public, they can even play out having subtle magical duels! Just be careful with players who go overboard: Mall security can be frighteningly quick to crack down on potential threats; none of the stores wants to have their customers scared away.

Most malls have limited hours of operation, so you need to plan your venue appropriately. If you live in a large college town or downtown in a city, you may have access to stores and restaurants that stay open late. In more rustic settings, only daytime will suffice.

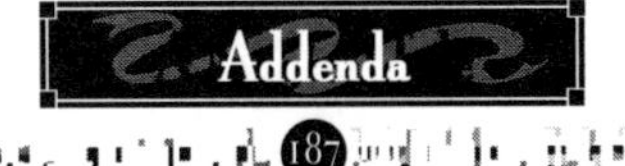

Remember to use identity tags, so that players don't accost random shoppers. It's also recommended that you set up a Storyteller's office in some easy-to-meet location, so that you can have players meet with you every two hours or so in case you need to make announcements, changes or scene rulings.

All of the usual caveats for sub-types of places in malls — stores and restaurants — apply, as well.

Private Residences

Benefits: Privacy

Drawbacks: Few players willing to provide

Gaming inside of a private home is, of course, the recommended venue. In a private residence, you can set up all the decorations, special scenes and unusual costuming that the host allows. Your players can be as boisterous and as deeply into their roles as desired, as long as you don't disturb the neighbors. Such gatherings often look to the neighbors like just another evening party, too, so you can get away with a lot, especially if you keep the really odd props, costumes and sets indoors.

Few people, however, will open their homes willingly and repeatedly to game nights. Large LARPs can cause a lot of mess, and some less-than-reputable sorts use this as an excuse to get a little light-fingered. One bad incident can turn a host off — and perhaps cause the host and friends to leave the game, too.

Always make sure to close off any "off limits" rooms and denote them clearly with a sign.

Hotels

Benefits: Private and meeting rooms available

Drawbacks: Expensive

Large-scale, convention-style games generally take advantage of hotels. A hotel is, essentially, a private residence that you just use for a few days. Within the individual players' rooms, anything goes, so long as it doesn't violate the hotel's rules: This makes it perfect for splitting up characters to meet by Tradition or cabal. At the same time, you can usually rent out a party or meeting room for your formal game site itself. If the Storyteller has a suite, the outer room can also serve as a special location for the game. This allows a wide variety of settings for play. Most hotels include a restaurant and are within driving distance of just about all of the other settings described here, too.

Unfortunately, hotelling is *expensive*. Unless your troupe has very deep pockets, chances are you won't be able to afford a hotel regularly.

Churches

Benefits: Very atmospheric; spacious

Drawbacks: Generally hostile to LARPs

A group with strong ties to a real-world church might be able to gain access to the church facilities as a club organization. Doing so outside of normal church hours can sometimes even guarantee a private set of rooms for use. This is in addition to the fact that many churches just *look* too cool, and thus provide a great setting for **Mage** games.

Unfortunately, roleplaying games have had a bad reputation with certain religious elements. While some pastors may be more tolerant than others, this is definitely a case of "find out beforehand." Never, ever try to sneak a LARP into a church without all parties knowing what's involved. There's too much risk of alienating the community.

Industrial Parks

Benefits: Often have a good World of Darkness feel; spacious

Drawbacks: May be hazardous; hard to arrange

Large industrial corporations use industrial parks and lots — factories, steel mills and junkyards. Such locations often have a barren, technological look to them, which plays into the World of Darkness perfectly. Plus, they often have a great deal of space available, from gravel yards to abandoned factories.

Acquiring the right to use such space can be difficult, though. Without proper connections to the owning company, using such space is generally considered trespassing. More importantly, old steel mills and factories often have *very* hazardous areas around them. A group that does manage to secure a site is best served by doing their gaming only in the outdoor gravel lots and small management sheds; don't risk losing players inside the bowels of some factory.

Traveling Venue

Benefits: Wide range of scenery

Drawbacks: Very difficult to coordinate

One experimental form of venue is the traveling venue. In this form of play, your troupe splits up with Narrators, each of whom stays in touch by radio or cell phone. Each piece of the game is free to travel where it will. You can delineate specific areas and give them World of Darkness equivalents. This lets your players move from place to place with actual travel time taken into account, and lets you play up the separation between groups when they move out for different tasks.

Unfortunately, this is extremely difficult to coordinate. Every group needs a Narrator with it. Every Narrator needs a way to communicate with the central Storyteller regularly and consistently. You may find a need to suddenly pull people back together, such as when someone *Correspondence* steps to a friend; this can be hard to do when they're 20 minutes apart in the real world.

Traveling venues are best done as an experimental one-shot until you get the hang of them.

Decorating Your Venue

Once you've settled on a venue location, it's also up to you to make sure it fits the game style you're trying to promote. A little decoration goes a long way; the World of Darkness subsists on mood, not just on buildings.

Your first and most important task is, of course, to figure out just how far you plan to go. Perhaps you don't have enough money to completely redecorate your house, or maybe you don't have the time or inclination to put up huge Styrofoam plinths and flashing techno-gadgetry. That's fine — although, of course, the more you immerse your players in the game, the more they'll probably enjoy it.

The immersion factor of your site can't be overestimated. The more your site pushes players into the spirit of things, the more they're likely to remain in character. It's much, much easier to keep a sense of character when the world actually *feels and looks* like the world the character's supposed to be in. A site that doesn't fire the imagination risks players feeling out of place or bored, which leads to out-of-play chatter.

Obviously, if you're using a public site, you have strict limitations on what you can and can't do. Private sites fare a little better, especially if you have a few hours of prep time.

Mood Music

Some venues like to use music to help set the feel of a specific location. This is good so long as it's not overdone. One of the biggest problems of the nightclub-format venue is that players often can't even *hear* one another over the music. Music shouldn't be intrusive; it should be an audio cue that helps to set mood.

You'll probably want to avoid music with lyrics. Stick with pure instrumentals, otherwise conversations wind up fighting over the words of the music. Your choice of music has a strong effect on the environment, and can make it discordant, eerie or pleasant. Remember that music doesn't always have to be soft tones and slow melodies. You can use instrumental rock, trance, grunge or techno to provide a more fast-paced, tension-filled atmosphere. Conversely, a Technocratic base might have elevator music designed to set visitors at ease (and make their minds open to manipulation). Strong classical music is almost always in vogue, unless you're talking about a game purely dominated by modern computer junkies and techno-wizards.

Remember, the players don't necessarily have to easily hear all of the music. If some of it drops off and isn't quite audible, that's all right. The music is an accompaniment; it's not supposed to intrude.

Lighting

Most of the time, your site will have strong overhead white lighting or sunlight. This is fine for a typical game, but specific settings might call for something different.

A good way to generate a more "spooky" atmosphere (such as an old Chantry) is to diffuse your light. Remove the bulbs from overhead lighting, and instead rely on lamps scattered about the room in various corners. If a room has white walls, try draping fabrics; this cuts down on the reflection and makes the light softer. Such diffusion gives more shadows, more areas of overlap and less of a sunlit atmosphere. It's a bit more cloistered and claustrophobic.

Colored lighting's a neat trick, but be careful not to rely on it exclusively. For one thing, it's annoying when it makes reading difficult or a costume impossible to see. Blue or violet lights can make for a soft, nightlike atmosphere, but they also render dark print hard to read, which can hurt the ability to use character sheets, books and references. Dark red lights work a little better, and they create a more menacing tone. Yellow lighting seems more naturalistic and works well for scenes in the Middle Umbra. Green lights offer some of the same problems as blue, but also tend to project an oceanlike or unwholesome pallor, and make people look unhealthy; they're perfect for blighted places or nasty parts of the Umbra.

Specific lighting, instead of just general room lighting, can also make a difference. Perhaps your high muckety-muck Hermetic mage has a small lamp stand next to his chair where he keeps a dim red lamp. This will cause the mage to seem sinister and out-of-place with respect to the rest of the room. Technocrats may have light strips around specific doors or on walls, indicating hazards or directions.

Players can carry light, too — you can cheaply buy glowsticks at hardware stores and use them to represent magical light. A procession of mages at night, all holding different colored glowsticks, can make for an eerie sight. With a little work you can also place a glowstick inside of a prop, making for a simple torch or lantern without the hazards of using real fire.

Aromas

Few games pay attention to scent, but it's a powerful memory trigger. Scents cause memories of similar situations to come to the fore, and thus can create a vivid sense of connection between a game scene and real events.

Usually your site will have a neutral scent: Lived-in, visited, not particularly scented. Clever use of aromas and incense can change this.

If you want to get across the idea of a Technocratic area, try cleaning tile floors just beforehand and spraying disinfectant about. These sharp smells will remind people of sterile, universitylike environments. For a hospitallike feel, put some rubbing alcohol near the doors and air vents; anywhere that there's air motion will cause the alcohol to evaporate, bringing its smell to the players who pass by.

Tradition areas tend to have other strong scents. You want to avoid anything that will cause nausea or problems for players and visitors, of course, so using various items that Tradition mages count as foci — like blood, dung or ash — is right out. The scents from those can overwhelm your players and cause the game to suddenly become a little too strong for comfort. Instead, try safer smells that bring up Tradition images. Incense is, of course, the first one to spring to mind, but it's not the only possibility. Different types of incense might represent different Traditions. A lodge or living room can benefit from the use of a fireplace, which generates a musty, wooden smell; this has connotations of comfort and home. Restaurants tend to have the sharp smell of mustard and spices, which bring out a kitchen atmosphere and heighten the appetite. Some bookstores also sell aromas, and you can use perfumes to give a place a masculine scent or a smell like fresh rain. Even scented air fresheners can affect your environment.

As with music, scent shouldn't be overwhelming. Just a little bit is enough to trigger memories.

Food and Refreshments

Aside from making sure that your site has access to bathroom facilities (since most games last for several hours), you might consider bringing foodstuffs as well. Mages eat just like anyone else, after all!

Just like other facets of your venue, your choice of foods influences the appearance of the game. Neatly arranged sushi and rice dishes clearly tell the players "Akashic Brotherhood," while barbecue and chips set the tone for more of a modern American trailer cook-out. An afternoon gathering with light snacks doesn't feel as serious as a full dinner or potluck.

Similarly, you can offer incentives for the players to bring foods according to their Tradition cultures. While not everyone's a good cook, a few people will probably rise to the challenge, and you can always let someone bring a salad or simple dish from the supermarket's deli counter. The "taste of a Tradition" helps players to feel more in character as they indulge in the character's specific culture — or find it alien in spite of their Tradition training.

What you serve has a strong effect on what you say about the game's location, too. If you serve only coffee, you establish a more office-like atmosphere. Fruit juices give a picnic feeling, while sodas are more in line with a restaurant or home location. If you have heavy, elaborate meals, you generate more of a sense of permanence — the location seems to be more like a house or store, some place where one would find such foods; having only light snacks enforces that the characters are on the run or highly mobile.

Signs and Pictures

Sometimes you can't be bothered to build a replica of Stonehenge in your back yard. That's OK — your players can imagine that they use magic; they can imagine the location as well.

Signs and pictures are a good compromise. Generally, having a visual is better than just having a description. For the aforementioned Stonehenge, you might copy a picture of the circle of stones onto a piece of paper, and label it "Standing Stones" underneath. Stick the picture on the end of a wooden post, and place a post for each stone — voila, you give your players a good approximation of the site, the locations of the stones and the appearance.

Signs help indoors, too; having access to computer-printed signs greatly improves the look of your site. A Technocratic door with a laminated "No Entry" sign and a biohazard symbol is far more menacing than a 3" x 5" card with the same words hand-scrawled in pencil, and it's only slightly more effort to make.

You can tie a sign in with scent, too. Just apply the appropriate scent to your sign. Then, when your players interact with it, they get a sense of the location from more than just a picture. For instance, instead of digging a grave in your backyard, you might put down a small cardboard cut-out in the shape of a headstone with a picture, and anoint it with an aroma like that of moist loam. Players who examine this will not only quickly realize that it's an open grave (from the picture and description), but will smell from the sign the cues that come with the site.

Umbral Locations

As mages grow more experienced with *Spirit* magic and with the histories of their Traditions, an eventual push into the Umbra is nigh-inevitable. Umbral Realms offer chances to play in just about any imaginable type of site. Also, in the Umbra, mages can quest to find mentors or information long since lost to the real world. With the Umbra's lesser restrictions on magic, it's also a very tempting place for mages to do a lot of their work.

Keeping the Umbra in Check

In spite of its obvious advantages, the Umbra isn't a place for mages to stay forever. Many a mage would retreat to the Umbra for all business if it were possible. After all, magic's more powerful and Paradox less threatening there! So what keeps mages in the real world? Several things:

• Normal Sleepers can't survive unaided in the Umbra. While it's possible to bring people there, and some Realms are self-sustaining ecologies, it's a very dangerous place. Marauding spirits, enemy mages and collapsing realities can all threaten Sleepers, who have *no* special defenses in the Umbra. Is your mage really going to take his family somewhere that a random, wandering Umbrood might eat them all?

• It's hard to affect the material world from the Umbra. Mages must exert their powers across the Storm and into the realms of Unbelief to send magic from the Umbra to the physical world. In most cases, it's easier just to do the magic on Earth.

• The Umbra has less impact on the consensus. Mages know that the Umbra reflects the real world, so if all the Traditions flee to the Umbra and the Technocracy completely takes over the Earth, the Umbra will soon follow. To make meaningful changes, mages *must* fight for belief on earthly battlegrounds.

• The Umbra is downright *dangerous!* Spirits, demons and other malefic entities roam free in the Umbra without the threat of Unbelief to limit their powers. Many of these creatures are far more powerful than any mortal mage will ever be. This isn't even counting the environmental hazards of places that are hostile to human life: Realms of fire, protean places where the laws of reality shift at whim, primordial forests full of terrible dinosaurlike creatures and cannibals with barbed spears — at least the material world is a bit more predictable. Sure, you can always run into a mugger or get hit by a bus. In the Umbra, though, there are thousands more ways to die.

Storytellers should be sure to play up some of these inconveniences of the Umbra from time to time, just to keep mages on their toes. The Umbra is not a safe haven, nor is it a place to effectively do battle for wars on Earth, nor is it an easy trip. Nevertheless, it's a useful stopping ground for mages willing to brave its dangers. Like most magical endeavors, the mage risks much for the opportunity to gain much.

Your key point should be this: Mages don't just jump into the Umbra for a quick jaunt. Umbral travel is an important, powerful journey, requiring preparation and forethought. While a fast vulgar effect might suffice to slip through in some occasions, most Umbral travel relies on ceremony. Consider the hero striding down a long stairway in a damp cave as he closes in on the Underworld, or laying out a circle of stones in the deep woods to open the path to the Penumbra. Such travels should always have a sense of mystery and duty to them.

When to Use the Storm

If your game assumes the existence of the Avatar Storm — which doesn't always have to be the case — you've probably already run into arguments about when to use it and when not to use it. In simplest terms, the Storm causes injury to mages because shards of Quintessential power are drawn to the strength of the Avatar, and these shards flense the mage's Avatar, spirit and body. Thus, the Storm causes damage when the mage passes the Gauntlet, and it distorts magical Effects that penetrate the Gauntlet.

A mage who simply projects his mind through other realms (with Master-level *Mind*) never actually takes his spirit or body through the Gauntlet, so he's safe from the Storm.

Stepping into or out of the Umbra triggers the Storm's effect once, as the mage crosses the Gauntlet. Once inside, the mage has crossed the Storm and is safe (at least, as safe as someone can be, in the Umbra).

Effects cast from the Umbra to Earth or vice versa generally don't hurt the caster, but they do damage the Effect. Such Effects become "Storm-tainted" and have a tendency to degrade. In general, a Storyteller can require anywhere from one to five extra grades of success for the Effect to penetrate at all, and these grades are stripped from the Effect, lowering its duration and potency. Furthermore, Effects often *warp* in

some strange way. If you're not sure how to warp the Effect, you might try drawing a card from a prepared Paradox deck and generating a suit-based phenomenon (see p. XX).

It's possible to cross into the Umbra at a Shallowing, a site where the Gauntlet drops between worlds. No Gauntlet, no Avatar Storm. Anyone can cross there, even Sleepers and spirits. Unfortunately, mages tend to fight hotly over Shallowings as a result of this, and they're dangerous places because you never know what will come through.

Reaching across the Gauntlet to thwack a spirit or pick something up does cause Storm damage. Just peeking across usually doesn't, although there may be exceptions.

It's sometimes possible to find a "backdoor" through which a mage can reach the Umbra; for instance, a mage might slip into a Demense (p. XX) while asleep, then walk from dreams to the Umbral Dream-Realm and thence to the Umbra itself. This does bypass the Gauntlet, but it's a hazardous journey at best.

You may find it easiest to set down a checklist of things that might trigger Gauntlet crossing and Storm damage, and then figure it out for your own game. For instance, in your game you might decide that floating around as a disembodied consciousness with *Mind* still draws Storm damage, but that mages can project their senses across with *Correspondence* and *Spirit* without risk, or you might even decree that for some reason the Digital Web is isolated from Storm effects (which will turn it into a popular jumping-off ground).

The Penumbra: Reflections

As noted in **Laws of Ascension**, the Penumbra reflects all of the physical world. It is, in a sense, a mirror image of the real world, but viewed in a lake that sometimes has ripples, distortions or images from the past.

Penumbral travel is pretty simple, and it's probably the least risky area of the Umbra. With but a step in all but the most Gauntlet-heavy areas, the mage can travel back to reality. Since the Penumbra contains reflections of the real world, you don't even need to make special sets and locations for it. Simply have your players indicate Umbral travel by placing one hand, palm facing down, against the chest.

The Penumbra offers useful clues and travel opportunities. Since it reflects places in the material world as their Resonance shows, you can use the Penumbra to give hints about the real issues with a site. If a building has twisted cables that spark with energy and drip with slime,

for instance, this is a clear indication that even if the place looks normal in the real world, something is terribly wrong with it. By the same token, a Node isn't necessarily immediately visible, but the area of the Umbra near it will probably seem vibrant and full of energy, which is a good indicator if the characters have lots of *Cosmology* or *Node Lore*.

If you want to have a highly spiritual game, you can try adding props and scenery to show off parts of the Umbra. Give them a prominent purple tag or handkerchief to indicate that they're in the Velvet Shadow. That way, players can ignore them until they use *Spirit* sight or travel. Of course, you probably don't want to set out too many important clues this way — otherwise some players might be tempted to metagame....

The Penumbra has one other important function as far as mages are concerned: It offers pathways to other parts of the Umbra. By following the Penumbra through the heart of a city and down a paved road surrounded by skyscrapers, for instance, a mage can reach the realm of Dystopia. Similarly, sticking to the deepest shadows and losing the trail to blindly walk in places of decay may lead to the Chasm. For a mage without a guide, this is the only way to really find other Realms. Mages (and Sleeper visitors!) can become lost in the Umbra, though; not all paths are marked, and sometimes walking into a place doesn't also mean easily walking back out.

Note especially that the Technocracy tends to use *Dimensional Science* to protect its installations. Not only is the Gauntlet preternaturally high in such areas, but a few field generators can easily erect shielding that prevents mages from simply "walking" through building security into a heavily fortified installation and then dropping off bombs across the Gauntlet.

The Astral Umbra: Ideas

Unlike other areas of the Umbra, most astral travelers don't rely heavily on *Spirit* magic; rather, they are travelers of the *Mind*.

The Astral Umbra represents abstraction and ideas. You don't even necessarily have to have a room to use it; players can be placed in a convenient quiet corner and run the scene all through narration. After all, the Astral Umbra is all in the head.

If you want to make a place that has an Astral Umbra impression, try using a small, white room. Remove as much furnishing as you can, except for a single spartan item. Go for the feel of the surreal rooms inside Dave Bowman's mind at the end of *2001: A Space Odyssey*. Items

or creatures suddenly appear in response to the mage's thoughts, but they are only ephemeral things, without true substance. They are the patterns from which things form. With magic a mage can give them substance, but things with substance do not belong in the Astral Umbra and "fall" out to somewhere else (usually the Penumbra).

The Astral Umbra is a place for confronting ideas. A mage can run into an idea given form here (try dressing someone up in plain white to personalize an idea). Other travelers of the mind sometimes meet, and time occasionally flows strangely here; it's a place to swap ideas of history as well as thoughts of the future.

Some other supernatural creatures sometimes frequent the Astral Umbra. In this place, combat doesn't take place physically. Attacks generally rely on Mental Challenges, with the loser suffering Willpower Trait loss. A character who runs out of Willpower finds himself ejected from the Astral Umbra.

In places where the Astral Umbra intersects with the Penumbra, Astral space has some level of "reality" to it, but visitors who concentrate on the thoughts of the place quickly move up into the realm of abstraction. Eventually it's like a Zen riddle: Nothing but emptiness wrapped in ideas. Fortunately, leaving the Astral Umbra isn't difficult; the traveler simply needs to let his mind lose hold of the ephemeral and sink back into the material — a sort of metaphysical slow descent back to the Penumbra.

The Dark Umbra: Ghosts

The Dark Umbra is a hostile place to mages. As noted in the crossover rule guides on p. XX, mages who visit find their powers weakened, and those who die here have no recourse.

The Dark Umbra comprises two separate but coexistent layers: The Shadowlands and the Tempest.

The Shadowlands are a sort of "negative Penumbra." Take all the vibrancy of the Penumbra, the building up of things spiritual and the emotional outpouring that affects its structure. Now, send it through a negative filter, like a piece of film. That's the Dark Umbra: A reflection of the physical world, but one tattered, sullied, decayed and overcome with despair. Travelers in the Shadowlands find that landscapes are bleak and crumbling, everything's falling down. Negative emotions are amplified, and places of brightness and hope seem washed out. Some mages do use the Shadowlands for quick jaunts, but this is risky. Since the Shadowlands sucks away energy, a mage who isn't careful can find himself trapped if he can't perform a ritual strong enough to step back into the physical world. And, of course, ghosts lurk here, and they often resent the living.

Metaphysically "below" the Shadowlands is the Tempest, a rampaging storm of primal matter. If the Penumbra is dynamic energy and growth reflected from reality and the Shadowlands are decay, the Tempest is the storm of raw primordialism from which all things sprang and to which they will all one night sink again. The Tempest itself generally seems like a strange plain of congealed soil and viscera, beaten by an ever-blowing wind that propels dust, grit, bits of flesh and chunks of forgotten detritus. Somewhere in the Tempest is a dark sea that seems to be the beginning and ending of all the land of the Tempest itself. Underneath the "soil," tunnels and caverns crisscross, entering caves with sleeping monstrosities. In a few rare places, pockets of the storm subside, and in these sanctuaries ghosts raise citadels and sanctuaries. The Tempest is a nightmare for mages — very little other than powerful *Forces* and *Entropy* magic can shield against its energies, and the nightmare winds send flaying shards that will rip body and spirit apart. *Things* lurk out there, too: Not only ghosts, but plasmic creatures spawned from the not-quite-nothingness left over from the effluvia of Creation, and twisted memories of creatures and places that never were. As these things have no hold on "reality," a mage cannot even rely on taking them across the Gauntlet to study; they are, in a sense, closer to the nothingness from which the cosmos originally came — and they all see intruding life as a cancer that must be cut out forever.

Moving between Shadowlands and Tempest isn't too difficult for ghosts, who do so as a matter of course. For mages it's a matter of following paths, just as one might follow a Penumbral path to a Realm. The mage can follow sinkholes and places where reality seems to crack at the seams, often by dropping into pits, cracks in the ground or decaying streets. Coming back *up* from the Tempest is much harder: The Byways between safe citadels are not always consistent, and the mage may have to use *Spirit* magic just to pull himself back "up." Once something falls toward the heart of Oblivion, the pull of utter vacuum is loath to give it up.

Mages might visit the Dark Umbra to gain information from ghosts, or in search of memories, or reflections of things destroyed. It's said that somewhere in the Tempest one can find anything that ever died or was broken. That's a powerful incentive for a seeker of lost knowledge.

Realms: Other Worlds

As a mage moves beyond the reflections of earthly reality, the Umbra takes on other, stranger shapes. At the Horizon, the boundary of imagination, it forms Realms, or places where specific images of reality hold sway. These Realms sometimes look like bits out of the real world, and other times are places that defy imagining. Some mages argue that Realms may have once been part of the world, but the Consensus ejected them to the Umbra when they were believed "unreal" by too much of humanity. Other mages argue that Realms are simply parts of the Umbra that respond to deeply imbedded urges and dreams of humanity.

Realms offer you a very exciting level of flexibility with **Mage** play. Since Realms can mimic just about any place you could imagine, you can take your **Mage** characters into a welter of different settings — near-future dystopia, sci-fi, fantasy, savage exploration, nihilistic tribalism or anything else you can imagine. Depending upon what your players want to do with their characters, you might make such trips a one-time deal for a little flavor, or a large part of the chronicle. You could even have your game set mostly in the Umbra or half-and-half split between Realms and reality.

Very powerful mages can actually create their own Realms, but doing so typically requires access to a Node. The Quintessence flow of the Node is moderated by the mage and sent into the Umbra; the mage uses his power to direct it into creation of a new place. Out on the Horizon, where the Umbra reflects space, the emptiness can be turned into anything a mage can dream of. In the past, Chantries would form Umbral Realms specifically for their members, using the power of their hosting Nodes. Unfortunately, the dearth of skilled mages in the modern age, combined with the difficulty of sustaining a Node's power across the ever-strengthening Gauntlet, makes it harder and harder to keep up a Horizon Realm now.

Realms can range from tiny to near-infinite. A mage with a yen for privacy and a small Node might shape a tiny, one-room Realm on the Horizon, a place where he can shut himself away from outsiders and cloak it with all manner of spells to avoid detection and entry (probably using *Correspondence* and *Spirit*). Legendary Realms of the past were said to house entire *planets* of their own; mages could visit whole worlds-that-might-have-been.

Of course, some Realms seem to sustain themselves. These highly prized places are stable within the Umbra; mages can make use of them

at whim. Unfortunately, their rules are their own — a mage can't step into a pocket Realm and simply reshape it as desired, but must rather accept its version of reality. That's why so many mages prefer to make their own Realms; sculpting a Realm allows the mage to make up its rules.

Shard and Shade Realms

Most Tradition mages know about the Shard Realms: Umbral reflections of the planets that correspond to specific Spheres. Each planetary body has a Sphere attuned to it, according to magely lore. Arguments still rage about whether this indicates some underlying cosmological truth to the system of Spheres, or whether the widespread acceptance of the Spheres caused their projection onto the Shard Realms.

Mages visit the Shard Realms to gain specific understanding of a given Sphere. A mage who wants to learn more about the nature of *Time*, for instance, can visit the Shard Realm of Time. There, the laws of the Sphere become manifest. In strange ways, the Sphere's power comes to the fore and becomes visible to visitors.

A Shade Realm, by constrast, is an Umbral reflection of the cosmos, as cast through the lens of a given Sphere. The Shade Realm of *Life*, for instance, is an entire universe filled with life and living things, with only tiny places here and there containing *Forces* or *Matter*. These Realms also offer insights into their Spheres, but are very dangerous to visit. Magical protections are a necessity so that the traveler can breathe, survive the forces at work and even comprehend the altered cosmology.

When you set out to use a Shard Realm in play, you should prepare a special setting in advance. Shard Realms have very strange characteristics that definitely set them apart from normal Earth. Therefore, you should take pains to dress up a room or outdoor garden specifically in the way the Shard Realm would look. If possible, try your best to use lighting and scent to increase its exotic appeal (see previous notes on those). You can use strobing, crashing red-and-yellow lights for the Realm of *Forces*, for instance, or softly pulsing yellow lights for *Life*. Always make sure that the surroundings play up the fact that it's an alien place.

Sol: The sun is the "Shard Realm Infinite," the beginning and ending of magical power. No portals or paths lead to it now; travel is seemingly impossible.

Characters from Realms

Are the human beings of other Realms as valid and "normal" as the people from Earth?

Yes, if you want them to be.

Realms are places that don't tie directly to the Consensual Earth that humanity decided to live in. This doesn't make their components less "real," though. A sword taken from Concordia to Earth is still a sword, and still functions and has solid mass (as long as it's made of something that would exist on Earth). Similarly, a person born in Dystopia who makes his way to Earth might be shocked by the low technology and the open spaces, but would otherwise be a normal person.

You can even allow people to play characters who come from these other Realms. The benefits and drawbacks of doing so should be immediately apparent. Characters from Concordia, for instance, have Renaissance-era sensibilities and technical know-how, as per the *Anachronism* Flaw. People from Dystopia have *Enhancements* but may suffer from *Agoraphobia*.

The rule of thumb: If it enhances the fun of game play, *and* it doesn't give the character anything for "free," run with it.

Note, of course, that Realm characters aren't necessarily appropriate for all games. A down-to-Earth, very street-level game probably won't benefit by having a pair of characters from Concordia and one from the Chantry on Cerberus.

Mercury: The Shard Realm *Correspondence*. Travel to and from this Shard Realm is difficult at best, because it seems to occupy a level of *Correspondence* understanding that surpasses the way *Correspondence* works in conventional three-dimensional space. The Shard Realm is a place where distance and direction are nearly meaningless; navigation is impossible to anyone without *Correspondence* knowledge and difficult even to those mages.

Venus: The Shard Realm *Life*. In the Umbral reflection of Venus, the planet is a verdant, hot jungle. Mages sometimes visit to explore its reaches for special herbs or spores, but it's also the home to spiritual predators of great size and danger. Below its surface are tunnels filled with all manner of crawling things. The dusty layer of the planet is actually an organic soup. Travelers risk disease and parasitic infection if they do not have *Life* magic protection.

Mars: The Shard Realm *Forces*. The most famous Chantry of Tradition history, Doissetep, once resided here. The Umbral reflection of Mars is a barren land torn with lightning, earthquakes and roiling skies. The temperature reflects reality: Burning during the day, freezing at night. Here all extremes of forces come to bear. Some evidence indicates the presence of Bygones on the Shard Realm, although none can say with certainty if these were simply things that passed to the Umbra from Unbelief, or creatures that actually thrived on Mars before humanity.

Jupiter: The Shard Realm *Matter*. As a tremendous body of swirling matter in the physical world, Jupiter casts an Umbral reflection of a huge place of caverns, rocks, magma and metal. Due to its sheer size, a great variety of possibilities emerge. Mages sometimes visit this Shard Realm specifically to look for rare elements or unusual compounds for magical research.

Saturn: The Shard Realm *Time*. Saturn's Shard Realm may be the most cryptic of all. It seems a place devoid of spatial dimension; rather, travelers in it find themselves altering their relationship to the time-stream, causing passage of time for themselves or changing when they come back. For this Shard Realm, you may simply want to use a very small room with blacklighting and violet wall hangings — it's so esoteric that even mages have trouble navigating it. Saturn's Shard Realm is a place where desperate mages go either to study *Time* Mastery or to hope to be catapulted into another era. Nobody yet knows how to control the flow of Time here to successfully predict the exit point.

Uranus: The Shard Realm *Spirit*. Essentially, this Realm is a large "reflection of a reflection." Here, spiritual power is unfettered by any ties to the material world. Binding spirits is difficult, and all Resonance is pronounced. Emotional states flare up in auras, and a person's spiritual nature becomes visible in a halo or aura. You might choose to double the effects of all Resonance in this Realm. More eerily, if you have a bunch of colored glowsticks on hand, try passing them out to the players with colors that seem to match their personalities — red for hot-tempered, blue for serene, green for sullen and so on. In the Shade Realm of *Spirit*, all spirits become untethered: Spirits are no longer trapped in fetishes and the Avatars of mages accompany them side-by-side. Each spirit keeps a thin cord that binds it to its housing, but this can easily be broken — and things can be ejected, spiritless, from the Shade Realm.

Neptune: The Shard Realm *Mind*. Much like the Astral Umbra, this is a place of thoughts. Mental states come to the fore, but unlike the Shard Realm *Spirit*, they don't simply appear in halos — they can actually cause subtle changes in the environment. In the Shade Realm, this is even more pronounced, and mental states can dramatically shift the landscape. Some mages consider the Shade Realm to be essentially a *tabula rasa* that forms an entire mindscape around every visitor. Other mages theorize that the Shade Realm of *Mind* is, itself, a tremendous consciousness — perhaps the universal unconscious.

Pluto: The Shard Realm *Entropy*. At the edge of the solar system lies the tiny world devoid of light and heat, where all things freeze and crumble. In its Shard Realm, the Euthanatos have one of the few remaining powerful Umbral Chantries (placed on the Umbral reflection of Cerberus, a moon of Pluto). The archmaster Senex continues to teach the power of *Entropy* as students survive inside the walls of a place where, just beyond the protective barrier, the world is devoid of light, heat or anything but slowly cracking ice, crumbling dust and energy-sapping vacuum. The Shade Realm of *Entropy* is even more of an enigma; old journals describe it as a place of utter darkness that makes the Shadowlands look well-lit by comparison, where nothing has form or structure.

Space and the Dimensional Barrier

Some mages mistakenly believe that, beyond a certain point, outer space becomes the Umbra. This isn't *quite* true, although it's close. Past the asteroid belt, the Gauntlet becomes staggeringly low; it's very easy to cross between "our" space and the other dimensions at that point. Still, the Umbra remains separate — that's why mundane astronomers on Earth don't see giant ruined castles on Mars; Doissetep existed in the Umbral reflection of the planet.

Sons of Ether, Void Engineers and the occasional travel-minded Virtual Adept do make jaunts out into space itself. As the Gauntlet thins (to about a 2), it becomes possible to very easily slip into other Realms. Tradition mages attribute this to space remaining largely unmapped and unknown and thus analogous to areas of the Umbra; the Void Engineers simply claim that outer space is free from the distortion shadows cast by Earth-bound technological signatures and therefore open field for warp effects and dimensional travel.

Games taking place in outer space have their work cut out for them. Unless you're in the movie business, you'll have to fake a whole lot — or set all of your action on the inside of a station or ship, such as the

Technocracy's recent Mars base, Ares City. Remember that space expeditions are still very much like early submarine excursions: Quarters are cramped, regulations are strict, and one false move could kill everyone! Players should always have the overwhelming sense that they're *way* out of their element, in a hostile environment that's waiting to kill them.

You probably don't need specific rules for explosive decompression and such. Suffice to say that an unprotected mage in space suffers just like anyone else. Sure, a magical Effect can turn the void into breathable, habitable ether, but the mage had best be quick about it.

Assume, if you must, that characters unprotected in space take two levels of aggravated damage automatically each turn, due to pressure change, radiation and the boiling/ freezing of bodily fluids and tissues.

Other Realms

Of course, the Shard Realms aren't the only places out there. Nor are the reflections of the Umbra. As noted before, many places exist that predate magely intervention — and that exist without mages' input.

The trick lies in keeping the Umbra mysterious and unknowable. While the descriptions here provide some leeway for playing in various Realms, there should *never* be a "complete catalog to the Umbra" or an easy map. New places form; old places change. No mortal will ever fully comprehend the depths of the Umbra. Some mages might become familiar enough with a given Realm or two to feel comfortable there, but no traveler should ever be totally confident that he's seen all of the Umbra or that he always knows what to expect.

The sample Realms presented below encapsulate some ideas of things in the Umbra as described in the **Book of Worlds** for **Mage**. They are, however, by no means the only places, and even Storytellers who use that resource should not consider it the be-all end-all of everything Umbral.

Chasm: The Realm of Things Lost

Become lost in the Penumbra, follow the cracks and the shadows, and there's a chance you'll end up at the Chasm. The Chasm is essentially a tremendous rift that stretches as far as the eye can see in either direction, surrounded by barren, wasted plains. Supposedly, everything that's lost (but not broken) eventually makes its way here.

Just looking at the Chasm is dangerous: It has a hypnotic effect on the viewer. A mage who looks over the edge of the Chasm and into its

depths must make a Static Willpower Challenge (difficulty of six Traits). Failure means that he becomes hypnotized by it. On the following turn, he must make another challenge; failing that, the mage leaps into the Chasm. If friends don't save the mage within a turn — using magic, rope, whatever — the mage falls into the darkness beyond viewable range and is gone.

Several paths lead down into the Chasm itself. Watching the path while descending seems relatively safe; it's only looking into the unfettered Deep that carries the hypnotizing, self-destructive weight. Mages can follow paths of Iron, Gold, Silver, Soil — each path seems almost metaphorical as well. Typically, the mage follows a narrow crevice or channel limned with a specific material. The paths seem, in some ways, to apply to metaphors of Ascension; the path of Iron has jagged rock and treacherous footing, while the path of Gold tempts with lost relics and jutting bits of valuable-looking crystals and minerals. Mages who can't master their own desires may find the paths too difficult to walk safely.

Beyond a certain distance down, the gloom of the Chasm becomes impenetrable. The Chasm itself sucks away magical energy; only a few hundred feet down and all magical Effects fail. This means (also) that mages have no way to see the path or to fly out if they fall….

Since all things lost end up at the Chasm eventually (if they don't wind up in someone else's hands), there's always potential to find a lost relic or bit of knowledge here. The price may be too high, though. It seems that nobody ever leaves the Chasm without making some sort of sacrifice.

Concordia: Hopes Shattered

In the Renaissance, the Traditions gathered their most powerful resources and, with the help of Nodes donated by every Tradition, created one of the most enduring and powerful Horizon Realms ever known. Called Concordia, the Realm was (and is) an entire world, complete with people, ecology, landscapes and cities. In the midst of it was Horizon itself — the Traditions' centerpiece Chantry, the seat of their archmages' power and the show of all that mythic strength could create.

Horizon was betrayed and destroyed. The Tradition archmasters and Primi scattered in its wake. Technocrats crushed the stronghold and set up powerful barriers to shut Concordia out from the power of its earthly Nodes. Still, with the arrival of the Avatar Storm soon after, the Technocracy lacked the resources to co-opt or destroy Concordia completely. Horizon itself became little more than a decrepit shell, occasionally visited by a daring member of the Traditions, while Concordia slowly fell apart around it.

Without the power of earthly Nodes to sustain it, Concordia is coming apart. Its people and creatures sicken, and the land cracks and shakes. In some places, the world itself breaks off and reveals the endless night-void of the Umbra. Because the world was built as a reflection of the Renaissance, its inhabitants don't understand what's happening; they only know that their paradise is dying, and that the powerful wizards who once protected them have died or fled.

Only desperate or hopelessly idealistic Tradition mages come here now. In some ways, Concordia once exemplified the best impulses of the Traditions: The Renaissance's cultures and arts all came together in a world where the Traditions blended their instincts and beliefs. Now it's a Realm suffering from the Traditions' hubris.

Dystopia: The Realm of the City

Some mages think of Dystopia as the near future. Others assert that even the Technocracy would never allow the world to come to this fate. This is a Realm crafted in the image of *Metropolis* and *Blade Runner*. A Realm where the great, technologically advanced but socially decadent cities sprawl over a dessicated landscape in a world where progress' effluvia permanently blackens the sky.

When mages travel along Umbral roads between sprawling skyscrapers, they sometimes approach Dystopia. The city itself is nearly limitless; it's as if civilization had spread endlessly across the face of the planet. Skyscrapers rise up from asphalt and black soil, while in between them low, neon-sign-covered buildings huddle with their patched roofs and metal-corrugated walls, barely keeping out the acidic rains. Sunlight is wan at best, and nightfall lit by the burning of multitudes of glaring lights and giant screens.

In the depths of the streets and below them, squatters eke out a precarious existence from the trash and rubbish that trickles down. Entire villages, buried by new layers of technology, exist under the cities. Above them, the masses work and live in cramped apartments, staring at glazed computer screens in cubicles. At the tops of the skyscrapers, above the toxic clouds, are the arboreal palaces of the few and privileged, who live in the sky with the sun.

Pattern-based spirits are common in Dystopia, though they usually take the form of small robots or computer programs. Mages must be cautious: Technology for tracking strangers is much better than Earth's, and mages have none of the identity cards, chips or numbers that Dystopia's citizens take for granted from birth. Even the Technocracy shuns this place; its bleak take on social structure and its polluted wreckage are signs of a failed technology.

Citizens of Dystopia often have small *Enhancements* (as the Background): Many can plug into computer terminals or have small cosmetic modifications. The people who live Down Below are often mutated aberrations, by contrast, turned squalid by their living conditions.

The streets of Dystopia often seem eerily familiar. That's because they're borrowed from the streets of the most teeming cities the world over. A vendor's cart from Hong Kong may stand in front of a Calcutta alleyway in which lurks a tin shack used as housing in New York.

Mages in Dystopia are recommended to leave as expediently as possible. Unfortunately, the only sure way out is to either get above the cloud layer and use magic to leave (a tricky proposition, because of all the guards and protections on the upper class), or to pay off a local spirit to guide one out and hope that it doesn't signal an alarm.

The Digital Web

Perhaps the most infamous of magely Realms is the Digital Web: the magical reflection of the connections behind all computer, telephone and similar communication devices. While Sleepers can experience the Web in its mundane internet form, mages with the right Effects or devices can actually enter the Digital Web and see an entire computerized world of virtual reality.

When entered holistically or with sensory input, the Digital Web resembles some sort of strange cross between *Tron*, *Johnny Mnemonic*, *The Matrix* and just about every other vision of cyberspace out there. Bright lines of light connect distant vistas; travelers can enter these vistas and find themselves in mini-Realms ("sectors") that have patterns and rules just like any other Realm. It's possible for a web sector to seem like a haunted castle, a Victorian manor, a high-tech spacecraft or just about any other imaginable setting; it all depends on the whims of the mage who "formatted" the sector and programmed it.

While in the Digital Web, mages interact through their "icons" — digital representations of themselves. Mages who enter solely with *Mind* magic often take on a sort of abstract representation or simple image; mages who enter holistically (in body, using *Correspondence* and *Life*) have "physical" reality in the web as well. Actions in the Web reflect things going on in the internet: For instance, a mage can "see" layers of things not visible to Sleepers. A mage doesn't see a website as a static, flat thing, but rather an object floating in the air with images according to its design. Because the mage exists in a more detailed dimension of webspace, it's possible for the mage to also do tricks that seem impossible to Sleepers, like easily rearranging websites, booting Sleepers from the 'net, even providing streams of real-time information from sound and video that seem implausible to Sleepers.

Within the Web, everything's a construct of *Forces* — energy given a virtual form. Thus, mages must use *Forces* to control, create or destroy "objects" in the Web. A mage who enters holistically can bring items with him but must use *Matter* and *Forces* to give them virtual equivalents. Conversely, a master of *Forces* can create items at a whim.

Of course, the Digital Web isn't all fun and computer games. People who experience the Web for long periods of time tend to suffer repetitive stress injuries, headaches, eyestrain and back trouble — all signs that the Web slowly pulls a trickle of Quintessence from its users to sustain itself. Some programs in the Web can be dangerous, and Nephandi and worse also lurk in the digital byways. Plus, there's the danger of a crash. During the Reckoning, the entire Web crashed and "whited out." As a result, dozens of web-spinning mages died, their Avatars torn into fractal patterns and scattered across webspace. Entire sectors were lost; in some places, pieces of original programming patterns shone through, making haunted areas. And, of course, more Sleepers become hooked up every day, and they're always becoming more skilled. Eventually they may reach the same level of skill that mages have with the web.

Entering the Web

A mage can experience the Web in multiple different forms. Using *Mind* magic, a mage can send his mind into the Web itself. In this form, the mage has a translucent icon indicating that he's essentially a projected sensory presence. The mage can experience the Web but can't actually affect it without doing magic.

Using *Life* and *Correspondence*, a mage can holistically shift into the Web. *Spirit* can do this as well; mages theorize that the Web is, in some senses, a manifestation of *Correspondence* space (the "space between spaces," if you will) and therefore that *Spirit* isn't always necessary. A physically-present mage literally vanishes from the "real" world and appears inside the Web, and can move around, interact with things and

cause repercussions just as a result of picking things up, breaking them, setting them on fire, etc.

Mages experiencing the Digital Web holistically do cross the Avatar Storm (unless you don't want to use the Storm, or want to make the Web a popular stomping ground).

Typical foci used for entry include virtual rigs (for sensory entry) or full-body virtual suits like those in *The Lawnmower Man* (for holistic entry).

Representing the Web

Representing the Web in your game is much like representing any other Realm. You can use a separate room and place players there when their characters visit the Web. Dress it up with colored lighting, especially strip-lighting and glow sticks; use computer parts from second-hand stores to add to the technology appearance. Some special sites might have ground rules that make them look like a different Realm; you'll want to use a slightly off-colored light to make these places seem a little "odd" even if they're meticulously designed to match up with what they seem to be. (Note how in *The Matrix* a green filter's used for all scenes that take place in webspace.)

You can also use IRC and similar internet chat programs for Web reps. A tech-savvy player can set up a mIRC room, and mages can drop by there to chat. In the Digital Web, such private havens can take on the appearance of actual rooms, and the mages can see each other and converse (or even fight!) normally. Just make sure that a Storyteller is on hand to moderate!

For a much more detailed look at the Digital Web, see the sourcebook **Digital Web 2.0**. This gives example locations, some rotes and chronicle ideas revolving around the Web.

OTHER SUPPLEMENTS

Laws of Ascension Companion
WW5033 $17.95 U.S.

Laws of the East
WW5016 $17.95 U.S.
Rules for playing Asian vampires.

Laws of the Hunt Revised Edition
WW5032 $19.95 U.S.

Laws of the Hunt Players Guide
WW5010 $14.95 U.S.
More rules for tracking and tricking the undead in live-action games.

Laws of the Wyld West
WW5004 $14.95 U.S.
The live-action worlds of werewolves and the Wild West, combined!

Liber des Goules: The Book of Ghouls
WW5006 $10.95 U.S.
The *Mind's Eye* rules for playing vampires' human pawns.

Mind's Eye Theatre: Book of the Wyrm
WW5029 $15.95 U.S.
Rules for creating and playing the enemies of the Garou as the Apocalypse looms.

Mind's Eye Theatre: Dark Epics
WW5027 $12.95 U.S.
These new streamlined rules for mass-combat, power crossover and tabletop conversion (to name a few subjects) have been developed and tested by the Camarilla, White Wolf's official fan club.

Mind's Eye Theatre: The Camarilla Guide
WW5017 $14.95 U.S.
New rules and tricks specifically for Camarilla vampires. A supplement to *Laws of the Night (Revised)*.

Mind's Eye Theatre: The Changing Breeds (Vol 1)
WW5019 $14.95 U.S.
The source for creating and playing one of the Changing Breeds: the Nuwisha, the Corax or the Bastet.

Mind's Eye Theatre: The Changing Breeds (Vol 2)
WW5024 $14.95 U.S.
The source for creating and playing one of the Changing Breeds: the Mokelè or the Gurahl.

Mind's Eye Theatre: The Changing Breeds (Vol 3)
WW5034 $17.95 U.S.

Mind's Eye Theatre: The Sabbat Guide
WW5018 $14.95 U.S.
New rules and tricks specifically for Sabbat vampires. A supplement to *Laws of the Night (Revised)*. Tradeback.

Mind's Eye Theatre Discipline Deck
WW5181 $14.95 U.S.
Almost 100 cards detailing the powers from the revised *Laws of the Night*.

Mind's Eye Theatre Journal #1
WW5401 $7.95 U.S.
The quarterly magazine of new rules, plots and ideas for *Mind's Eye*.

Mind's Eye Theatre Journal #2
WW5402 $7.95 U.S.

Mind's Eye Theatre Journal #3
WW5403 $7.95 U.S.

Mind's Eye Theatre Journal #4
WW5404 $7.95 U.S.

Mind's Eye Theatre Journal #5
WW5405 $7.95 U.S.

Mind's Eye Theatre Journal #6
WW5406 $7.95 U.S.

Mind's Eye Theatre Journal #7
WW5407 $7.95 U.S.

Mind's Eye Theatre Journal #8
WW5408 $7.95 U.S.

Mind's Eye Theatre Prop Deck
WW5180 $14.95 U.S.
All the cards you need to wield as weapons and influence in-game.

The Shining Host
WW5009 $15.00 U.S.
The essential rules for playing live-action faeries, based on the *Changeling: The Dreaming* Storytelling game.

The Shining Host Players Guide
WW5030 $15.95 U.S.
Rules for playing the lost changeling kith and houses.

Vampire Storyteller Guide
WW5021 $15.95 U.S.
This book combines new Thaumaturgy paths with extensive advice on creating a chronicle.